Schoolteacher

SCHOOL-TEACHER

A Sociological Study

Dan C. Lortie

With a new Preface

The University of Chicago Press Chicago and London

For Pam, Pete, Paula, and Philip

The University of Chicago Press, Chicago 60637
The University of Chicago Press, Ltd., London

© 1975 by The University of Chicago
New Preface © 2002 by The University of Chicago
All rights reserved. Published 2002.
Printed in the United States of America

20 19 18 17 16 15 14 13 12   4 5 6 7

ISBN-13: 978-0-226-49353-4 (paper)
ISBN-10: 0-226-49353-9 (paper)

Library of Congress Cataloging-in-Publication Data

Lortie, Dan C. (Dan Clement), 1926–
    Schoolteacher : a sociological study / Dan C. Lortie;
with a new preface.
        p.   cm.
    Includes bibliographical references and index.
    ISBN 0-226-49353-9 (alk. paper)
    1. Teaching—Vocational guidance—United States.
    2. Teachers—United States—Social conditions.
    3. Teachers—Psychology.   I. Title: School teacher.
    II. Title.
LB1775.2.L67   2002
371.1'0023—dc21
                                        2002020788

♾ This paper meets the requirements of ANSI/NISO
Z39.48-1992 (Permanence of Paper).

Contents

Preface 2002

Education does not change at a rapid pace—the major structures in public education are much the same today as when *Schoolteacher* was written in 1975. This preface deals primarily with continuity in teaching work, but there have been changes and some promising developments to which I will also allude. For readers who are interested in suggestions on how further research might center on both change and continuity, permit me to refer you to my article in *The International Handbook of Educational Change*, edited by Andy Hargreaves, Ann Lieberman, Michael Fullan, and David Hopkins (Dordrecht: Kluwer Academic Publishers, 1998), vol. 1, pp. 145–62.

Apart from the suggestion that teachers might get more involved in research on their work, this book does not advance recommendations for action or implications for policy, but is devoted to description, analysis, and interpretation. I sought to write as objectively as I could to avoid confusion with advocacy for a particular program of reform. I am quite ready, however, to suggest how teaching and learning might benefit from this research *if* readers realize that tracking implications and making suggestions for action are inevitably speculative and based on personal values and preferences. As opinion, these thoughts have no claim to scientific validity—their use, however, can be found in their capacity to stimulate thought, provoke fresh ideas, and produce lively debate. I hope they do.

I address three audiences in this preface: first, those engaged directly in teaching work; second, school administrators; third, those who make policies and administer resources that shape our public schools. With a few exceptions, the ideas presented are rooted in the text of *Schoolteacher.*

I.

Two important trends in recent years have expanded the circle of those directly engaged in teaching work. First, "professional development"—activity focused on helping experienced as well as beginning teachers strengthen their teaching capabilities—has had remarkable growth. Not long ago, school districts rejected plans to spend time and money on staff development, arguing that this was the responsibility of state agencies, and that it made little sense to invest in teachers who may move away. Today we find an increasing focus on such undertakings at the local level.

The second trend is a largely increased emphasis on analysis of the tasks and choices teachers make in the course of their working day. "Reflective practice" describes the process in which teachers think longer and harder about what they do and work to guide their activities accordingly. As a sociologist, I believe that such introspection works most effectively when associated with interaction among peers who can also personify different types of teaching and provide examples of alternative practices. The emerging focus on analysis has been developed by leading centers of teacher education and has spread to settings that bring teacher educators and classroom teachers into closer and more productive association. The comments in this section are directed, then, to teachers, university faculty members who work closely with them, and persons engaged in staff development.

Schoolteacher provides some starting points for thinking about and discussing issues of practice. Spotting such points may be easiest when we encounter alternative ways of thinking about teaching as found in the discussion of goals in chapter 5. There it is noted that teachers usually "add" objectives to those attached to the formal curriculum and do so in various ways—they may emphasize moral objectives, focus on "connecting students to school and learning," or talk about a particular concern with ensuring that all the children are learning. Teachers reading this book can ask themselves important questions at this point: What do *I* want to emphasize? What underlies that choice? If challenged, how would I defend it? At a time when "high stakes testing" presses teachers to focus on tested material, are there ways to fit in additional goals that I care about? Does the setting I work in make any particular goal especially significant? Does the grade, subject, or specific students I teach make some goals more relevant than others?

Thinking about a particular purpose and its complexities can also be productive. Take, for example, the objective of moral education—helping students to distinguish right from wrong and learning to choose the former. There are many run-of-the-mill situations that are not problematic but there are other situations where the right choice can prove to be ambiguous. It may be necessary to select from two good options that are in conflict or to decide which of the two undesirable ones is, in fact, the lesser of two evils. These more complex decisions are examples of areas where the different components in our educational system can work together closely to help teachers. Teacher preparation programs can give teachers experience in analyzing moral questions not only in general terms (i.e., classes in the philosophy of education) but in specific contexts—using teaching cases that are based on a variety of actual situations and events can serve that purpose; cases have been developed, in fact, that deal specifically with ethical issues. Local staff development programs can provide opportunities for the exploration of such questions, as can teacher associations and unions.

There is a risk in focusing on personal reflection—it could be construed as implying that improvement rests entirely on teachers working alone with their students and their consciences in their separate classrooms. But there are impediments to effective teaching that lie outside the classroom, in the organizational context. Despite the many years of experience we have had with operating schools, it is still difficult to mobilize and sustain the energies of a few adults and large numbers of children to be productive day after day, year in, year out. Our society is marked by much cultural variation, making the common socialization of children, always potentially contentious, especially so. Those and other realities make it difficult to ensure that organizational arrangements per se do not hamper the efforts of students to learn and teachers to teach. They are mentioned here to make it clear that I am not saying that changes in individual teachers are all that is necessary to remedy problems in schools or that teachers can ignore the organizational settings in which they work. In fact, I urge teachers and those who work with them to identify as fully and carefully as they can the points where organizational considerations inhibit their functioning and reduce the chances of success with students. For example, do grading and grouping practices "tell" some students that they cannot learn? Are student cliques in high school allowed to depreciate and reduce the self-confidence of other students? Do the adults in the school convey mixed messages to students about what is expected from them? Are resources needed for teaching distributed in ways that are both fair and effective? Analysis by teachers and their associates should extend, then, to studying the culture and operations of the school in which they work, and they should, I believe, press to have their observations and perspectives play an important part in the decision making of the school.

"How am I doing?" The answers that teachers give to this question—and the processes they use to form their answer—are, in my view, of vital importance for several reasons. Teacher rewards are, in general, aligned with school objectives—their core psychic rewards come from feeling that their teaching efforts are successful. Positive and accurate answers to the teachers' self-assessment question are associated, then, with a higher level of school accomplishments. In addition, although there are other indicators of student learning, teachers have an intimate, unique knowledge of the students and classes they teach that adds a special awareness, a human dimension, to the evaluation of student outcomes. While "supervisors" may be helpful in guiding teacher behavior, their responsibilities are normally such that they can pay only limited attention to any one teacher or group of students. Thus teachers make many decisions in the course of a day, week, or month without consultation; it follows that effective self-evaluation produces better overall monitoring of instruction in the school. Finally, the complexities of teaching can produce doubts about one's efficacy, which produces a loss of psychic rewards even when such feelings are not justified. Not only is any possible subsequent decline in morale undesirable in its own right, it may produce other unfavorable consequences. Teaching is unusual in that teachers play a very large part in recruitment through example, and a drop in their morale will make the occupation seem less desirable to those considering the occupation.

Chapter 6 discusses the fragility and complexities facing teachers when they try to answer the how-am-I-doing question. It reveals that large numbers of teachers find it difficult to even answer. The extent of these difficulties suggests that increasing the ability of teachers to discern what is happening with students and classes is of great importance and that those who prepare teachers and those who work with experienced teachers should make strong efforts to help them solve the problems involved. A few modest proposals follow.

• Teachers have been shaped in turn by their own teachers and by their personal responses to those teachers—such influences stretch over many years. The result is an accretion of views, sentiments, and implicit actions that may be only partially perceived by the beginning teacher (See chapter 3). Whatever can be done to help future teachers make implicit dispositions explicit will free them to become more aware of what they do while teaching and to more readily consider practices to which they have not been previously exposed. Having students write at length about former teachers and share those observations with peers might begin the process—sharing such materials and discussion with others could help individuals recognize some themes from what they emphasize in their recollections and the meanings that might be attached. Recalling and reviewing particular classroom incidents could provide occasions to use newly learned concepts from a variety of courses and disciplines. Ingenious teacher educators can, and I hope will, come up with approaches that will help beginners increase their awareness in ways that advance self-evaluation and the willingness to consider a broader range of alternatives.

• Upon being asked to discuss how she assessed her performance, one elementary teacher in Five Towns responded with enthusiasm and laid out, in exceptional length and detail, the various ways in which she dealt with "that difficult question." Yet the cellular organization in schools creates boundaries that prevent colleagues from sharing in the kind of expertise displayed by this remarkably articulate teacher. Although there are schools where a sense of professional community exists, mutual isolation during most of the day is the rule at many schools. (Readers with an interest in colleague relations among teachers will find useful material in recent studies by sociologists and others who have examined the "professional communities" in which some teachers participate.) More ways should, I think, be found to reduce the mutual isolation of teachers and the resulting loss of valuable knowledge. Those in professional development help when they bring teachers together, and principals are also in a position to increase opportunities for teachers to work together and to share know-how.

• Evaluation and self-evaluation could benefit, I believe, from the wider use of technological tools that are already available. My impression is that while videotaping gets some use, it is not extensive. Would it help if highly articulate and effective teachers showed tapes of their classrooms to other teachers and provided running commentaries on what influenced their instructional decisions? For example, what cues from students do they trust and which have they learned to ignore?

Marketing experts employ various devices to test responses to commercials; could such techniques be put to better use by helping teachers test and improve their communication skills?

II.

I owe to my late friend, the economist Charles Benson, the fundamental insight that *time* is the most scarce resource in schools. A major challenge to school administrators is to manage the use of time wisely to achieve the best possible outcomes. Scholars studying instruction have established that "time on task" plays a significant role in student learning. The consequences are obvious—poor allocations of time, by wasting the most valuable resource, reduce teaching effectiveness and student learning.

In chapter 7, teachers report on the changes they believe will allow them to do a better job, and, in another question, they talk about changes that would increase their satisfaction. The responses are surprisingly similar—the modal answers to both questions revolve around the use of time. The specifics are likely to vary somewhat from place to place but the central thrust, I believe, remains the same—teachers want more "potentially productive time." This term recognizes that although there are uncertainties built into teaching, there is no teacher-induced learning whatsoever when time is spent on paperwork and other tasks not directly connected to teaching.

There are two aspects to this emphasis on using time to teach. The first is connected to the production of learning—it appears that teachers are right to link time and student outcomes. The second is symbolic. When school schedules and administrative actions displace teachers' core tasks, teachers can interpret this as depreciating the importance of teaching, and they resent the administration. There are times, it seems likely, when administrators cannot avoid interrupting teachers or face obstacles in arranging schedules that maximize teaching time, but one wonders whether they pay as close attention to such considerations as they might. For example, I have been escorted around schools by principals who did not hesitate to interrupt classes to introduce me—a courtesy that was in no way necessary and that I, knowing how teachers might feel about this, found uncomfortable. Public address systems, it seems, apparently offer an irresistible temptation to some principals and their assistants; teachers, despite union contracts intended to prevent it, still complain about "unnecessary" and "overlong" meetings called by the principal. Administrators should be aware that actions seen to deny the central importance of teaching retard the sense of common purpose that organizational theorists tell us is so important in establishing trust in leadership and in achieving shared goals.

Lest superintendents and their staffs think I am placing exclusive blame on principals for producing the sense of wasted time among teachers, let me relieve them of that notion. Some time-use problems in schools originate in central offices. For example, central officials may proliferate requests for reports from principals who, in turn, must ask teachers to provide details. (Principals are particularly disturbed when they have previously supplied the information and know that it could have been simply retrieved from central office computers had it been properly stored there.) Anomalies in bus scheduling that force curtailment of curricular and extra-curricular activities usually originate in the central office; principals may be less available to assist staff when principals, sounding much like teachers, complain that "unnecessary" or "overlong" meetings keep them away from their schools.

The current emphasis on "leadership" can mislead school administrators into overlooking the central importance of effective management; management is sometimes derided by leadership theorists who make the word "manager" sound worse than "bureaucrat." There is research, as well as common experience, that underscores the importance of management skill in directing activity toward achieving goals. An example is Glenn McGee's dissertation at the University of Chicago that establishes, with considerable sophistication, that the best predictor of whether new technology will be widely used hinges primarily on the principal's managerial acumen in introducing and supporting it. Those of us engaged in the preparation of school administrators (as I was for many years) should also accept some of the blame when time is used poorly in schools. It seems to me that we have not paid enough attention to enabling time to be the ally rather than the enemy of teaching and learning.

III.

I wish to conclude by addressing readers involved in the governance of schools or the disposition of funds for public education. I will focus on projects and programs that seek to raise the quality of instruction, advancing a working hypothesis that we need to think about change in non-hierarchical terms.

A distinctly American culture influences our schools in many ways by shaping our very notions of how to bring about change. This culture is influenced by two strong forces. The major influence seems to come from the management style of American businesses, a tendency identified years ago by Raymond Callahan in his classic study of scientific management and school administration, *Education and the Cult of Efficiency.* A visit to the local bookstore will quickly reveal that almost all the writings on organizations, change therein, and leadership are addressed to readers in business firms. Those books, usually hortatory in nature, build on the assumption that the hierarchical distribution of rank and power found in corporations is the natural and appropriate way to "get things done." Widely read publications such as general news and business magazines highlight the importance, nay grandeur, of the successful CEO. The other major force—large governmental organizations, including the military—shows a similar structure based on differences in rank that allocates the right to make decisions in a decreasing ratio from top to bottom. In neither corporations nor federal bureaucracies do those who work at the lower ranks have significant influence in setting the direction of the organization or, for that matter, the tasks they are expected to perform on a day-to-day basis.

There are many ways in which schools and school districts require effective management by people skilled in such work. Yet it seems that in our educational planning, we tend to rely too heavily upon the idea that all situations should be administered in the same way. Some school boards, for example, eager to participate in the movement toward more professional development, think instantly in hierarchical terms and appoint a central official—perhaps an assistant superintendent for professional development—expecting that person to conduct professional development with the usual top-down, bureaucratic methods. Government agencies and private foundations are likely to think in similar terms, requiring that innovative programs follow the usual vertical authority lines, citing the need for "accountability" and assuming that there is only one way to ensure it. I submit that alternative leadership patterns are needed in organizations that, like schools, need frontline individuals to make wise decisions in a situation where close and constant supervision is neither possible nor desirable.

The data in *Schoolteacher,* particularly in chapters 3 and 8, underscore the limits of vertical authority in influencing teacher classroom behavior. Official curricula are accepted as blueprints for action, but when teachers seek advice, they are considerably more likely to turn to each other than to administrators; at the same time, they tell us that in considering whether to adopt new ways of teaching they frame any such decision in terms of its match with their own personalities and teaching styles. We have seen that they feel free to select personal goals to add to those established by their schools. Reliance on strictly vertical controls, then, is likely to be ineffective given teacher preferences for lateral influence from peers and independence of mind in deciding how and when to change their teaching practices.

I would like to cite some undertakings that I believe are consistent with what teachers tell us. They suggest that effectiveness in fostering change can occur without reliance on the usual hierarchical authority.

• Professional development schools, in my view, constitute one of the most promising developments in both pre-service and in-service education in recent years. Those I have in mind feature regular students and outstanding teachers—the latter guide the efforts of beginners and provide opportunities for experienced teachers who wish to gain new levels of skill and insight. They build on our understanding that teachers prefer to learn from peers, particularly when those peers can demonstrate their effectiveness with students. These schools may also include faculty members from universities who not only qualify as outstanding teachers but who also bring the latest research and the ability to elicit intelligent reflection to the creative mix.

• A project that dealt with the beginning years of school flourished quietly in a group of Chicago schools in low income areas for several years. Year after year the schools received highly favorable evaluations. The project combined two special features. The first was space for parents do what they wished during the school day—there was little by way of a formal program, but parents and teachers had chances to interact. The second consisted of special arrangements for teaching. Each teacher worked with the same group of students for two or three years and each teacher had the freedom to design the teaching program and the resources to purchase whatever was necessary to carry it out. In this case, the support given teachers included an unusually high amount of freedom to act—it also expressed trust in the ability of teachers to make good decisions. The close relationships that developed with the parents meant additional support for the teachers and the children.

• Another project that received strong outside endorsement (in this case, by highly respected evaluators from Columbia University) looks remarkably simple. Funds were made available to hire persons to link teachers and others working in schools to outside sources of research and analysis. Those persons talked with members of school staffs to ascertain what problems they encountered in the course of their daily work. When staff members expressed interest, those hired for the project would conduct searches in ERIC and elsewhere to find materials that might be helpful in solving the problems mentioned by individuals. They then delivered the materials to those who had cited the issues without any effort to shape their response—their job was simply to provide information. The enthusiasm generated, given the simplicity of the program, is almost amazing—interviews with "clients" left no doubt in the minds of the evaluators that their work had been positively affected by the information with which they were provided. The outcome also throws doubt on the talk we hear about the alleged "resistance" practitioners show to research and other professional writing. My guess is that part of the success of the project rests in the complete lack of compulsion. It is a rare event for teachers (and perhaps people in other organizations as well) to receive useful information without any pressure to respond to it in a particular way.

A few examples do not a thesis prove. But as Everett Hughes once said, the burden of proof rests on the person who says that what happens once cannot happen again. There is considerable need, as I see it, for research and experimentation on how we can combine accountability with creative ways for teachers to go about doing and improving their work. As is clear, I am firmly convinced that we can enrich our organizational strategies well beyond conventional notions of hierarchy and vertical control. In this era of charter schools and choice within public education, the time may be ripe for considerably more organizational innovation than we have witnessed in the past.

As an author I have the privilege of stating my views first. But now it is your turn. As a reader, it falls to you to accept or reject my contentions—to subtract, add to, or alter the ideas presented here. I invite you to do so.

Preface

Public schools shape our young and influence their life chances. Elementary and secondary schools consume billions of dollars each year and employ one-quarter of the nation's public servants. And education mobilizes vast amounts of political energy on issues such as racial segregation, collective bargaining, church-state relationships, and inequality. Professional educators today confront research and development styles of thought which challenge them to rethink their traditions and to justify choices from a range of competing alternatives. Public schools, in short, are among our major social, economic, and political institutions; they seem headed, moreover, for the trauma Max Weber called "rationalization."

Despite their pivotal role, public schools have received relatively little sociological study. Schooling is long on prescription, short on description. That is nowhere more evident than in the case of the two million persons who teach in the public schools. It is widely conceded that the core transactions of formal education take place where teachers and students meet. Almost every school practitioner is or was a classroom teacher; teaching is the root status of educational practice. Teachers are making strenuous efforts to increase their influence on how schools are run. But although books and articles instructing teachers on how they should behave are legion, empirical studies of teaching work—and the outlook of those who staff the schools—remain rare. Changes are proposed and initiated without sure knowledge of the settings they are presumed to improve. Without a clear picture of school reality, efforts at rationalization can dissolve into faddism and panacean thinking. I hope that this book will add to our knowledge about schools and stimulate others to undertake empirical study.

This volume deals with a variety of issues in the organization of teaching work and inquires into various sentiments teachers hold toward their daily tasks. The unifying theme is a search for the nature and content of the ethos of the occupation. By ethos I mean the pattern of orientations and sentiments which is peculiar to teachers and which distinguishes them from members of other occupations. It cannot be asserted, of course, that teachers are unique in every respect; we find numerous points where their problems and sentiments resemble those of others. What *is* unique is the particular constellation found in the occupation—the special combination of orientations and sentiments which prevails among teachers. As we shall observe, that pattern derives from both the structure of the occupation and the meanings teachers attach to their work.

The nine chapters fall into four distinct parts. Chapter 1 is a chronological review of selected structural features of teaching in which I explore the balance of continuity and change over three centuries of American history. The second part is made up of chapters 2, 3, and 4, each of which is devoted to a major process of occupational perpetuation: it deals with recruitment, socialization, and the distribution of career rewards. In each instance I relate the ways these issues are resolved to their implications for orientations among teachers. Three major orientations receive repeated reinforcement from the structure of the occupation.

Chapters 5, 6, 7, and 8 compose the third section. It is organized sequentially; unlike the second section, where each chapter is largely self-contained, the argument stretches over four chapters. The emphasis is on the meanings teachers give to their tasks and the sentiments they generate while carrying them out. Chapter 5 examines teacher goals and chapter 6 the problems which complicate their realization. Chapter 7 discusses the general sentiments of classroom teachers, and chapter 8 focuses on teachers' preferences about their day-to-day interactions. The final chapter is also a discrete section: it centers on three scenarios which might unfold in the future. It demonstrates certain connections between the analyses done in the book and practical action; it also proposes points where additional research should prove of value.

Public schools and classroom teachers have been part of the American scene for generations; though studied too little, they are extremely familiar. Familiar sectors of society present special problems for the sociologist. To gain fresh understanding, he must penetrate the conventional definitions which enmesh his object of study; he needs some way to cut through the "hand-me-down" depictions and interpretations which permeate the culture. Success in attaining such perspective is always relative, but there are research strategies which help. Among those I have employed is a stance which combines naiveté with skepticism—a questioning approach toward what is commonly said about teaching and teachers. It is also useful to limit one's control over responses; consequently, this study relies greatly on open-ended inquiry which lets teachers describe their world in their language. I have occasionally found it helpful to devise original analytic schemes to interpret data. I believe, however, that the most useful strategy in studying a familiar, highly defined sector like teaching is comparative method. Time and again it has been helpful to recall that teaching is one way among many in which people earn a living; time and again the analysis has been advanced by contrasting teaching with other occupations.

Several approaches and methods are used in this book; it includes historical review, national and local surveys, findings from observational studies by other researchers, and content analysis of intensive interviews. I have sought to match the method to the type of problem under examination. Some of the data permit quantitative analysis, but in other instances constraints of sample size and representativeness limit analysis of subgroups and generalization. Understanding the subjective world of people within a given field of work calls for long, detailed, and open-ended interviews which are costly in time and money: the benefits of intensity are purchased at the cost of scope. Yet it is surprising how much one can learn about an occupation without using complex measures; simpler tools such as the mode and the marginal distribution (even without concern for ordinality) are very useful in uncovering the ethos of a social group. The data used here (except for the historical summaries) range from the early 1960s to the early 1970s; although studies over that period indicate little change, subsequent investigators may wish to study the influence of recent changes. Such suggestions are offered throughout the book, but particularly in chapter 9. My interest here is in the central characteristics of teachers and teaching as found in conventional school arrangements, the base from which further development will have to take place.

Willard Waller, in the preface to his classic *Sociology of Teaching*, laid great stress on the importance of social insight. I like to think that this study lies in that tradition and that the methods used provide persuasive documentation of genuine insights into the nature of teaching as an occupation.

Acknowledgments

One of the more civilized practices of scholarship is the public thanking of those who have helped in the course of research and writing. I find this a particularly pleasant task; few have been more fortunate than I in the support they have received from those around them.

I began the research which eventuated in this book while teaching at the Harvard Graduate School of Education. Francis Keppel—that dean *sans pareil*—provided tangible and intangible support at a crucial point. Donald Mitchell and his colleagues at the New England School Development Council gave financial help and supplied access to school systems. Colleagues in the Graduate School of Education were both stimulating and responsive; I want in particular to mention Charles Benson, Bob Marden, Dave Tiedeman, Charles Cogan, and the late (and deeply missed) Vince Conroy. Herold Hunt was a considerate senior colleague. I was particularly lucky to have the help of Anne Trask as interviewer, research assistant, and colleague; her unwavering enthusiasm and fresh ideas played a vital part in this undertaking. Sally Skoug helped me as I formulated the Five Towns questionnaire. Arthur Wise and Nancy Doyle were outstanding interviewers and imaginative colleagues.

Associates at the University of Chicago Department of Education have been generous in abetting my efforts. Roald Campbell, both as director of the Midwest Administration Center and as chairman of the department, assisted me at every turn; the same can be said of Vern Cunningham, Alan Thomas, and Edwin Bridges. Emil Haller and Carol

Kronus helped code and recode the qualitative data; their subsequent research in their own right underlines how fortunate I was to have their help. Bob Panos guided me through the mysteries of the computer world; Irene Anderson and Romelle Livingstone reaffirmed their competence as typists. I thank those who read the manuscript; they include Frank Chase, Bob Dreeben, Jack Glidewell, Irving Harris, and David Street. Benjamin Wright shared his data without hesitation. I gained much from many delightful conversations with Philip Jackson.

Conventions of anonymity prevent me from naming the many teachers and school administrators whose assistance is the sine qua non of studies like this. They can be assured of two things: I am deeply grateful to them and have strived to merit their trust by respecting the data only they could have provided.

My wife, Eunice Jensen Lortie, contributed in more ways than I can identify. She moved with me through the demands imposed by each stage of the work, bolstering and stimulating and responding throughout. To top it off, she tactfully but firmly edited the next-to-final draft, supplying me with an operational definition of when I was, in fact, finished.

1

The Hand of History

By showing institutions in the process of transformation, history alone makes it possible to abstract the structure which underlies the many manifestations and remains permanent throughout a succession of events.

Claude Lévi-Strauss,
Structural Anthropology, p. 22

Occupational pasts are not all alike. Some, particularly in technological fields, are short; of those with longer histories, some display comparative stability and continuity while others feature sharp turning points and considerable change. It is important to consider such histories; as Lévi-Strauss points out, "only the study of historical development permits the weighing and evaluation of the interrelationships among the components of the present-day society" (Lévi-Strauss 1967, p. 13). In this instance, we will trace the development of selected characteristics of teaching to provide background for later analyses and to ascertain the balance between continuity and change within the occupation. An estimate of that balance will help us to understand the social system which prevails in public school teaching.

Although my debts to historians will become evident, the approach taken here is more sociological than strictly historical. Good history captures the spirit of an era, connecting events so that we perceive unities in otherwise disparate happenings. The developmental strategy used in

1

this chapter, however, sacrifices that advantage to a search for continuities and discontinuities in the evolution of an institution. Perhaps we should call the method "structural chronology" rather than history, for we shall move across time periods and restrict our focus at any given point to particular considerations. The goal is to achieve an overview of how teaching has come to be the kind of occupation it is today.

The rubrics used to organize the several chronologies derive from the sociological study of institutions and occupations. (For examples, see Caplow 1954; Gross 1958; E. Hughes 1958; and Taylor 1968.) The first deals with the position of teachers in the authority structure of public schools. The second and third refer to economic matters; whereas one is general, the other deals specifically with the different meanings monetary rewards have for men and for women. In the fourth section, the social position of teachers is discussed, with special attention to their social rank and the way society has regarded them. Succeeding sections discuss the growth pattern of the occupation and arrangements governing admission and training, and are followed by a brief recapitulation of associational bonds within teaching. The chapter concludes with some comments on the relative balance of change and continuity in the development of the occupation.

The Organizational Imperative

American teachers, especially since the early nineteenth century, have generally worked in organizations.[1] Fee-for-service instruction by individual teachers has been limited to tutoring the children of wealthy families and teaching special skills like music and dancing. Transactions between teachers and their students have usually been mediated by a third party; in public education, that party has consisted of a school board composed of elected or appointed citizens. Such boards have participated in raising funds, provided physical facilities, and supervised the instruction of children in a given geographical area. The fact of school board authority has been a constant, but its exercise has changed in interesting ways. And changes have also occurred in the methods teachers have been permitted to use in asserting and sustaining their authority over children.

Schooling and teaching were neither uniform nor institutionalized during the first century and a half of europeanized life on the American continent. We must, as historians caution, avoid projecting current conceptions onto different times (Bailyn 1960; Cremin 1970), but we can find some patterns in the descriptions of colonial schools found in Elsbree's book on teaching (1939). Those who taught school (most were men) were hired by local authorities for designated periods to perform stipulated duties for predetermined salaries. Those who taught were likely to do other kinds of work as well, for occupational life was considerably less specialized than it is today. Officials in the community assessed the would-be teacher's moral standing and his knowledge of what he was expected to teach—clergymen figured prominently in such screening. Once under contract the teacher performed his schoolhouse duties single-handedly. Local communities developed strategies for monitoring the performance of the teacher: the usual procedure was to visit the school periodically and demand recitations from the students. Elsbree's judgment is that this overseeing was little more than "superficial appraisal" (p. 71). He contrasts such arrangements with those prevailing in city school systems during the 1930s: noting that "there was no hierarchy of officers common to our present city school systems," he concludes that "the teacher was perhaps more nearly his own boss at this time [the colonial period] than at any subsequent period." There was little restraint on the teacher's authority—physical means ("rule by ferule") were fully accepted. Since the schoolhouse was physically separated from the community, the teacher had considerable privacy in the conduct of his day-to-day work.

The citizen governing board emerged during the colonial period and became a key building block in the system of mass schooling that was constructed during the nineteenth century (Tyack 1967). Originally a subcommittee of selectmen, it grew into a distinct body with unique rights and responsibilities. Although the formation of the Republic placed education under state authority, de facto powers moved to local school boards which gained authority over most facets of the schools. The formal structure which emerged during the nineteenth century was monolithic: unlike the federal government's division of power between executive, legislative, and judiciary branches, all formal powers were concentrated in the citizen governing board. One fails to find, for example, any clear distinction between "administrative" and "professional" domains in the school systems which grew out of the Common School Crusade. As school systems multiplied in number and grew in size, they became more bureaucratized. By the twentieth century the superintendent had become the chief administrative officer responsible for implementing school board decisions. The outcome of bureaucratization was to divide the "third party" [the governing body] into two layers, one consisting of part-time citizens, the other of full-time administrators. Through time, administrators increasingly stood in for boards in supervising teacher activities and affairs.

Urbanization resulted in the development and spread of multiple-classroom schools during the nineteenth century. The teacher's working conditions and status were naturally affected. He lost some of the privacy which had enhanced his independence during colonial times. Furthermore, a teacher was no longer *the* teacher: those instructing the young became members of a category of persons so employed in the local school. Larger units required coordination and other administrative tasks, which were assigned to principals and superintendents and, later, to their assistants. (One must not forget, however, that in many rural areas the one-room schoolhouse was sustained well into the twentieth century. As late as 1956, there were 34,964 one-teacher schools in the United States [Tyack 1967, p. 470].) Thus the dominant mode of schooling in twentieth-century America has consisted of thousands of school districts with a hierarchy of offices and some degree of bureaucratization (Bidwell 1965; Lortie 1969). Teachers became employees supervised by full-time, physically present administrators acting on authority delegated by school boards.

Authority relationships between teachers and students have also shifted. Earlier teachers, as was noted, were expected to use physical force to control their charges; gradually, however, the role of the student was redefined as new conceptions of the proper treatment of children arose. During the latter half of the nineteenth century and the early decades of the twentieth, laws and school custom changed; increasingly sharp limits were placed on the teacher's use of physical punishment. There is a paradox in this transformation of values and practices: the teacher's use of physical coercion was limited at about the same time compulsory education became the rule. The presumption that students attended school voluntarily became void just when teachers were forced to maintain their authority through persuasion and other leadership qualities. Discipline took on a different coloration under such conditions: teachers had to learn how to "motivate" students regardless of whether they or their parents wished them to be in school.

The hierarchization of schools and the diffusion of compulsory attendance produced dual "captivity" in the relationship between teachers and students. Students were assigned to particular schools by place of residence, and once in school they were allocated to specific teachers by school administrators. Teachers, having accepted employment in a given school district, were assigned to a school by the superintendent and to particular students by the principal. Thus neither student nor teacher had much to say about their relationship: each was forced to come to terms with an externally imposed requirement of cooperation. It is a truism of sociology that formal requirements can induce informal evasions, and some parents undoubtedly manage to influence the placement of their children. Teachers, moreover, have fought hard to gain seniority rights in the matter of transfer within school systems, and this grants some freedom in the kinds of students experienced teachers will teach. Such choice, however, remains categorical rather than individual; unlike fee-for-service professionals, teachers cannot build a clientele of selected individuals.

Whatever the reasons, American teachers have not seriously challenged the conception of school governance as the proper province of part-time citizens. Yet the actual capacity of boards and administrators to wield their legal powers has not been constant throughout the years of the modern school system. Important change has occurred in the century or so since Mann and others led the Common School Crusade. Elsbree's judgment of the situation in the 1920s and 1930s appears accurate; it seems that the subordination of teachers was greatest then (Elsbree 1939, p. 71). Callahan (1962) has described the ideologies of school officials of that time. Importing imagery from business and "scientific management," they saw teachers as similar to factory hands—as agents charged with implementing detailed specifications developed in central headquarters. Despite considerable stability in the formal powers of school boards and officials, power relationships have changed over the last four or five decades, and such changes were well under way before collective bargaining attained genuine potency. Although they have rarely challenged the authority system in principle, teachers have worked together to offset the capacity of boards and administrators to *use* their formal rights.

In the early days of the modern school system, school boards certified teachers, hired and fired at will, and paid individual teachers as they thought appropriate (Elsbree 1939, p. 338). Certification was centralized, however, at the turn of the century; it became the responsibility of state officials acting under publicly enacted rules and regulations. Teachers managed to introduce and amplify the concept of permanent tenure for classroom teachers of all kinds, and legislation became general which made it increasingly difficult for employers to dismiss teachers after they had served their initial probationary period (Elsbree 1939, p. 476). Teachers backed single-salary payment schedules which aligned payment with such "objective" qualifications as years of education and service. The diffusion of these three changes took time, but once they were general, each limited the power of school authorities. Boards and administrators could no longer define who was or was not "a teacher." They lost the power of hiring and firing at will and the leverage they had possessed by paying teachers individually. We have of course seen additional changes with the advent of widespread teacher bargaining. As I shall argue later, some of those changes fulfill the same function of limiting hierarchical authority. The assertions of teachers have not emphasized their "positive" collegial powers, but they have increased their "negative" powers. They have, in short, been able to achieve structural changes which reduce the power of superordinates by restricting the capacity of officials to affect the personal goals of teachers. Teachers have not pressed to reorder the hierarchy in which they find themselves: at least publicly, their associations continue to honor the idea of citizen control over schools. (Only in isolated instances have they attempted to replace administrative powers with teacher groupings.) Although the pyramid of authority in today's school looks much like that found a century ago, the powers of those in superordinate positions have been somewhat reduced. But today as yesterday, teachers continue to work in settings where formal authority is vested in board members who do not belong to their occupation and are therefore beyond the reach of its internal controls.

On Income

Public school teaching takes place under the aegis of corporate bodies located in the public sector. Parsons states that the incomes of persons working in the public sector—at similar levels—are lower but more secure than those earned in the private sector. He sees a trade-off between the amount of money received and the amount of risk entailed (Parsons 1958). Teacher incomes today fit the model of public sector employment, but formal employment security did not occur until relatively recently.

Given the novel and complex situation facing the early colonists, Bailyn portrays their discovery of means for financing schools as an impressive achievement (Bailyn 1960). The forms of support they knew in Europe did not work in the wilderness. After decades of experimentation with various combinations of contributions, fees, taxes, rents, and so forth, they settled on the local taxation of property holdings. Such taxation was incorporated into the common school model developed during the nineteenth century; subsequently it has provided most of the money needed to operate the public schools. In recent years, however, state governments have augmented their contributions and the federal government has begun to use its taxation resources to assist local school districts (Campbell, Cunningham, and McPhee 1965).

The form of financial support developed by the colonists and subse-

6

quently extended into the system of mass education developed later did more than permit the existence of public schools: it shaped them in fundamental ways. Bailyn notes that "the piper came to call the tune," as financial arrangements underscored the power of local citizens over the schools. The use of property taxation held down levels of expenditure, for as Benson indicates (1961, p. 18), it is a highly visible and relatively painful kind of tax. Those who determined the level of expenditures for schools (normally school boards with review by local governments) were, being local, accessible to the population of taxpayers and likely to give serious consideration to complaints about excessive costs. The preponderant share of school expenses has always been teachers' salaries. Fiscal arrangements, therefore, have exerted conservative pressures on teacher income.

Historians who discuss teacher income tend to use adjectives like "low" and "underpaid." Elsbree, after heroic efforts to uncover the comparative income of colonial teachers, placed the average at about that earned by skilled artisans—above that of common laborers but below the incomes of ministers, physicians, and lawyers (Elsbree 1939, p. 97). Tyack reports that incomes received by teachers in 1841 "were below the wages paid to artisans . . . and often below the earnings of scrubwomen and day laborers" (1967, p. 414). One suspects that the tendency of historians to see teacher incomes as too low springs from a "just wage" approach; teacher incomes seem discordant in terms of usual ideas of social rank. Economists may argue that teachers have been paid "the going rate," but many in our society have considered teacher incomes as somehow inappropriate given the importance of education. Until "teacher militancy" and the forceful action of the last few years, newspaper editorialists frequently prefixed the word "teacher" with the adjective "underpaid."

Benson's observations on teacher income support the application of Parsons's comments to teachers (Benson 1961*b*, p. 289). Although the level of payment has risen steadily over the last eighty years, the climb in income has not changed teachers' relative position within the economy. Benson reports that teachers receive (on the average) five to seven thousand dollars less per year than four other college-based occupations. He also points out that teaching salaries display a low, fixed ceiling; the typical salary schedule projects an ultimate income which is no more than twice that received in the first year. The latter pattern is more characteristic of public than private sector income profiles.

Elsbree points out that colonial teachers possessed security advantages over those who did not work for salaries or have annual contracts—they could count on a stipulated, predictable amount of money in return for their work (p. 96). But the assurance that one's employment was secure for years in advance did not come until tenure provisions became widespread during the first half of this century. Before then, teachers could be dismissed easily not only for incompetence but for a variety of infractions against morality stringently defined. As we shall see throughout this book, the economic realities of teaching play an important role in its nature: they undergird its social class position and the shape of careers within the occupation.

The Differential Value of Money Rewards

Continuities and changes in the sex composition of the teaching force have played an important part in the development of the occupation. Since the economic implications of these shifts have been particularly significant, we shall give them particular attention.

The modal teacher of the colonial period was male, a schoolmaster who taught in a "petty school" where basic reading and arithmetic were learned. Less frequently, he taught in the more advanced "grammar schools" of the day (Cremin 1970). Women teachers existed, but apparently constituted a minority. They taught primarily in "dame's schools" in which pupils studied in the teacher's home. Some women also taught in the summer sessions of the regular schools. Elsbree reports that the salaries earned by women teachers were "consistently lower than those awarded men" (p. 96).

Thousands of schools were created as public education expanded during the nineteenth century, and it was not long before the schools were staffed primarily by women. By 1870, for example, there were 123,000 women teaching and 78,000 men; year after year thereafter, the proportion of women increased (Tyack 1967, p. 470). By 1930 there were five times as many female as male teachers, and the men who did teach taught primarily in the higher grades.

Butts and Cremin do not find the feminization of teaching mysterious; they see the cause as economic, since women could be hired for considerably less than men (Butts and Cremin 1953). Teaching was comparatively attractive to women: they had, after all, few alternatives. The major options they faced were domestic service, employment in factories, and types of work which were extensions of feminine functions in the home—such as laundering and baking (Ogburn 1933). The widespread use of the typewriter and the accompanying explosion of office employment opportunities for women did not occur until the turn of the century, and nursing, social work, and library positions did not become numerous until the twentieth century. The vigorous industrial and commercial expansion which followed the Civil War, on the other hand, reduced the relative attractiveness of teaching for men; those were, one recalls, the years of the famous advice "Go West, young *man.*" It is tempting to use Linton's ideas to account for the increase in women teachers during the nineteenth century and the early part of the twentieth (Linton 1936, p. 117). He argued that societies tend to assign work roles to men or women; shifts toward women predict that men will withdraw even where economic reasons are not compelling. But the generalization has not been true in high schools, where teaching became and remained evenly distributed between men and women. The latter division persisted through the introduction of "equal pay for equal work" in the twentieth century. Nor does Linton's proposition fit the developments which occurred after World War II: during the decade or so following the war, the trend was reversed rather rapidly and the proportion of men entering classroom teaching increased (Tyack 1967, p. 470).

Linton's emphasis on sex as a basis of allocation is more applicable to administrative rank within school hierarchies, as males have continuously outnumbered females in such positions. The official positions opened by bureaucratization during the nineteenth century were filled almost exclusively by men. The pattern thus established persists today in the career aspirations of members of the two sexes. Mason found, for example, that whereas most beginning male teachers expected to stay in education but to work in positions other than classroom teaching, most beginning women teachers who projected futures in education tied them to classroom work (Mason 1961, p. 103). Teaching, it appears, is institutionalized as temporary employment for men and continuing employment for women. Seen in this light, sex segregation takes the form of stages within the work career. Teaching is suitable lifelong employment for a woman, but for men it is acceptable primarily "on the way up."

Teaching is somewhat special in its distribution of money rewards by sex. Despite decades of talk about equalizing opportunities for women who work, this occupation is one of the very few where substantial numbers of women perform the same work as men and in fact receive the same compensation. It is trite to note that society holds different expectations for men and women and that men are accorded the role of principal breadwinner. Yet that commonplace has repercussions which are sometimes overlooked. Specifically, the demands encountered by

9

men and women throughout their working lives differ markedly. Most women who persist in teaching and do not marry do not meet sudden, sharp increases in their financial responsibilities—they can often use additions in income as they please. But most men who stay in classroom teaching marry and have children—their income expenditure profiles typically show a period during which costs rise sharply while income increases gradually. For most men teachers, therefore, similar incomes have less "value" than for women teachers: they represent a less useful contribution to the performance of their principal roles. We see confirmation of this in the high proportion of male teachers (and the considerably lower proportion of women) who find it necessary to take on additional employment (National Education Association 1972, p. 75). We will have several occasions to observe the consequences of this difference in the value of money rewards for men and women.

Special but Shadowed: The Teacher's Social Position

Teaching seems to have more than its share of status anomalies. It is honored and disdained, praised as "dedicated service" and lampooned as "easy work." It is permeated with the rhetoric of professionalism, yet features incomes below those earned by workers with considerably less education. It is middle-class work in which more and more participants use bargaining strategies developed by wage-earners in factories. We can gain insight into some of these ambiguities by reviewing the development of the role in our society.

I shall advance the following interpretation of the available evidence: teaching, from its inception in America, has occupied a special but shadowed social standing. The services performed by teachers have usually been seen as above the run of everyday work, and the occupation has had the aura of a special mission honored by society. But social ambiguity has stalked those who undertook the mission, for the real regard shown those who taught has never matched the professed regard. Teaching is a status accorded high respectability of a particular kind; but those occupying it do not receive the level or types of deference reserved for those working in the learned professions, occupying high government office, or demonstrating success in business.

The origins of the status in colonial times involved themes which have proved remarkably persistent. We recall the Old Deluder Satan Act which symbolized the linkage Puritans felt between literacy and salvation. Schooling was God's Work (Tyack 1967, p. 15). The status of teachers in colonial America reflected the connection between their activities and the core values of that society. Yet that status also reveals a shadow thrown by the peripheral quality of the connection. It was, after all, the clergyman who stood at the center of things—at the very heart of matters of piety. The teacher, almost-but-not-quite a minister, was off to the side. The proximate but peripheral standing of those early teachers is seen in the duties they performed, in the ways they were selected and supervised, and in the social composition of the occupation. The texts and materials used were heavily religious in content. The usual nonteaching work of teachers consisted of marginal (even menial) tasks in the domain dominated by the clergy. Teachers rang the church bells and swept up and, on the other hand, taught Bible lessons and occasionally substituted for an ailing pastor (Elsbree 1939, p. 63). Those who wished to teach had to accept stern inspection of their moral behavior, and more often than not the inspector was a clergyman—we have noted that ministers were usually represented in the visiting committees which evaluated the teacher's work. It appears that some young men aiming toward the ministry took on teaching duties along the way. For such persons, teaching can be seen as an apprenticeship to be discarded after one acquires credentials for a more significant position. Cremin (1970) feels that this explains why some teachers possessed outstanding educations for the time: higher learning, in short, was likelier within the ranks of the clergy than within the ranks of teachers.

Elsbree's effort to fix the social standing of colonial teachers matches this view of a special but nonstellar standing (1939, pp. 109-22). Using four indexes available in historical records, he finds that two point to higher status and two to lower. Forms of address and pew placement in church were associated with higher rank; the social ranking at Harvard and Yale of the sons of teachers and levels of wealth indicate lower standing. One can view the evidence as discrepant, but there is another way of thinking about it—the indexes might refer to status in divergent circles. Forms of address and pew placement can be seen as referring to *local* standing, especially in the religious community, whereas rank at college and total wealth were symbolic resources in the wider society of the time. Seen in this perspective, teachers were valued members of local congregations and neighborhoods, but could not command deference when they competed with men of broader cosmopolitanism and prominence. Charters suggests that teachers were part of the sacred order of society, a point with which I agree (Charters 1963, pp. 764-73). But it is not likely that the sacred order completely ruled the sensibilities of colonial Americans or fully determined the bases on which they accorded deference to others.

The position of teachers changed somewhat as urbanization, seculari- zation, and school expansion occurred during the nineteenth century. Teaching became work performed by young women, and given the relative position of the young and the female in the nineteenth century this probably reduced rather than augmented its social rank. Teachers became more abundant, making the individual teacher less uncommon and prestigious. Yet we find that the teacher's social position retained some of its earlier characteristics. Although purportedly secular, the Common School Crusade did not entirely eschew the rhetoric of previous times, a rhetoric which implied an exalted definition of teaching. Secularization did not seem to empty teaching of its special moral qualities, for teachers continued to be held to a severe set of special controls over their personal lives (Waller 1961, p. 43). Teachers were expected to participate in church activities. One suspects, however, that these controls (so excoriated by modern writers) may have served unrecognized functions within the social system. They may, for example, have made it feasible for parents to permit their daughters to live away from home without threat to the girls' moral acceptability. The moral controls surrounding teaching set it apart from the dominant alternatives of factory and domestic work. Whether better paid or not, teaching was demonstrably "respectable" employment and closer to middle-class standards.

The "special but shadowed" theme has persisted into more recent times. Consider, for example, the problem of teachers' subordination to others. Whereas earlier teachers were symbolically and literally outranked by preachers, later teachers have found themselves in a similar position vis-à-vis school administrators and professors, both within their immedi- ate field and in the disciplines. The principal and superintendent emerged as persons of presumed greater expertise and standing during the latter decades of the nineteenth century; during the twentieth century, some professors of education became spokesmen for schooling and leaders in various pedagogical movements (Cremin 1961). The specialist high school teacher emerged at the same time that colleges and universities expanded manyfold; those teaching particular subjects at the secondary level were placed in a less expert position than those teaching the same subjects in institutions of "higher" learning. Thus teachers never did gain control of any area of practice where they were clearly in charge and most expert; day-to-day operations, pedagogical theory, and substantive expertise have been dominated by persons in other roles.

There is evidence, however, that teaching continues to be defined as work of more than routine interest and importance. The best national data we have on the social position of teachers remain the National Opinion Research Center (NORC) studies; these two studies, done at two distinct times, place teachers below the established professions, top government officials, and business executives, but above craftsmen and some others whose earnings exceed teachers' (National Opinion Research Center 1953; Hodge, Siegel, and Rossi 1964). Teaching is somewhat unique in terms of sex, for it is the highest ranked occupation where women constitute a majority. A corollary study conducted simultaneously with the first NORC survey disclosed that Americans consider the services offered by an occupation a critical factor in assigning it a particular rank (National Opinion Research Center 1953). It seems that teachers derive status benefits from a generally favorable view of their functions and tasks. Education is defined as a proper and good thing and those who dispense it have a standing which has apparently persisted throughout much of American history.

It is conventional to connect the term "middle class" with schoolteachers, and although that class is now so large as to reduce its descriptive value, it may have particular usefulness in depicting this occupation. It connotes some of teaching's more characteristic features, such as respectability, stability in life-style, and income predictability, and it also points up the presumed necessity for continued employment. Teachers receive a certain level of respect and have the advantage of being able to plan ahead; though they are not truly affluent, their assured income permits them to undertake purchases (homes, cars, etc.) which certify their middle-class standing (National Education Association 1972). Unlike those engaged in business enterprises, however, teachers have faint hope of economic breakthroughs, of gaining that large fortune which releases one from the necessity of earning one's living. But teaching has attracted many persons who have undergone the uncertainties and deprivations of lower- and working-class life. As we shall see later, it has provided a significant step up the social class ladder for many Americans.

The Pattern of Cellular Growth

The human ecologists in sociology have taught us to look for connections between the distribution of institutions and the characteristics of the population in a given community (Hollingshead 1957). Less attention has been given, however, to ecological patterns involved within the development of particular institutions or occupations. The discussion in this section links ecological patterns to the organizational features of public schools and to the career system we find in teaching. I shall argue, that is, that the way schools grew—the "cellular" pattern—articulated both with the school as composed of multiple self-contained classrooms and with chronically high turnover in teaching ranks.

Colonial teachers were employed in separate establishments dispersed throughout settlements which were in turn distributed over extensive and sparsely populated territory. Most teachers must have gone without association with other teachers for long periods of time, except perhaps in a few large communities like Boston. Each teacher, moreover, spent his teaching day isolated from other adults; the initial pattern of school distribution represented a series of "cells" which were construed as self-sufficient.

As cities grew in size and number, school patterns changed. The previously separated cells were combined under one roof and students were assigned to separate classrooms according to age. There were some deviations from the classic pattern (such as the short-lived Lancastrian system), but the model developed in Boston soon dominated the urban scene (Elsbree 1939, p. 196). The creation of schools composed of multiple distinct classrooms, however, did not result in a sharp increase in task interdependence among teachers, since individual teachers either taught all subjects to a particular group for a year or, as later developed in the higher grades, taught a single subject to the same group for a stipulated period of time. Nor did the multiple classroom model completely replace the one-room schoolhouse with students of various ages led by one teacher: such schools, we have seen, remained numerous in rural areas well into the twentieth century. Some teachers have begun their careers in one-room schools and moved on to urban multiple-room schools without, so far as one hears, experiencing serious difficulties. Teachers' work, in short, was not radically altered by the development of the multiple-unit school. The principalship emerged, of course, and the beginnings of a hierarchy of officials took place. As before, the teacher continued to work largely alone with particular students but under the general surveillance of a full-time administrator appointed by the board of education.

It took well over a hundred years (the movement began, I believe, in the late 1950s) for serious opposition to arise to the "egg crate school." Such opposition is found today among those advocating team teaching and other arrangements in which the internal walls of the school are removed or circumvented. But throughout the long, formative decades of the modern school system, schools were organized around teacher separation rather than teacher interdependence. Curricula assumed such mutual separation and served coordinating functions by aligning the contributions of teachers in different grades and subjects to student development. Elementary education came to be seen as a matter of accretion—of serial learning in particular subjects. Secondary schooling, on the other hand, would mix notions of serial learning and contemporaneous study of different subjects. This type of organization meant that each teacher was assigned specific areas of responsibility and was expected to teach students the stipulated knowledge and skills without assistance from others. The pattern so developed remains dominant today, although there are increasing types and amounts of deviation from it. For example, teaming, open classrooms, individually programmed instruction, and other schemes based on a different interactive paradigm continue to be considered "innovative." The single cell of instruction has played a key role in the devlopment of the American public school; like any persistent feature of a social system, it became interconnected with other parts of that system.

It is likely that the persistence of separation and low task interdependence among teachers is related to the circumstances affecting the growth of schools and the demographic characteristics of those attracted to teaching. The great expansion of schools initiated in the nineteenth century continued for many decades—steady growth has been the rule in the emergence of mass public schooling. Expansion, moreover, was accomplished under somewhat special constraints; namely, the maintenance of a more-or-less fixed ratio between teachers and students. More students has meant more teachers, a connection which has not occurred in fields (e.g., agriculture and manufacturing) where technological developments have permitted fewer persons to produce greater quantities. Mass schooling has inexorably produced a larger and larger occupation.

Continued growth of the public school system required the services of thousands upon thousands of young, single women. This pool of personnel has never produced a high proportion of teachers ready to commit many years to work outside the home; and the problem of turnover was compounded by school board policies which ruled out the employment of married women. (Such restrictions prevailed well into the twentieth century.) In short, teaching was *institutionalized* as high turnover work during the nineteenth century and the modern occupation bears the marks of earlier circumstance. During many crucial decades of its development, teaching required annual infusions of many new members in order to meet the demand created by expansion and high turnover.

The growth pattern and organization of public schools have accommodated to these conditions. It was easier for those governing schools to see them as aggregates of classroom units, as collections of independent cells, than as tightly integrated "organisms." They could cope with expansion of the student population by adding new classrooms and new teachers—it was not always necessary to create new schools to absorb increased numbers. They could deal with the steady loss of experienced teachers without severe organizational shock. Assuming the teacher left at the end of the school year (and norms developed which made it reprehensible to leave during the year), new teachers could readily be placed in the former teachers' classrooms with new groups of students. Such flexibility was possible as long as teachers worked independently; but had their tasks been closely interwoven, the comings and goings of staff members would have created administrative problems.

We can see the connection between independence of effort and high turnover from another vantage point—the difficulty of constructing a closely knit division of labor when teachers' average service was short. Task interdependence would have required that each teacher find and accept a particular role within the matrix of interpersonal relationships in the school. This is difficult enough in favorable circumstances, and teachers would have had to sustain such subtle relationships under conditions of low cohesion. Therefore the continual coming and going of staff members militated against the development of that easy familiarity which permits people to mutually adapt their actions and tasks. It would have required great effort on the part of administrators and teachers to develop the necessary teamwork. It does not seem surprising, in this light, that the division of labor selected was based on gross characteristics such as age and subject matter and that coordination was minimized by assigning tasks so that each teacher worked for long periods of time without heavy interaction with colleagues.

The pattern of low task interdependence persisted after schools employed married women and the average time of service increased. But another phenomenon supported the earlier patterns: we shall explore later how married women find it difficult to expend time and energy beyond the formal work schedule. Schools where married women predominated could not count on the faculty to spend long hours on coordinative or organizational efforts.

There are other connections between the ecology of schools and personnel realities which merit mention here. The distribution of schools on the neighborhood principle, for example, matches the circumstances of married women who teach in elementary schools; dispersion throughout the community, and location in residential areas, makes it easier for such women to economize on travel time. The temporal ecology of schools (five-day weeks, short days, numerous holidays, and long summer vacations) provides more time for household duties than is available in most other lines of work; it also coincides with the schedules of school-age children. One can also argue that such schedules have provided a kind of "subsidy" which permits men to teach. The hours are such that many can take on additional employment and thus resolve the economic difficulties in teaching. What we see here is familiar to sociologists—social patterns which prevail over a long period of time encourage vested interests and resistance to change.

Eased Entry

From the perspective of more than three centuries of schooling, the creation of formal arrangements for training and certifying teachers is relatively recent. For almost two hundred years, those who taught school received no special preparation. Although provision was made for such instruction around the middle of the nineteenth century, it was at least seventy more years before most teachers had special training. The system of formal preparation and induction which developed has some note-worthy characteristics, particularly when we put it in the context of professional rhetoric which pervades public education.

Teaching was not a "regularized" occupation during colonial times; considerable variety prevailed in the qualifications of those who taught. Cremin (1970) writes that some of the grammar school teachers possessed first-rate college preparation, but it seems that most teachers, particularly those working in petty schools, had considerably less schooling. Certain general expectations were held for teachers: acceptable moral character, proficiency in the subjects to be taught, and maleness—the last being thought necessary to wielding the rod of control. There was an abortive attempt to introduce certification in the colonies, but it appears that this effort was directed primarily toward ensuring that teachers conformed to prevailing orthodoxies (Elsbree 1939, pp. 46-51). School boards "licensed" teachers a year at a time, a curious practice in which the employer attested to the qualifications of those hired. There were no general or established criteria for controlling entry—selection was made individual-by-individual by such school decision-makers as selectmen, ministers, and other leading citizens.

The preceding patterns prevailed well into the nineteenth century. But gradually the idea that women could control students took hold, and they gradually replaced men. The first normal school appeared in 1839 and was followed by the establishment of many others. Tyack believes, however, that such schools prepared only a minority of teachers before the turn of the century (1967, p. 415). High schools were anything but common during the nineteenth century, and those employed to staff the enormous expansion of public schools usually had grade-school educations. Late in the century, certification by school boards was replaced by state review and certification. Although this was initially based on a system of direct examination of candidates, states came to rely on the completion of prescribed courses of study in colleges and universities. Today the beginning teacher is normally a college graduate with special courses in education and some experience in practice teaching. The expectation of college graduation, however, is recent; Elsbree (1939) points out that in 1921 most states had no specific scholarship requirement for teaching, fourteen required only high school graduation, and a smaller number required some special work in education (p. 351). A big change had taken place by 1937, however, for by then thirty-two states required more than high school preparation, ranging from one to four years of college; it seems that the Depression permitted school boards to raise their demands. Corwin (1965) indicates, however, that it is easy to exaggerate the relative significance of these changes in teacher schooling, for the general gains in schooling in the population make it doubtful that teachers improved their standing in relation to the public at large.

Colleges and universities began to establish chairs and departments of education late in the nineteenth century, and as these increased in number liberal arts colleges became an important source of teachers for the burgeoning high schools. But the bulk of classroom teachers continued to come from other sources: by 1928, for example, all but five states had created normal schools or state teachers' colleges. These public institutions are of special interest because they symbolized a particular public policy toward the occupation. State governments played an important part in facilitating entry to teaching by creating low-cost, dispersed, and nonelitist training institutions. They thus enhanced recruitment to an occupation in which monetary rewards were, to put it cautiously, limited. It is as if the society, acting through governmental agencies, sought to offset the limited incentives of teaching by making access easier; tax funds were more readily available to train teachers than to pay them higher salaries. This policy is still evident; thousands of teachers are prepared in publicly supported college units of education not noted for their high selectivity. Federal agencies, moreover, seem more interested in facilitating the entry of disadvantaged individuals than in raising admission standards or increasing teacher income. In any event, one finds programs for training teachers in the preponderance of

18

four-year colleges; this is one of the most widely accessible types of vocational preparation conducted at the college level.

Another characteristic of the system has facilitated entry—the pattern of "contingent schooling." Many teacher preparation programs are arranged to be accessible to persons already teaching in schools; we see the results of such arrangements in the large percentage of teachers whose educational qualifications have increased greatly since they began to teach. School systems provide an incentive by paying teachers for additional study. The system is "contingent" in this sense; those who persist in teaching can choose to increase their investment in professional training while those who expect to work only for a limited time can restrict their investment to the minimum needed for employment. Minimum requirements for entry have not risen much in the last decade or two, but persisting teachers have been encouraged to increase their formal study.

I shall close this brief discussion (chapter 3 deals with these matters in more detail) by pointing out that whereas state governments have spent funds to prepare teachers, local school districts have not, to any considerable extent, engaged in large-scale in-service training programs for teachers. I am not sure why this is so; local school districts may have been unwilling to spend local resources on teachers who might move away from the home district. Other possible reasons are the dampening effect of preexisting state involvement and the limited funds available for school operations. But whatever the reasons, the lack of large-scale training of teachers at their place of work has had, as we shall see, important consequences for the development of teaching as an occupation.

The Associative Factor

Combativeness by schoolteachers is a recent phenomenon; when three centuries of teaching are taken into account, we see that the existence of associations of teachers is a recent development. We can discern three stages in the bonding together of those who work in schools: (1) near inactivity, which prevailed for more than two centuries; (2) a period of burgeoning activity, marked by "inclusiveness," in which all "professionals" belonged to the same general organizations; and (3) the recent shift to differentiated associations and forceful tactics. I shall present a brief overview of those stages in order to set current events in the context of the development of the occupation.

Associational activities were close to nonexistent from early colonial

19

days to late in the nineteenth century. Physical isolation and diversity prevailed during the colonial era; geographic barriers and extreme localism in school affairs inhibited the creation of bonds among those who worked in schools. Elsbree was unable to uncover any record of voluntary associations of teachers before the Revolution (1939, p. 246). With the advent of urbanization and the concentration of teachers in communities and multiple-unit schools, educational associations began to appear. But the groups created in the early decades of the nineteenth century proved to be ephemeral and insignificant (Elsbree 1939, chap. 20). The voluntary associations which made a difference—propaganda societies formed to promote the Common School Crusade—numbered teachers among their members, but leadership was in the hands of others, particularly lawyers. The societies advanced the concept of public schools. They did not concentrate on the occupational interests of teachers. Occupational associations did emerge, however, just before the Civil War, and these beginnings included groups on the local, state, and federal levels. Reading the accounts of these initial attempts, however, leaves one with a strong impression of elitism: for example, at the very time when women had begun to outnumber men in school work, the associations either barred women entirely or placed severe restrictions on their participation.

Associational life increased after the Civil War and accelerated during the early decades of the twentieth century. The National Education Association, initially organized so that it favored the dominance of administrators, underwent important reforms during the early years of the century. For that or other reasons, rapid expansion followed: it grew from ten thousand members in 1919 to two hundred and twenty thousand members thirteen years later (Elsbree 1939, chap. 33). State teachers' associations grew quietly between 1845 and 1900, then expanded rapidly between 1910 and 1930, hiring full-time officials and building their membership of teachers from 15 percent in 1910 to 70 percent in 1937. It appears that similar growth occurred in local teachers' associations during the second decade of this century.

The forms of association developed during this period of expansion stressed the common interests of those employed in schools rather than the differences between them. The National Education Association consisted of many subunits, and some were organized around occupational roles (e.g., distinct groupings for superintendents, principals, and teachers). State associations, though less complex, also included "all ranks" within the membership, and inclusiveness was the practice of local associations. There was talk of "an integrated profession," and of "strength through unity"; all who worked in schools were presumed to benefit from such coordinate activity. Critical and scholarly inquiry is needed, however, for we know little about the internal stresses which may have marked the years before World War II. The record indicates, however, that inclusive bonding was at least formally successful in eliciting teacher participation, since they joined by the tens of thousands. The alternative conception advanced by teacher unions failed to generate widespread commitment until after World War II and, in fact, well into the fifties. The American Federation of Teachers, founded early in the century, sought to convince teachers that their interests lay in opposition to administrators (as "employees" working for "employers"), but the message convinced few; only in a small number of large cities did teachers choose to join unions (Havighurst and Neugarten 1957).

During the fifties and sixties changes unfolded rapidly. Some dramatic union victories, particularly in New York, signaled the new mood—a mood which enveloped teachers within the National Education Association and its state affiliates. Teachers no longer defined the superintendent as their major representative to the board and the community, but took things into their own hands and demanded salary increases and other benefits through collective bargaining strategies. Teachers moved sideways, so to speak, to form stronger lateral ties as members of a common occupation whose economic interest excluded school management. Somewhere along the line the ideal of an all-inclusive organization lost its élan; in some states and some other associational activities, superintendents reacted to teacher aggressiveness by loosening their ties to inclusive associations.

It is not simple to learn where associational affairs stand at any given time, for we have no reliable or complete system of national reporting on such affairs (Lortie 1973). It seems, however, that we are witnessing a process of occupational differentiation within schools—a centrifugal movement breaking apart the almost familial ties developed during the years of inclusive organization. There is also a shift from the more passive, consensual politics of earlier decades to reliance on strikes and allied sanctions. The affairs of teachers are evidently moving in a direction similar to those of unionized workers in factories and the crafts, but it is too early to tell whether that format will become all-encompassing or whether teachers and school boards will develop unique relationships. I shall discuss some of these issues in chapters 8 and 9.

The Tilt toward Structural Continuity

Any judgment we make on the balance of change and continuity in teaching will depend partly on what area we assess. A focus on intellectual history, for example, concentrates attention on changes in curricula and pedagogical theory; emphasizing the preoccupations of successive eras leaves an impression of dynamism in matters of schooling. But when we center on structural aspects of the occupation the results are different; on that level one is impressed by the relative dominance of continuity. The range of such stabilities, moreover, is broad; it includes the disposition of authority, the status of teachers inside and outside the institution, the organization and nature of core tasks, the rate of technical change, and the conditions which surround entry to the work. Let us summarize each in turn.

Although the specific details of authority disposition have varied somewhat over the decades, the central locus of authority has not. American schools developed under the aegis of local citizens who selected representatives to supervise the schooling of their children; to this day schools are governed by representatives of the citizenry. Schools are operated on the assumption that citizens have the obligation and capacity to support and rule them; one rarely hears anyone put forth an alternative ideology of authority in school affairs. Public schools, unlike universities, have not created explicit divisions of authority among board members, administrators, and faculty. Formally and officially, all powers of governance rest in the hands of boards of education and state legislatures. Some of the specifics may be undergoing change (we will examine the role of state governments, for example, in chapter 9), but the principle of citizen control has not received serious challenge. No one argues that today's superintendents are any less vulnerable than their predecessors; school administrators possess little authority which does not depend on the continued favor of school boards. Teachers have not gained the legal right to govern their daily work affairs; they do not possess the explicit rights, for example, gained by professors, physicians hospitals, and clergymen in the armed services.

status of teachers within schools and within society at large has remained relatively stable over the years; in this respect, perhaps teaching illustrates our growing awareness of the rigidity of social rankings in general. Although teachers have managed to dull the edges of administrative power, they continue to be employed subordinates. The subtleties implied by the phrase "special but shadowed" have survived changes in contextual particulars; the shadow cast by the clergy was replaced by the favored position of professors and school administrators. The economic rank of teachers has changed little, and prestige indicators also point toward continuity. Although the average teacher today works for a longer period of years than teachers in the nineteenth century, some observers continue to lament that teaching is not a lifetime career or, in fact, a full-time commitment for many of those engaged in it. Thus, if professionalization requires sharp changes in status, it seems premature to claim that it has taken place in teaching; teaching is only partially professionalized (Lortie 1969).

The organization of teacher tasks has undergone limited modification since colonial times; one of the most important changes was the emergence of the multiple-classroom school during the nineteenth century. Despite the proximity it introduced, however, the subsequent work relationships of teachers have been marked more by separation than by interdependence; most teachers still spend most of their time working alone with a group of students in a bounded area. In industry, hundreds of occupations have come and gone over the past century; patterns of cooperation have followed technological requirements which reorder relationships among workers. The same process has occurred among the members of some professions (e.g., medicine and engineering) where new technologies have fostered new specialties and complex new interconnections among practitioners. As we shall see, the persistence of cellular organization has produced important consequences for teaching; it is itself connected with high turnover, habits of curricular thinking, and the commitments of those drawn into teaching.

Basic teaching techniques have also been extremely slow to change. The principal modes of instruction (lecturing, recitation, demonstration, seat work, small group instruction, etc.) were known and used years ago; they continue to dominate despite the increased range of possibilities (Goodlad 1970). The contrast with other occupations is impressive; one thinks, for example, of the fundamental changes in farming over the last fifty years and the associated gains in productivity. We can see the absence of any important gains in teacher productivity in similar teacher-student ratios; teachers do not claim that they can now teach more in less time.

Among the occupations of above-average social rank, teaching has continued to be marked by easy entry. During the sacred era, it was easier to teach than to preach; since the advent of secularization and the emphasis on professionalization, teaching has presented fewer obstacles than professions or some would-be professions. Entrants need not take the risks involved in acquiring a fee-for-service clientele, and admission to professional preparation has been relatively simple. Society, it seems, has preferred to get teachers by easing access rather than by offering higher rewards; thus, while other fields seeking professional recognition have been able to raise entry standards (calculating that status and income gains offset increased costs for the newcomer), the educational qualifications required of teachers have simply kept pace with general trends in the society. Those who persist in teaching, of course, acquire additional credentials; "contingent schooling" facilitates entry while encouraging those who continue teaching to add to their qualifications.

When we study the structural features of teaching, the balance tips toward continuity. Some readers, exposed to press and television accounts of recent events, may wonder, Isn't it true that collective bargaining, research and development efforts, and new financial arrangements are changing the occupation? There can be little doubt that teaching is undergoing transition; in fact, I will devote chapter 9 to these developments. But the direction of such change is by no means clear. Nor does it seem appropriate to claim, as some journalists have, that teaching has already been "revolutionized." But in an inquiry of this kind, the past is more germane than the projected future. As we shall have ample opportunity to see, the ways of teachers are deeply rooted in traditional patterns of thought and practice.

It is not likely that the continuities we have observed could have been sustained purely by accident; one does not, after all, expect institutional stability to prevail without supporting mechanisms. In the next three chapters we shall examine the principal ways teachers are differentiated from other workers in our society; specifically, we will inquire into processes of recruitment, socialization, and career rewards. From the perspective of the occupation, these processes are the means of its endurance: no occupation which fails to attract new members, inculcate its subculture, or sustain commitment through time can survive or maintain its identity. We shall find that the ways these processes unfold in teaching reaffirm much of its past. They also foster other orientations among teachers which contribute significantly to the nature of the occupational ethos.

2
Recruitment and Reaffirmation

There is nothing obvious about the ways people are routed into various kinds of work in modern society. In preliterate or caste societies it is relatively easy to predict what work a child will do; the division of labor is simple and the rules of inheritance are explicit. But in societies like ours the situation is considerably more complex. There are thousands of occupations in modern economies; individual choice not only is important but is upheld by our work ideologies. It takes inquiry, therefore, to learn how personal decisions interact with social constraints to produce the aggregate of individual decisions which result in movement into a given occupation. Can we discern regularities in personal choice? What part do ascriptive qualities (social characteristics visible at birth) play in the process? The general task of this chapter is to grapple with such issues in the case of classroom teaching; the goal is to understand as much as we can about allocation into this occupation.

Any occupation which fails to recruit new members will not survive. It is less apparent, however, that the *way* an occupation fits into the competitive recruitment system will affect its social composition and its inner life. Occupations compete, consciously or not, for members, and there is a largely silent struggle between occupations as individuals choose among alternative lines of work. Occupations proffer different advantages and disadvantages to those making choices, and people vary in their dispositions and personal circumstances—an occupation will attract some persons and repel others. Out of the combinations which ensue, an

25

occupation will come to be staffed by people of particular dispositions and life circumstances.

To draw in new members, an occupation must possess certain "recruitment resources." I wish to underscore the point that the term recruitment need not imply planning or strategy development by occupational leaders: recruitment is like the ecological processes described by Park, which operate without deliberate formulation or control (Park and Burgess 1924). Recruitment resources consist of the properties which assist an occupation in competing for manpower and talent. There are two major types of resources: attractors and facilitators. The first consists of comparative benefits (and costs) proferred would-be entrants; it includes money, prestige and power, and the psychic attractions of the occupational tasks. The second set of resources is less commonly noted; it rests on social mechanisms which help people move into the work (we have already encountered an example in the pattern of "eased entry").

We will seek to identify the recruitment resources of teaching, examining first the attractors and later the facilitators. In reviewing known attractors, we will analyze their content and examine the appeal they emphasize. Our discussion of facilitators will link them to the life circumstances of those who have entered teaching. Do recruitment resources in teaching attract particular kinds of people with particular orientations toward work and schooling? If so, how are such orientations likely to influence the ethos of the occupation? What connection, if any, prevails between modes of recruitment into teaching and the tilt toward continuity we found in chapter 1?

The Attractions of Teaching

We can find what occupational characteristics attract people to a given line of work by using a model of career decisions as choices among competing alternatives. In such a model a particular occupation is presumed to "win out" over competitors because it offers greater advantage to those making choices. To identify which characteristics elicit commitments, I questioned those within the occupation, asking them to describe the attractions they saw in it and to identify those which made it more attractive than the alternatives they seriously considered. I developed this approach during earlier work on legal careers (Lortie 1958).

This section has two major parts. In the first we will review data in which teachers described the attractions they saw in teaching; the data consist of intensive interviews in five towns in the Boston metropolitan area, hereafter referred to as "Five Towns" (for details, see Appendix A), and national surveys conducted by the National Education Association (NEA)[1] Although the interviews were conducted and analyzed before I encountered the NEA surveys, there is sufficient convergence for joint use. The second part of the section concentrates specifically on the material benefits of teaching and their differential meaning for men and for women.

Five Attractors to Teaching

The Interpersonal Theme. One of the most obvious characteristics of teaching is that it calls for protracted contact with young people. To cite this as an attraction seems almost tautological, but this is not so when we compare teaching with other kinds of work; very few occupations involve such steady interaction with the young. It led the list of attractions among Five Towns teachers, although it is interesting that some respondents did not specify that the interactions were primarily with children—they simply said they liked "to work with people."[2]

"Desire to work with young people" led the selections of NEA respondents: 34 percent of the 2,316 teachers answering the questionnaire chose it. It appealed equally to men and women in the total sample, but 10 percent more elementary than secondary teachers checked it as their predominant reason for choosing teaching careers (NEA 1967, p. 47).

Contact with young people helps teaching in its competition for members; on reflection, we observe that it occupies a favored competitive position in this regard. Unlike other major middle-class occupations involving children, such as pediatric nursing and some kinds of social work, teaching provides the opportunity to work with children who are neither ill nor especially disadvantaged. Those who want such contact can visualize it taking place under "'normal'" conditions which do not include sickness, poverty, or emotional disturbance. The psychological needs which underlie an interest in working with children are undoubtedly varied and complex, and there is no research which justifies the concept of a single personality type among teachers (Getzels and Jackson 1963). The care of youngsters is generally said to be especially consistent with the social definition of women's work in our society. It is interesting therefore that the data do not show that women have a marked preference for this attraction. Perhaps it is a matter of intensity rather than extensity; but we will need subtler measures before we can settle this point.

Some Five Towns teachers preferred to talk about teaching as "work with people," not emphasizing the age differences involved. This rhetoric suggests that they perceive interpersonal work as valuable.

27

Rosenberg (1957) found that a large proportion of college students sought work which offered much contact with people. It is provocative, moreover, that the highest-ranked occupations in our society (high government office, the learned professions, and positions of business leadership) reveal a gregarious cast. "Working with people" carries a certain aura, and to so define the work of teachers adds dignity and enhances the self-esteem of members of the occupation.

Teachers are involved with knowledge and its diffusion; their work has also been described as an "art" requiring special sensitivity and personal creativity. Involvement with knowledge and the call for creativity could quite logically serve as foci for attraction to teaching. It is therefore interesting that neither of these aspects of the role receives as much attention as the interpersonal. More than twice as many NEA respondents chose the interpersonal theme as chose "interest in a subject-matter field," the alternative closest to expressing intellectual interests. The NEA survey did not include interest in creativity as an option, an omission which is itself suggestive. And at most a handful of Five Towns teachers gave responses which could be construed as concern with creativity. Perhaps this points to conventionality in the sense that classroom teachers are closer to popular culture and less differentiated than, for example, artists and certain categories of intellectuals.

The Service Theme. Although their status has been shadowed, teachers have been perceived as performing a special mission in our society, and we see the continuation of that conception among those engaged in the work today. The idea that teaching is a valuable service of special moral worth is a theme in the talk of Five Towns teachers.[3] Respondents in the NEA national survey chose the option "opportunity for rendering important service" in 28 percent of the instances, making it the second most frequent response. Women were a little more inclined to stress it than were men, selecting it 29 percent of the time compared with 25 percent among men; and elementary teachers were even more inclined to favor it, with a percentage of 32 compared with 23 percent of the secondary teachers.

One can argue that teaching as service is grounded in both sacred and secular aspects of American culture. To Christians, Jesus is "the Great Teacher"; teaching has been an honored vocation within the Roman Catholic church for centuries; the Jewish tradition is steeped in the love of learning. Thus those who define work as an expression of their religious faith can connect teaching with their beliefs; this gives teaching a resource of considerable potency. As we saw in chapter 1, Americans respect the secular version of the service ideal, ranking occupations partially in such terms. The definition of teaching as service to others is a recruitment resource of some significance.

The service appeal of teaching, however, cannot be described as universal, for to see teaching as service, one must attach a certain degree of efficacy to it. It makes little sense to define teaching as service if one is skeptical about its conduct or value. One might, of course, enter teaching to change it; but as we shall see later, it is difficult to find members of the occupation who so describe their entry. One can infer that teaching as service is more likely to appeal to people who approve of prevailing practice than to those who are critical of it.

The Continuation Theme. Sociologists normally depict schools as socialization agencies charged with preparing students for adult roles in other parts of the society. It is clear, however, that some who attend school become so attached to it that they are loath to leave. Five Towns teachers talked of such attachments and referred to them as attractions to the occupation.[4] Some said they "liked school" and wanted to work in that setting; others mentioned school-linked pursuits and the difficulty of engaging in them outside educational institutions. A teacher might, for example, have affection for a hard-to-market subject like ancient history or be interested in athletics but not have the ability needed for a professional career in sports. Each can find in teaching a medium for expressing his interests. Some high school teachers told how teaching "came close" to a primary, but blocked, aspiration; an English teacher, for example, may substitute directing school plays for an earlier hope to act. Teaching can serve as the means of satisfying interests which might have originally been fostered and reinforced in school; this attraction has a built-in quality.

The NEA survey did not ask about continuing such interests, but perhaps some of those selecting "interest in a subject-matter field" fall into this category. That response drew many more high school than elementary teachers (23 percent versus 5 percent), but that could be a result of the wording, which designated specialized interest in one subject rather than general attachment to school.

A mass system of public schooling means that millions of young people move through the schools; it is hardly surprising that some develop lasting affiliations. Widespread contact with each generation is a powerful recruitment resource possessed by few occupations. Yet we must recall that the attraction of continuation is not universal among the young. The concept will probably be unattractive to those who look forward to new experience and novel challenges; to "stay in school" will strike some as surrendering their passport to engage in specifically adult activities. Is it not likely, therefore, that fewer of those who opt to continue with school will have a strong interest in the new and untried? It also seems probable that those who feel positive enough about school to stay with it will be more likely to approve of existing arrangements and will be less motivated to press for change. The continuation theme, in short, appears to have a conservative bias.

Material Benefits. There are reasons why teachers underplay the role of material rewards in their decision to enter the occupation. Historically the status has been defined as underrewarded; teachers addressing others may hesitate to cite material benefits when in the public eye such rewards are said to be inadequate. But I suspect that the emphasis on service, on teachers as "dedicated," is a more potent source of inhibition, since many people both inside and outside teaching believe that teachers are not supposed to consider money, prestige, and security as major inducements. Such normative pressures make it probable that material benefits influence teachers' decisions more than their answers indicate. There is indirect evidence, at least, that such normative inhibition is at work; we will discuss it after summarizing the direct data.

More Five Towns teachers were willing to list material benefits as attractions to teaching than as key factors in their decision to teach[5] (these benefits include money, prestige, and employment security). The NEA study included two benefits as possible "predominant reasons"; 6 percent chose "security" and only 2 percent "financial rewards." Men were slightly readier to cite security (8 percent versus 5 percent) and women, money benefits (2.1 percent versus 0.6 percent). The NEA options did not include prestige.

There are two aspects of teaching which make the few references to material benefits puzzling. Viewed in the context of occupations with a large proportion of *women,* teaching salaries are not notaby deficient, particularly when the relatively fewer working days per year are taken into account. The usual alternatives considered by women teachers normally offer no greater income and may, in fact, offer less. The other fact that leads one to expect greater emphasis on material rewards is that a significant proportion of men who teach come from homes marked by economic insecurity and low social status.

The thought that normative inhibitions reduce teachers' readiness to include material benefits among the major attractions gains support from indirect data gathered in Five Towns. Respondents were asked why *other* teachers were in the occupation—they were asked to project motivations onto unnamed others rather than to talk about themselves (question 39, Appendix B-1). Using categories for money, security, and prestige and an additional one for time compatibility, we find provocative differences in the distributions of self-ascribed and other-ascribed motivations. The theme of service increases on the "projective" item, suggesting that if normative inhibitions are indeed less there may be more references to idealistic considerations: 42 percent of the answers about others refer to service compared with 17 percent in the self-descriptive, major factors question. The most striking difference, however, refers to material benefits. In the projective item, the general category had to be subdivided to accommodate the more frequent mentions. Although all material benefits together were mentioned only 6 percent of the time on the self-descriptive item, each single benefit elicited frequent mentions in the projective question (money, 37 percent; security, 34 percent; and prestige, 12 percent). Respondents who were reluctant to depict material benefits as influential in their own cases show no such hesitation when interpreting the behavior of teachers in general. Interpretation of such a difference is hazardous— it might, for example, imply depreciation of colleagues rather than a projection of personal feelings. But it does at least suggest that these respondents are aware of the drawing power of material benefits.

The differences by sex in the question about other teachers' interests are also provocative. A category had to be included for those who said, one way or another, that "teaching is a good job for women." (The 19 percent involved included both men and women.) But men and women differed in their emphasis on money as an attraction; 54 percent of the women and 39 percent of the men alluded to it. The fact that more than half the women teachers saw money as a positive feature in attracting and holding others indicates that we should be skeptical about the 2 percent statistic in the NEA study. One is forced to wonder, in fact, at the reliability of subjective testimony on this matter. I suspect that the research we need to estimate the effects of material benefits on recruitment should focus on the decisions people make rather than on their later interpretation.

The Theme of Time Compatibility. The working schedules of teachers have always been special; although the length of the school year has increased steadily over the last century, most Americans are required to work considerably more days per year than the average teacher.[6] Teachers are sensitive to criticism about this, and one senses that reaction in the statistics their national association gathers to show that teachers actually work longer hours than formal school schedules require (NEA 1972, p. 34). The fact remains, however, that the teacher's schedule features convenient gaps which play a part in attracting people to the occupation. Work days which are finished in midafternoon, numerous holidays, and long summer vacations do not go unnoticed by young people comparing teaching with alternative possibilities.

As with material benefits, more Five Towns teachers listed the work schedule as an attraction than were ready to accord it a major role.[7] It figured prominently, however, in the question where respondents were asked to interpret the behavior of other teachers; in that context, 44 percent mentioned it, and women did so oftener than males—54 percent versus 26 percent.[8]

Five Towns respondents who said that schedules attracted them related working hours to other obligations and pursuits. The dominant obligations referred to were those associated with wifehood and motherhood; the schedule permits time for shopping, household duties, and so on, and matches the schedules of school-age children. Although a few men mentioned compatibility with family life as an attraction, more pointed out that teaching schedules allowed them to undertake further study or do other kinds of work.

The compatibility of teaching schedules is probably a potent recruitment resource; few occupations can offer men and women with other interests such flexibility. Yet it has some disadvantages. Teachers are sometimes criticized for having "easy jobs" (Vidich and Bensman 1958). Occupational leaders do not seem inclined to use this attraction to obtain recruits; they probably feel that it is inconsistent with the occupation's status as a service field and that treating teaching as a means to other ends tends to reduce its intrinsic value. One suspects, moreover, that those who are drawn into teaching primarily by this attractor are less likely to identify strongly with the occupation and its interests. One would not expect people who selected teaching because it made limited claims on their time to give long hours of extra service. If this is so, compatibility is also indirectly conservative in its effects; change in an occupation normally requires extra effort from its members.

The testimony of classrooms teachers makes it clear that the occupation possesses potent attractors. Teaching is special in at least two respects: few occupations can offer similar opportunities for protracted contact with normal children, and few can provide such compatible work schedules. The definition of teaching as service (the aura of its mission) sets it apart from many other ways to earn a living. Schools instill interests and attitudes which help recruit the next generation of faculty members.

Although muted, material benefits play their part in drawing persons into the occupation.

Analysis of the appeal of the several attractors, however, reveals important limits on their scope; taken together, they affect the distribution of values we would expect to find among new entrants. There is a reiterated emphasis on conserving the past rather than changing educational institutions, implicit in the themes of service and continuation. The tendency of teachers to stress the interpersonal suggests conventionality rather than a special, deviant point of view; the operation of time compatibility is probably indirectly conservative. We are speaking, of course, of propensities and probabilities rather than of absolutes, of a bias toward continuity rather than of a uniform predisposition common to all teachers. What makes these propensities of special interest, however, is that they reappear when we examine the circumstances which facilitate entry to teaching. Those circumstances and the accompanying facilitators will be discussed immediately after the next section.

Material Benefits and Sex Differences

The reluctance of teachers to link their entry to material benefits need not deter us from trying to understand how such attractions affect recruitment and, in particular, influence the sex composition of the occupation. In chapter 1, I pointed out that the types of material benefits proffered by teaching are likely to operate somewhat differently for men and women. Although each attracts members of both sexes, each appears to vary in the meaning (and possible intensity) it has for them. I will review three kinds of material benefits from this point of view, using data from Five Towns and from national surveys.

Money Income and Alternatives Foregone. Occupational choice is an either-or decision where one selection rules out others, most likely permanently. Economists have a useful concept which they use as part of the calculus of rational choice—the idea of "alternatives foregone." We can extend the concept and think of any given selection as being more or less subjectively costly to individuals (and categories of individuals) when we take into account the aspirations set aside when, for whatever reasons, they enter a given line of work. When we make this transposition into a social psychological definition, we need not assume that rational choices were made or, in fact, that the sacrificed aspirations were indeed assured. Approached this way, it turns out that entering teaching is subjectively more costly for men than for women.

Approximately three-quarters of the Five Towns teachers considered another occupation before entering teaching (question 9, Appendix B-1). *All* the alternatives they mentioned were middle-class and upper-middle-class occupations, and 59 percent were interpersonal work with some element of public service. They were not aiming low in their work aspirations. But men and women did not choose teaching from the same list of possibilities. Whereas the men considered business administration and the professions, women thought about semiprofessions (nursing, library work, and social work), office positions, and the performing arts. Except for a small number of women who entertained hope of working in the high-prestige professions, there was no overlap in the alternatives men and women considered. Teaching is the one occupation on which both sexes converged.

It is evident that men and women will feel that they sacrificed different levels of income (and prestige) in order to teach. With the exception of the performing arts, the women's alternatives are marked by similar or lower earnings. One can become rich and famous in the performing arts, but such success is rare. Young women who opt for teaching (or parents who influence them to do so) are not usually following a course which involves material sacrifice. Men who enter teaching, however, find it less difficult to avoid feeling that their teaching careers have brought them less than the alternatives would have yielded; the lifetime earnings of business executives and professionals (and their social positions) clearly exceed those of classroom teachers.

Economists will argue that what has been said will make teaching less attractive to men than to women and that this will perpetuate female dominance of teaching ranks. Granted. What I wish to point out, however, is that some men do become teachers and that their sense of loss has a depressing effect on the recruitment of younger men. We can reason that male teachers will have greater material motives for regretting their fates and are thus less likely to project high enthusiasm for their work. We will see later that identification with teachers plays an important part in recruitment and that young men and women tend to identify with members of the same sex. To the extent that a subjective sense of deprivation makes male teachers less acceptable as models, there is a systematic tendency for the occupation to attract more women than men. The differential distribution by sex of material rewards of money and prestige therefore probably has effects beyond its role in the original calculus of choice.

Social Mobility. The special mission of teachers gives their occupation a standing somewhat higher than we would expect solely on the basis of income. We have just alluded to the limits on the prestige of the occupation when it is compared with the highest ranked fields; it is useful, however, to examine the other side of the stratification equation. Teaching is clearly white-collar, middle-class work, and as such offers upward mobility for people who grew up in blue-collar or lower-class families.

Although it is a truism that teaching has benefited from its position as a mobility ladder, it remains difficult to obtain precise information on how many teachers have ascended by entering the occupation. There are thorny technical problems in making estimates on the matter, especially in classifying the original social rank of teachers whose parents were engaged in farming. [9] We can, however, confirm the presence of considerable upward mobility by making conservative use of available data.

A national sample study conducted by the NEA reveals that "the social backgrounds of teachers come close to representing a cross-section of the American public," except for a slight upward bias (NEA 1963, p. 15). Thirty percent of the teachers sampled came from homes where the father was a blue-collar worker. A crude index of mobility within teaching, therefore, is provided by the difference between offspring and their parents; since teaching outranks blue-collar occupations, the sons and daughters of blue-collar parents have climbed significantly by entering teaching (National Opinion Research Center 1953). The procedure is conservative, however, in that it disregards mobility among those who came from lower-status rural families. Using the 30 percent figure, we can estimate that in an occupation now numbering over two million members, somewhere around six hundred thousand persons have crossed the boundary between blue-collar and white-collar work. Teaching appears to be one of the more important routes into the middle class.

Men and women do not benefit equally from these mobility gains. The NEA data disclose that women teachers typically originate in higher-status homes than men in the occupation; for example, more men teachers' fathers were blue-collar workers.[10] Perhaps the disparity stems in part from the differential opportunities perceived by women and men. We noted that within the usual framework of possibilities considered by women, teaching ranks high; it can appeal, therefore, to relatively advantaged women. With their wider range of possibilities, men are less likely to choose teaching if they have socioeconomic advantages. But whatever underlies the disparity, teaching is a more important medium of upward mobility for men than for women.

The subtle differences in the meaning of mobility and prestige for men and women in teaching makes it risky to assign it much greater salience for one or the other. From available data we can infer that mobility as such draws in more men. Yet the acceptability of the occupation for women of higher social background also facilitates their entry. It seems, then, that the social rank of the occupation recruits differentially among men and women, influencing members of both sexes but producing recruits of somewhat different social class backgrounds.

Employment Security. American work ideologies tend to denigrate impulses toward employment security, and occupations are sometimes derided by calling their incumbents "security-seekers." This ideology seems a poor description, however, of the economic behavior of many who voice it: the readiness to take protracted risk does not appear abundant. Our task here, however, is not to analyze the gap between ideology and reality in American society, but to uncover some of the meanings security has for men and women in teaching. Employment security is basic to other work rewards; the unemployed earn none.

Anyone studying teaching during the sixties was bound to encounter men whose fathers were on the fringes of the economy during the Great Depression of the thirties. Teachers who grew up in those years (particularly in working-class homes) can have sharp recollections of the pain of economic insecurity.[11] The NEA survey I have referred to makes it clear that a noteworthy proportion of male teachers came from homes where the breadwinner had little protection against unemployment or under-employment during the depression. It seems highly probable, therefore, that some of these men, upon being discharged from the armed services at the end of World War II, chose to use their educational subsidies to prepare for work which was more secure than their fathers'. The flow of veterans into teaching during the postwar years is therefore related to the depression; college education was an unexpected boon for some, and although they may have dreamed of higher-income occupations, it seems likely that they valued the security proffered by classroom teaching.

Women have somewhat different reasons to appreciate the security of teaching. Fewer women grew up in economically vulnerable homes and even fewer would have expected to play the role of principal bread-winner. Employment security can, however, be meaningful to both single and married women. The single woman is assured of a predictable income without having to compete aggressively with men. For those who marry, the economic aspects of security are probably less important, but there are psychological and family-connected benefits. The absence of employment anxiety after tenure has been attained helps to make teaching compatible with marriage and motherhood. If these married women were forced to compete actively to hold their jobs, it would be considerably more difficult for them to balance the rival claims of work and family. Employment security makes it easier for married women "to keep work in its place." If they must miss time at work, as when a child is ill, they need not fear discharge. Given the complexities which confront women who combine marriage and motherhood with full-time employment, security gives leverage in an intrinsically delicate situation.

Security is an important recruitment resource for teaching, and I suspect that it exerts more influence than teachers are ready to accord it. The NEA survey indicated that more men than women were ready to assign it a key role in their entry, but the difference was only 3 percent. Since it serves valued purposes for members of both sexes, it is not critical in perpetuating the predominance of women. But we should not be surprised when teachers react strongly to perceived threats to their economic security—a case in point is the New York strike of 1968 (Mayer 1969).

Among the material benefits of teaching, it appears that money most clearly differentiates the appeal of teaching for men and women. Men place teaching salaries in a different comparative context, and they are thus considerably more attractive to women than to men. What makes great change unlikely is that the marginal utility of additional salary is greater for women than for men; attempts to draw in more men by raising general salaries are likely to produce a greater number of highly qualified women applicants. Employers are faced with a dilemma: Are there controlling reasons to hire men even where their qualifications are less impressive than those of available women? Even if some employers were so convinced, could they implement such policies in view of the adverse public sentiment symbolized by the Women's Liberation Movement, laws proscribing discrimination against women, and the collective power of women in teacher organizations? It seems most doubtful. Traditional modes of compensating teachers are likely to enhance the continued preponderance of women in classroom teaching.

Two General Facilitators

We observed in chapter 1 that entry to teaching has been facilitated by such mechanisms as highly accessible training and nonelitist admission standards. Two other ways entry to teaching is eased have something in common—each broadens the pool of potential candidates for the occupation.

Chapter Two

The Wide Decision Range

Some occupations have a narrow "decision range" because they are not visible to the very young or because they require that the first of a mandatory series of decisions be made at an early point. Few youngsters, for example, are sufficiently aware of actuarial science to choose it at an early age; at the other end of the scale, it is difficult to become a concert musician or a physician if one has not taken the preparatory steps early in life. Occupations which discourage early decisions or constrict later ones will at any time have smaller pools of potential candidates than those with wide "decision ranges."

People can decide to become teachers at any of a number of points. Since the occupation is ubiquitous and highly visible in the lives of children, it can easily figure in their fantasies about adult occupational activity; even young children can make persisting decisions to enter teaching. At the other end of the continuum, it is possible to decide on teaching late and still implement the decision: in Five Towns, for example, several people decided in their thirties to enter teaching. There are supports for decisions made both early and late; since teaching is perceived as among the more accessible occupations, adults feel less pressure to protect youngsters who wish to teach against their possible disappointment; and training institutions have been ready to admit, and school systems to hire, "older" people.

There are indications in Five Towns and in other samples that variations in the age of decision are patterned by sex and school level. Thus 63 percent of the women teachers in Five Towns decided before they graduated from high school, but only 24 percent of the men did so; 41 percent of the men, in fact, waited until their last year in college or later to commit themselves to teaching (question 6, Appendix B-1). Kronus found a similar sex difference in her sample, and Benjamin Wright found that women considered teaching earlier than men did (Kronus 1969, p. 23; Wright, personal communication). With sex held constant, elementary teachers in Five Towns and in Wright's sample decided earlier than secondary teachers. Women, especially those who select elementary teaching, are the most eager recruits; men are more hesitant.

A wide decision range has other consequences in addition to enlarging the candidate pool: one is heterogeneity in patterns of entry. One might expect early decisions to show more affective properties than those made by older people, who have more information; late decisions, on the other hand, may point to considerable "compromise" as hopes and plans are realistically assessed (Ginzberg et al. 1951). Some teachers, therefore, will talk about teaching in glowing terms, as a "calling" they chose early and have given unwavering commitment; others will talk about their choice as a compromise with reality's demands. This is a potential source of cleavage among teachers since those at each extreme may be uncomfortable about the others' valuations of teaching. The heterogeneity of entry patterns indicates that teaching is not, in this regard, standardized by professional consensus, nor is its membership carefully screened through shared criteria for admission. Consequently there is considerable *self-selection;* the motivations, orientations, and interests candidates bring are not systematically assessed to eliminate those whose characteristics fail to fit a particular model. As we shall note in later chapters, the diversity so permitted has important consequences for the inner life of the occupation.

The Subjective Warrant

Licenses to practice regulated occupations are issued by governments after candidates have passed the stipulated examinations. But this is the culmination of a longer process during which individuals have played a critical part by qualifying or disqualifying themselves; those who sustain an ambition have tested and retested themselves in terms of a personal conception of what their goal will demand, and have in their own eyes passed those tests. We find examples in adolescent boys' testing their dexterity to see whether they have "surgeon's hands" or arguing with peers to see whether they might succeed in law. It is instructive to know what people think is required for success in a given work role, for this indicates the subjective filters associated with the occupation—its "subjective warrant." Occupations with stringent warrants will lose more would-be members through self-discouragement than will those with permissive warrants.

Given the tendency to ease entry into teaching, we might expect to find that subjective tests are also less than stringent. We can examine this possibility with data gathered in Five Towns, where teachers told what personal qualities they thought suited them for teaching (question 11, App. B-1). Analysis produced three types of answers: (1) statements of personal preference; (2) references to interpersonal capacities and dispositions; and (3) allusions to intellectual interests and abilities. A quarter of the responses fell into the first category, with such answers as "I liked children and wanted to work with them." The modal response, however, dealt with personal characteristics like patience, a sense of humor, leadership ability, and a calm and self-possessed nature (slightly over half selected those). The third category, intellectual strengths and interests, was mentioned least, getting fewer than a fifth of the responses. These responses included knowledge of a subject, intelligence, being well-organized, and enjoying learning. Interpersonal qualities and preferences were mentioned more than three times as often as intellectual attributes in Five Towns; such differences, even in a limited sample, command attention. This emphasis on the interpersonal is consistent with the themes of attraction we examined earlier.

The subjective warrant implied by the Five Towns data is not stringent. The preferential responses are logically circular: wanting to teach becomes justification for doing so. Interpersonal qualities, even though not possessed by everyone, suggest a plastic rather than a resistant warrant—one which an individual can shape to suit his purposes. It is difficult, after all, to be sure one does *not* possess the cited qualities. Intellectual criteria, on the other hand, are rendered "scarce" by academic grading systems which depend upon ranking. The question is not whether respondents selected "the best criteria" but rather the effects of using a particular set of criteria. The attributes teachers chose—preferences and interpersonal characteristics—were less likely to force self-elimination than would more stringent standards of self-assessment. The data suggest that there is a social psychological correlate to structurally eased entry; in both instances the hurdles are set at the lower notches.

A final comment. It is interesting that the permissive warrant fits so neatly with the existence of early and late deciders. It prevents those making early decisions from seeing the aspiration to teach as ridiculously high. It also helps those making late decisions to avoid worry about their lack of protracted and specialized preparation for the role: since personality and preference rule, other considerations are secondary. One also observes that the content of the warrant has a "feminine ring"; it emphasizes expressive qualities which, as Parsons and Bales (1955) point out, are presumed to differentiate women in the American division of labor between the sexes.

Specific Circumstances and Special Facilitators

People may join an occupation for reasons besides its desirable qualities; personal circumstances can play a vital role in their occupational fates. Sociologists use the concept of "life contingency" to refer to such conditions and have contributed this perspective to multidisciplinary efforts to develop theories of occupational choice (Ginzberg 1951). One need not deny the importance of rational components in occupational selection to note that options can be constrained or individuals be unwilling to make cool and calculated choices. In this section we will identify circumstances which are associated with entry to teaching and examine the recruitment resources they imply.

In both Five Towns and the national NEA survey, some respondents made it clear that personal circumstances played a major part in their entering teaching. In Five Towns, some "jumped the logic" of quesions to do so; they disregarded inquiry into the attractions of teaching to describe how others influenced their decision or to mention constraints which made the attractions of secondary importance. Other resondents denied the premise of choice among alternatives; they told of "always wanting to teach" and denied that they had given serious consideration to other possibilities. Such respondents corrected for the rational bias built into the interview and revealed the limitations of any model which assumes entirely independent, unconstrained, and carefully weighed decision-making.

Those who designed the NEA survey were not committed to a particular decision model; they included personal events in the list of responses presented to respondents. Thus we find 6.4 percent of those responding chose "A tradition in my family" as the main consideration in their decision.[12] An additional 6 percent selected "Example set by a favorite teacher," a response referring to processes of identification rather than general characteristics of the occupation.[13] Shirley Stokes's study of Ontario elementary teachers revealed that they thought classroom teachers and family members had played a large part in their entry (Stokes, n.d.). Wright and Tuska (1968) have analyzed the occupational choice of teachers in terms of complex processes of identification within the family. The factor of constraint in decisions to teach is frequently mentioned within public school circles, but it has received little or no research attention; the NEA list, for example, did not give respondents an opportunity to talk about the absence of alternatives. The closest was a self-incriminating "Unsuccessful in another line of work" which, unsurprisingly, drew only 0.4 percent of the responses.

This section is based on the analysis of recurrent themes in Five Towns. I will present specific circumstances which emerged in the course of analyzing the entire entry section of the interview. I will begin with relatively "affective" kinds of choice situations and then turn to those in which external constraints played an important part. My primary purpose is to find the ways people move into teaching and to explore their implications for recruitment resources.

Chapter Two

Early and Affective Decisions

It is not easy to visualize an eight- or ten-year-old child engaging in an informed search of all occupational alternatives and rationally weighing relative costs and benefits before making a choice. The image strains imagination; even the presumption of information, much less the capacity to evaluate, violates what we know about children. Confronted by early occupational decisions, therefore, it makes sense to use models which do not assume pure rationality. What emotional experiences attract children to a given occupation and solder them to an early commitment?

Early decisions do occur in the teaching occupation; this has been established by several studies (Kronus 1969; Wright and Tuska 1968). The fact itself is interesting, for it demonstrates that teaching possesses recruitment resources beyond its relative attractiveness in cost and benefit terms. We know that identifications with teachers and with family members who teach contribute to entry; there is also evidence that familial reinforcement contributes to the decision. Identifications and reinforcement are psychological processes, but they rest in turn upon sociological conditions. Identification cannot occur without appropriate models, and reinforcement cannot occur without environments which support the aspiration to become a teacher. These surrounding conditions will dominate our attention. (Others are better qualified to analyze the psychodynamics involved, particularly the role of unconscious psychological processes [Wright and Tuska 1968].)

The discussion is based on analysis of the transcripts of women elementary teachers in Five Towns. Early decisions were markedly more frequent in that subgroup, and there is reason to believe that this is general.[14] The three kinds of entry we shall review are based on what appears to be the primary process in each individual case; any such classification, however, ought to be seen as tentative, since it could mask the extent to which the processes described are more general, and since each type of entry involves a complex combination of influences. I shall note some promising connections which, because of the small number of cases, must be seen as hypothetical at this time. This area needs more research, and I hope that these hypotheses will be helpful to other investigators.

Identification with Teachers and the Marginality Hypothesis. Among those reporting an early decision and an enduring commitment to teaching, some respondents emphasized how strongly they identified with

42

a single teacher or with teachers in general. Sometimes the respondent was unable to pick a particular point of decision, saying that she "always wanted to teach" and "never considered anything else." Others did recall a particularly dramatic point in their early lives. The following is an example:

I decided in the first grade of school. Absolutely, too. I couldn't understand a word of English. I went home to my mother and said "I'm going to be a schoolteacher." [What do you think attracted you to teaching?] I think the teacher. Most first grade teachers do influence their pupils, and I liked it. I didn't understand a lot because I couldn't speak English, but I did enjoy being with the youngsters and having fun and learning something. [Did the teacher take special interest in you, do you think?] No. I don't think so. Although I was a novelty because I was of Greek descent and I was the only Greek girl in the school....But I do remember one strange incident. You know my name is very difficult to pronounce in English. So she got as close to it as she could and called it——, so I've been——ever since. *That's how I was named an American.* [#20, F-54-1st][15]

The quotation illustrates another theme which was linked with early identification with teachers—the theme of cultural or social marginality. Sociologists have long been interested in the social psychology of "marginal persons" who live at the intersection of two cultures (Stonequist 1930). The children of immigrant parents often experience such marginality as they try to cope with the divergent cultures of home and the community at large. Historians have pointed out that schools have played a key role in "Americanizing" the offspring of the foreign-born, but they have not, to my knowledge, discussed the potency of the teacher as a cultural symbol. The teacher can stand as an image of mastery of the world which is problematic for the marginal student; in the instance cited, the teacher performed the psychologically striking function— normally performed by parents—of naming the child. The teacher can serve as a personal link for the strange child in an alien community: the teacher possesses and shares the knowledge needed to escape that strangeness. It seems likely that teacher influence depends partly on parental reactions to such identifications; Five Towns respondents told of parental support.

We can hypothesize that some early deciders identify with classroom teachers in order to resolve sharp problems of identity induced by marginal status. Kronus's research on early-deciding high school teachers (primarily female) revealed that they (1) were more frequently the daughters of foreign-born parents and (2) more frequently had mothers who worked predominantly in lower-status occupations (Kronus 1969, pp. 88–90). One could interpret her findings in similar terms; the daughters of foreign-born women and women with low-status jobs may find them less than adequate as models and turn to the teacher as at least a partial substitute. It might also be worth inquiring into the possibility that marginality is only one circumstance which complicates identity-formation and that other difficulties might also make children identify with teachers.

Regardless of the specific circumstances which make such identification likely, it remains an important recruitment resource. We might choose to ignore the mechanisms in question, arguing that since millions of children pass through schools, even random tendencies to identify outside the home will produce a significant number of commitments to teaching. There is, however, another propensity which is relevant here—the tendency of children to identify with same-sex adults, a tendency exhibited both in Five Towns and in Wright's data.[16] The widespread contact of children with teachers fosters identifications which can turn into occupational decisions; by the same token, however, the distribution of men and women in the occupation, particularly the preponderance of women in elementary schools, provides many more potential models for girls than for boys. Quite unintentionally, one suspects, those who developed our system of mass schooling solved part of the recruitment problem for teaching in making school part of every child's experience. The sequence of events that made teaching in elementary schools primarily women's work initiated a self-perpetu-ating cycle in which identification produces more early, affective deci-sions among girls. Identification with classroom teachers, therefore, is another recruitment resource which fosters continuity rather than discon-tinuity in the occupation.

Continuity within the Family. One is not surprised to find that some children choose to follow the same occupations as their parents and other kin; not only does identification encourage such occupational inheri-tance, but occupational choices express values which are influenced by parents. Parents who see teaching as an avenue for expressing service to others are likely to instill the general value and to exemplify a linked occupational choice; family encouragement is a powerful recruitment resource.

As a massive occupation marked by high turnover, teaching has thousands upon thousands of former members (particularly women) rais-ing children as well as vast numbers who still teach and raise families. The result is that many families have a teacher in a position of influence; in Five Towns, one third of the respondents spontaneously reported that teachers were among their close relatives. (A standard question asked of all would probably have produced a higher percentage.)

A respondent who decided on teaching while in elementary school illustrates the process of identification within the family.

I think the fact that my father has always been a teacher had a great deal to do with it. I've always heard about teaching and so forth. I think that was the big thing—my father.

The nonrational nature of her decision was underscored:

I don't think I had any practical view in my mind when I was in elementary school. I may have changed my mind if I did. [Did your father encourage you?] Yes, very much so. [#39 F-31-6th]

The sheer size of the occupation, therefore, provides it with a large number of recruitment "agents" within American family life; such agents can serve as models or actively encourage teaching, or both. In instances where this influences people to enter teaching, elements of continuity are doubly apparent, for they include esteem for one's family as well as the emulation of teachers.

Labeling by Significant Others. Symbolic interactionists since Cooley and Mead have argued that personal identity is influenced by how others respond to one; one aspect of such influence is the labeling of a child's behavior and the attribution of occupational futures (Cooley 1956; Mead 1934). This process is likely to develop, reasonably enough, when others observe particular propensities in a person and attach specific meaning to them.

I just think I was pretty good at explaining things to other people and I was often called upon by my teacher to instruct, even in high school. It just came naturally, I guess. They used to say I was a born teacher.... When we played, I was always "the teach." [#3 F-69-3d]

Birth order might influence children to act in ways which elicit labeling as a future teacher and thus affect the timing and mode of entry:

I had always liked children. I adored children. I had a younger brother and sister. I was nine years old when my little brother was born and so I took a lot of care of him because just two years later my little sister was born; so while my mother watched my little sister, I watched my little brother grow up. I liked to be with little children and I liked to play with them and sing with them and tell stories and things like that. . . . My parents encouraged it. My mother used to teach school and many in my family were teachers so that I had associated with teachers. [#8 F-58-5th]

Many children play teacher, and one suspects that many voice teaching as a fantasy choice as Ginzberg (1951) theorizes. One would expect that girls are labeled as teachers more frequently than boys, if only because a wider range of their behavior will be so channeled. An obviously nurturant girl who enjoys the company of younger children can be so labeled; but so can a somewhat aggressive and dominant girl. Nurturance among boys is probably suspect, whereas aggressiveness can be taken as a token of future prowess in a wide variety of "masculine" occupations like business, law, or politics.

Before we leave the topic of early deciders, it is important to observe the absence of a particular phenomenon—a nonfinding. We found that two out of three of the major processes involved in early entrance rested on positive identification with teaching and thus reflect continuity with preceding practice. But what of negative identifications, of experiences with injustice or incompetence which could lead someone to teach in order to improve levels of performance? In short, where are the counter-identifiers?

If there are people who enter teaching because they wish to express negative sentiments through direct attack on conventional practice, they do not appear among the respondents in Five Towns; nor, in fact, are they evident in any studies I know of. If they do indeed exist they must be very scarce.[17] We could use specific inquiry to confirm the limited number of such persons in teaching, but assuming that if they were numerous they would appear, their absence has significance. It means, essentially, that the conservative force represented by teachers who entered with highly positive sentiments of identification is not offset to any appreciable degree by people favoring discontinuity and change toward other conceptions of teaching. Since positive identification appears to have the upper hand, so, apparently, does continuity.

Entry under Constraint

Models which stress rational considerations in occupational choice may lead us to overestimate the freedom enjoyed by those selecting work; psychological theories may also disregard life contingencies which make any particular selection something other than the pure expression of personality needs. Occupations recruit people who in different circumstances might have made different rational choices or found more congenial ways to express their personalities. To grasp the entire range of teaching's recruitment resources, we must examine entry where it has hinged on external constraints.

We turn now to circumstances in which Five Towns respondents, of both sexes and both school levels, found themselves less than free in their occupational choice. In our society such circumstances tend to vary with male and female status. And constrained entries do not necessarily point to current dissatisfaction with the occupation; the testimony of Five Towns teachers illustrates how psychological mechanisms can resolve dissonance in people's lives (Festinger 1962).

Socioeconomic Constraints and Undergraduate Education. American states, as we observed in chapter 1, established special institutions for preparing teachers during the nineteenth and twentieth centuries; in the state in which the Five Towns are situated, for example, the system of state teachers' colleges is an economically and academically accessible type of college instruction. Some respondents said their entry to teaching was heavily influenced by their earlier decision to attend colleges which stressed teacher training. For example:

As I told you, my father died when I was in the eighth grade and I'm the youngest of nine children....I intended to go to——and didn't have the finances. I would have liked to go to——or—— and it was also a question of finances. I was accepted at——State Teachers and at——and went to——State Teachers. It was what I could really afford paying my own way. I haven't regretted it for a moment. I didn't go into teaching because it was something I had wanted to do all my life. [#28 F-26-5th]

I never wanted to be a teacher, but I wanted an education and I went to——State Teachers....I was in teaching a couple of months before I found out...it was a good accident...because now I like it very much. [How did you happen to apply for a job?] Well, this system sent people for appointments up to——State Teachers. I figured I had gone through four years of college and everybody at home begged me to try it for a year and so I did, and that's how I came to be a teacher. But I'm not sorry. [#9 F-23-2d]

Some respondents said they came to enjoy the prospect of teaching only after experience in required practice teaching; they found that it was interesting work which they did well. It might be useful to find out what persons, though similarly constrained in their selection of college, did *not* elect to teach. (Ironically, it may be that those with the finest academic records—and therefore the best opportunities for further study—were less likely to enter classroom work.)[18]

This form of constrained entry is probably most frequent among women who teach in elementary schools. There are indications that women elementary teachers come, on the average, from somewhat less prosperous families than women who teach in high schools; if this is so, their economic resources more frequently rule out expensive forms of higher education, while social class attitudes among their lower-middle-class and lower-class parents would make attendance at a "vocational" college more acceptable (NEA 1963, p. 85; Stout 1966). One gets the impression that women who teach in high schools more frequently attended college as a matter of course; and we find that more of them made a last-minute decision to enter teaching.

Few occupations are in as good a position to take advantage of socioeconomic constraints which limit access to college education. The system of inexpensive and accessible colleges for teacher training turns out to be more than an institution of socialization—it also recruits. One finds a kind of "entrapment" as such colleges draw in students of limited opportunity whose initial interest in teaching is low. According to respondents in Five Towns, such entrapment may prove benign.

Parental Prohibitions and Dutiful Daughters. If it is true that "independence norms" are more frequently invoked for sons than for daughters, then parents intervene more in girls' occupational choices than in boys'. This holds for decisions made by Five Towns teachers: women were more inclined (55 percent versus 40 percent) to portray their decisions as influenced by parents (question 8, App. B-1). This may, however, reflect the tendency of male teachers to make their decisions at a later age.

Whatever the general effect of parental intervention, parental prohibition did play a part in constraining the decisions of some women teachers in Five Towns. The basis of such prohibitions was moral.

I really wanted to be an opera singer and my mother would have liked that—she had been an accompanist—but my father didn't approve. "Too many temptations in show business," as he put it. In fact, that's how I became interested in languages. [#79 F-60-Latin, languages]

I had no intention of entering teaching as a career until my last year in college. My idea was to go into theater work, but my folks strenuously objected to it. I think they had the old idea that theater people were wild and wooly and their dear daughter could not belong there. [#22 F-55-English]

I wanted to be a nurse, but my folks didn't want that. [#94 F-61-Physical education.]

In each of these instances, the original desire of the woman was blocked by parental opposition, which rested on moral disapproval of the choice as dangerously erotic or not respectable. The daughters made interesting adjustments, trying to get as close to the original goal as possible. The first quoted above became a language teacher, working with languages first learned for opera; the second directs school plays; and the third, a teacher of physical education, undertook special training in that field because it included hospital experience. In the past, moral acceptability has played some part as a recruitment resource for teaching. It is suggestive, however, that the respondents quoted above are older teachers. It may be that moral objections to popular alternatives have declined in recent years and may, in fact, play a small part in the future.

Blocked Aspirations and Convertibility. Students of occupational choice are familiar with the process of compromise. Whatever reigning mythologies may proclaim, many young people are unable to enter the line of work they most prefer (Ginzberg 1951). Teaching is somewhat special in that those who enter it as a second choice possess above-average educational qualifications. In that sense, teaching has an enviable competitive position; its accessibility fosters the entrance of people who might never have gone to college to become teachers.

About a third of Five Towns teachers reported that they had wanted to go into another line of work but were unable to do so because of external constraints. The major obstacle they reported was financial—they lacked the funds to pursue the additional training needed. (The lack of funds affected men more because their aspirations more frequently required extra training.) Teaching had a distinct advantage in competing for the secondary allegiance of those who could not pursue their primary goals; the undergraduate schooling they had already acquired readily qualified them for teaching.

Cases can be found in both sexes. A biology teacher, for example, said he hoped to enter medicine, but neither his parents' funds nor his own were sufficient to finance a medical school education. A social studies teacher was an ardent outdoorsman who hoped, after completing his bachelor's degree, to go into forest management; but depression conditions made that impossible. Today he uses his holidays and vacations for hiking, sailing, and so on. A few teachers are still bitter about not achieving their primary goals, but most are not. As Ginzberg (1951) argues, most people have a remarkable capacity to adjust to other than their fondest hopes.

It is easy to overlook the element of constraint in the decisions of some women who choose teaching for its compatibility with marriage. Some accept a change simply because it will make life easier:

> I majored in home economics and I was going into dietetics and then I met my husband and we planned to get married, and marriage and dietetics didn't seem to mix. I decided to go into education then. . . . [What was the most important factor in your decision to teach?] Probably my marriage. It was a horrible reason but I guess that was the reason. The hours gave me a chance to get home, make dinner, clean the house, vacation, and things like that. [#23 F-32-Homemaking]

Although the woman we just quoted is somewhat uncomfortable in reporting why she chose teaching, she apparently did not feel any particular loss from the switch in her occupational plans. Another woman, however, after attending a high-prestige university, was unable, for economic reasons, to carry out plans for doctoral study. She had to work if her husband was to realize his aspirations:

> And then in very practical terms, we were getting married the following summer and I felt there was no point in shopping around any further. I might have taken a year or two to explore other possibilities if it hadn't been for that, but my husband was going to medical school. [#92 F-23-English]

It is clear, therefore, that teaching sometimes obtains the services of people who attended college with other objectives in mind. Realizing that they will not attain these objectives, they use their education to enter teaching. At this point the special nature of teaching's status comes into play, for although it may not rank with the original choice in prestige and other emoluments, it is clearly middle-class, reputable work. People who cannot make it as doctors, business executives, or professors can at least avoid slipping into work of considerably less standing. Teaching functions, therefore, as a stratification safety net which allows people to land without severe damage to their status aspirations.

The recruitment resources of teaching maintain a delicate balance between eased entry and structured discouragement. Were teaching easier to enter, it might lose any special standing; were the obstacles higher, the pool of college-educated potential entrants would be reduced. Discussion about teacher training, it seems, often overlooks these questions. Some fret about facilitated entry for those who did not make an early decision to teach, fearing that it lowers the status of the occupation. Others castigate educationists for requiring anything more than mastery of the subjects to be taught. The former usually advocate more pedagogical instruction, but they rarely point out that this reduces the pool of college-trained candidates. And those who urge more substantive training for teachers are likely to ignore consequences such as increasing the proportion of late entrants.

Wise policy-making in the years to come requires more knowledge on the comparative performance and talents of early and late entrants. In terms of talent gains and losses for teaching, we should inquire into the *net* effects of recruiting those who originally intended to follow another career. Although it is too early to predict whether the recent oversupply of teachers will persist, it may usher in a new era of selectivity for those training and hiring teachers. Such knowledge could assist them to make informed rather than merely expedient decisions.

The Mixed Case of Second Careers. Some people decide to become teachers only after they have tried another line of work; in Five Towns, this occurred primarily with men who had begun careers in business or the priesthood. These instances are constrained in the sense that those involved have invested in an alternative and found it unsatisfactory.

In the instances found in Five Towns, two resources seem to figure in these career changes—the convertibility of prior education and the positive moral definition of teaching in our society. It is curious how this comes about. Those men who had tried the priesthood concluded that celibacy was not right for them; casting about for work which was both accessible and morally acceptable, they lit on teaching—it met both criteria. The men who had begun in business, however, usually reported that they were shocked and dismayed at the "venal practices" and "cutthroat competition" they encountered; they wanted accessible work which was morally superior to business. Teaching met their needs as well. The two groups converged on teaching from divergent directions but for similar reasons. There is, one suspects, a general tendency to see the moral worth of work as somehow associated with a sincere "calling," the tests of which usually require persistence through obstacles. But in these instances, teaching was both a "moral" and an "easy" choice.

Institutional Entanglements

It is easy to overlook the many ways an occupation interconnects with society at large; educational discussions, for example, often treat recruitment as if it is solely a matter of internal policies governing admission to training, the content of preservice education, and certification. Such an approach distorts reality; for, as we have seen in reviewing recruitment resources, teaching depends partly on contributions made by other sectors of society. Teaching has existed long enough, and has been sufficiently stable, to develop significant linkages to the values, institutions, and informal networks of American life. It is helpful to look at recruitment from that perspective.

The dependence of teaching on society is visible in the attractions it proffers. If teaching is to be defined as reputable and even honored service, the cultural context must uphold the service ideal and connect it with schooling. Not only does our society say that teaching is appropriate work for women, but the division of labor in family life makes teaching particularly attractive to women. The American system of social class "subsidizes" the occupation, in a sense, by making teaching a relatively inexpensive escalator into the middle class for those from lower-status homes.

We also see societal support in the facilitators which help people move into teaching. Those who rule the affairs of teaching, for example, permit would-be teachers to make decisions across a wide time range and do little to offset the permissiveness of the subjective warrants. Social considerations also play a part in the more specific types of facilitation. Early decisions are supported by the marginalities of a heterogeneous society and by the modeling encouraged by a mass education system with high rates of personnel turnover. Stereotypes of sex roles influence the young, particularly girls.

We can see society's hand in constrained decisions as well. The states have set up ready educational routes into teaching which snare some who cannot afford other kinds of higher education. General colleges admit students who will be unable to pursue study for the highest-ranked occupations, but societal arrangements permit them to convert their education into credentials for teaching. Our moral definition of work makes teaching acceptable to those who wish to leave both "higher" and "lower" callings; teaching is defined as reputable work for the daughters of those who are especially concerned about sexual conventionality. The accessibility of teaching, in fact, is a function of the ordering of opportunities within the occupational system; the obstacles set up by other fields help teaching to recruit new members.

Social dependence, however, can run the other way as well; teaching and our society stand in a symbiotic relationship. The conventional organization of middle-class family life, for example, is reinforced by the availability of teaching positions for wives and mothers; employment can be undertaken while other roles are honored. The social class system gains some of its potential for upward mobility from teaching as a route into the middle class. Colleges can offer curricula which might otherwise be condemned as impractical if graduates are employed to teach otherwise arcane subjects. Religious conceptions of service gain credibility when it is possible to attach them to specific lines of work. Elitist occupations provoke less hostility when disappointed aspirants can fall back to a middle-class alternative. Interdependencies of this type reveal the tendency for long-standing social arrangements—even in nominally discrete sectors of society—to move toward mutual adaptation and support. People and groups outside the occupation, therefore, can have vested interests in the continuation of established arrangements. The symbiosis which connects teaching to other sectors in our society, therefore, has important implications for prospects of change.

Recruitment as Reaffirmation

On the basis of what we have learned about recruitment into teaching, one could not say that it is highly selective or calculated to produce great homogeneity within teaching ranks. There are filters, but they are not fine. It would probably be naive, in any event, to expect an occupation with more than two million members to be composed of look-alikes. It is important to note that efforts to find a single teacher personality have not been successful (Getzels and Jackson 1963).

There are ways, however, in which the recruitment system is canted to favor particular kinds of entrants. The occupation is evidently more attractive to women than to men, since recruitment resources elicit more female than male candidates. Another bias is toward the perpetuation of the occupational status quo. I shall conclude the chapter with a brief summary of these two propensities of the recruitment system.

There are several respects in which the attractors and facilitators of teaching are more potent for women than for men. Economic incentives provide a case in point, but they are not the only one—other benefits (e.g., time compatibility) hold greater value for women. The subjective warrant comes closer to matching feminine than masculine ideals as defined by our society; it emphasizes qualities which are more widely reinforced for girls than for boys. The structure of schools fosters identification with teachers for girls more than for boys; girls encounter feminine models throughout the entire span of their schooling, whereas boys usually have few male teachers before the upper grades. Families are more likely to contain women who are or have been teachers. Girls are more frequently sent to undergraduate colleges oriented toward training teachers; they are also more likely to be the objects of moralistic concern. There are two major ways recruitment resources foster a conservative outlook among entrants.[19] First, they appeal strongly to young people who are favorably disposed toward the existing system of schools. The tendency for decisions based on identification to be linked with a traditional outlook is not offset, as far as I can ascertain, by the presence of any noticeable number of counteridentifiers who want to alter the nature and direction of school practices and modes of operation.

The second way recruitment draws in conservatively inclined persons is more subtle and encourages people who have only limited interest in the occupational affairs of teaching. We can see this clearly in the case of time compatibility; one would not expect people who choose teaching because it makes limited demands on their time to invest the effort needed to change either the context or the conduct of classroom teaching. Men tend to be transient members of the occupation, literally and psychologically, a phenomenon we will examine in detail in chapter 4. They are thus reluctant to project continuing futures in the classroom and to identify their interests with classroom teachers in general. Also, dissimilar entry patterns can have similar effects. While early deciders may act conservatively because they are living out identifications with figures from the past, late (usually male) entrants may lack the motivation to challenge historic patterns. Many male teachers, in fact, are upwardly mobile and likely to construe their interests as lying in the administrative domain; they may feel that their personal advancement depends on maintaining a hierarchy.

It is considerably easier, then, to see recruitment into teaching as leading to reaffirmation than as leading to challenge to the past. Recruitment is one of the key processes in any occupation; in teaching, it tips toward continuity rather than change. As we shall shortly see, other processes also sustain stability.

3

The Limits of Socialization

Occupations shape people. Scholars as diverse as Adam Smith, Karl
Marx, Emile Durkheim, Max Weber, William James, and Thorstein
Veblen have discussed the profound influence work has on human
personality. Modern sociologists and psychologists have provided us with
studies of how people are affected by their occupational pursuits.[1] We
have learned that conditions of entry play an important part in socializing
members to a given occupation; and we expect those who study work
institutions to pay close attention to both formal and informal processes
of induction.

Yet not all occupations influence entrants to the same extent. Some
organize the experience of the neophyte in ways which have profound
effects; others do not. Some inculcate complex and specific technical
cultures in their novices; others do not. Contrast, for example, pathways
to full participation in the Jesuit priesthood, quarterback status in
professional football, or diamond-cutting on the one hand with beginning work as a waitress, factory worker, or taxi-driver on the other.
Among the observable differences are the time it takes to qualify, the
arduousness of the preparation, and the complexity of the skills and
knowledge needed for full membership.

The comparative impact of initial socialization makes considerable
difference in the overall life of an occupation. Where such socialization is
potent, the predispositions of newcomers become less important through

55

time; the selves of participants tend to merge with the values and norms built into the occupation. The opposite holds where socialization experiences are weak; in that case, the attitudes, values, and orientations people bring with them continue to influence the conduct of work. The internal structure of an occupation is also influenced by the potency of socialization arrangements. Occupations with highly developed subcultures—that is, with rich, complex bodies of knowledge and technique—differentiate entrants from outsiders, laying the basis for a special sense of community among the initiated. The reverse also holds; where the content of initiatory stages is sparse, the significance of guild is low. Contrast, for example, the internal relationships found in medicine and in retail sales, in airline piloting and in driving delivery trucks, in certified public accountancy and in routine office work.

On the basis of what we have learned in the preceding chapters, we would not expect teaching to stand at the high end of the continuum of comparative socialization impact. Structures affecting entry have been kept loose to ease recruitment; the occupation does not filter candidates through a refined selection screen or subject them to a powerful induction sequence. We observed that "professional preparation" is comparatively recent in its development and that there are few evidences of major technical change in the conduct of instruction. Cellular organization retards rather than enhances colleagueship. Teachers, moreover, are subordinates employed in organizations where those who govern (board members) do not belong to the occupation; the workplace of the teacher—the school—is not organized to promote inquiry or to build the intellectual capital of the occupation. We begin, then, with the general expectation that initial socialization into teaching will be somewhat less involved than that found in the historic professions or arcane crafts, since the conditions we generally associate with a rich subculture do not prevail for classroom teaching.

The purpose of this chapter, however, is to go beyond such indirect observations and closely consider the issues of socialization in teaching. How do the stages of socialization compare with those found in highly developed occupations? What do teachers say about their shaping as members of the occupation? Does their testimony accord with claims of professionalization made by some occupational leaders? How do the beliefs and orientations of teachers connect with the socialization sequence? We shall deal with such questions using data from Five Towns, a survey conducted in Dade County, Florida (See Appendix A), and studies conducted by other researchers.

The Stages of Formal Socialization

One way to assess the impact of an occupation's induction processes is to examine the sequence of experiences that entrants typically undergo. Occupations vary in the complexity of their apparatus for inducting new members. It is reasonable to assume, other considerations being equal, that highly developed sequences will have a greater effect on neophytes than will simple ones. At first glance, such comparisons seem very difficult, for there are a bewildering variety of occupations and routes into them. Much of the apparent diversity, however, is rhetorical rather than real, since certain basic components are found in all systems of occupational induction. Those I can identify are: (1) formal schooling, (2) mediated entry, and (3) learning-while-doing. This universality permits us to compare any single occupation, component by component, with highly developed instances in other fields, thus achieving a rough but useful summative judgment on the overall complexity of induction into the occupation.

Two kinds of schooling are involved in work socialization—*general schooling* and *special schooling*. Compulsory education laws have set the minimum general schooling required, but there are significant variations above that level. Occupations increasingly tend to require at least high-school graduation, but there are kinds of work which can be begun with less (Berg 1970). Many fields insist upon college preparation; one of the principal trends of work in the twentieth century is the increased number of would-be professions which demand higher education. Less prestigious college fields require four or five years of total study in institutions of higher education, but some of the established professions demand four years of college *before* full-time specialized study is begun.

The amount of specialized schooling needed varies more than demands for general schooling. One may leave school and immediately begin work in a factory or as a retail sales clerk: where special schooling is required, it is measured in hours and days rather than months and years. We find the other extreme in medical specialist training, where four years of medical school is supplemented at both ends, by prescribed undergraduate courses and by study needed to pass board examinations after resident training. Much of the diversity in induction revolves around different types of special schooling, including such diverse arrangements as barber colleges, two-year technical institutes, correspondence schools, and night-school study. University education is frequently both long and diverse. It can involve study of basic sciences and other disciplines, special disciplines peculiar to the profession (e.g., theory of motors, stress of materials, pathology), and codifications of practice garnered over centuries of experience (e.g., law of contracts, principles of building design, practice of surgery). Highly developed special schooling features not only intellectual complexity but variations in setting; in medicine, for example, it includes classroom instruction, laboratory work, clinical rounds, and seminars. Compared with occupations in general, teaching requires relatively long general schooling. Today few teachers begin work with less than twelve years of school and four years of college, including some college study of education. (Some states now require five years of college.) Since teaching was one of the first occupations in America to possess special schools, we might expect it to require a long period of specialized study, but compared with other college-based occupations this is not true.[2] It is difficult to get precise and reliable information on what proportion of the average teacher's undergraduate study is centered on pedagogy and related courses, but it rarely matches the length of special schooling required of engineers, doctors, lawyers, clergymen, and other professionals. Although there is some variation by level (programs of elementary education tend to have more education requirements), education undergraduates probably spend, on the average, somewhere between one and two years of equivalent full-time study on specialized courses (Conant 1963).

Special schooling for teachers is neither intellectually nor organizationally as complex as that found in the established professions. The study of medicine and engineering is rooted in science; law and divinity can point to generations of scholars who have contributed to their development. Neither holds for education, for specialized study of the subject has a short history and an erratic connection with the mainstream of intellectual development in modern society. Early study of education was isolated from scholarship; attempts to integrate it with disciplines like psychology have lasted only a few decades. Nor do we find an equivalent to the centuries of codified experience encountered in law, engineering, medicine, divinity, architecture, and accountancy; no way has been found to record and crystallize teaching for the benefit of beginners. Law students have their precedents, and engineers have exemplars dating back to ancient Rome; physicians recall Galen and centuries of empirical treatment, and clergymen can pore over thousands of published sermons and exegeses. Architects can examine monuments of success and failure, and the beginning student of accounting, although probably unknowingly, is working with concepts dating back to medieval times and refined by generation upon generation of practical men. But what meaningful record exists of the millions of teaching transactions that have occurred since the City on the Hill?

The organizational simplicity of instruction in education is seen in its heavy reliance upon conventional classroom instruction: lecture and discussion are the bread and butter of education study. There are variants, of course—workshops, films, and occasional field trips, and some see promise in such innovations as television and "microteaching" (Dreeben 1970). But the study of education is mainly standardized around traditional classroom instruction and private study. It does not routinely feature the varieties of learning settings found in the established professions.

Mediated entry is probably the classic form of work induction. Apprenticeship, for example, was highly developed in medieval times and undergirded the entire system of guilds. Today we find mediated entry under various labels and in a wide range of occupations; it is manifest in the long formal apprenticeship of the building crafts, clerkships in law firms, internships and residencies in medicine, and the "management training programs" conducted by many corporations. In some instances, mediated entry means a protracted engagement in a complex series of steps, as in training to be an airline pilot or a certified public accountant. Such systems, regardless of their length, share certain features. Typically the neophyte takes small steps from simple to more demanding tasks and from small to greater responsibility under the supervision of persons who have attained recognized position within the occupation.

Compared with the crafts, professions, and highly skilled trades, arrangements for mediated entry are primitive in teaching. The only major device of this kind is "practice teaching," which is short and comparatively casual. Most states require some such experience before certification, but usually only a few weeks. The practice teacher normally observes the work of an experienced teacher and teaches classes as that teacher sees fit; mechanics of operation are worked out in conjunction with a degree program in education in a college or university. Reports on practice teaching frequently point out that its effectiveness depends in large part on the skill, involvement, and conscientiousness of the supervising teacher. There is little to suggest that it is conducted uniformly.

One of the striking features of teaching is the abruptness with which full responsibility is assumed. In fact, a young man or woman typically is a student in June and a fully responsible teacher in September. "Beginning teachers'' are on probation and usually receive more supervision than their experienced colleagues, but their daily tasks are essentially the same. It is no accident that some refer to this as the "sink-or-swim" approach.

Learning-while-doing has played a major part in the history of American business and industry. Before the recent emphasis on long general schooling and special study for business, young people entered offices or factories and succeeded or failed on the basis of what they managed to learn in the course of everyday work. (The process was glorified in the "office-boy-to-president" myth.) Many jobs are still filled this way, particularly in manufacturing and service fields. Those with few specialized skills may acquire them in training programs operated by the business concern or begin in positions requiring no distinct skills. Making provision for internal mobility has become an expensive and complicated matter in modern business, and millions of dollars are spent each year on a wide variety of special programs. The armed services are noteworthy in this respect; they have developed a multitude of training programs to staff positions "from the inside."

Teaching historically has relied heavily upon this kind of work socialization, since for the first two centuries of schooling in America no special preparation was available or required. Learning-while-doing continues to be important; we shall see that teachers believe work experience is highly influential in shaping their performance. Study by teachers is reinforced; salary schedules and promotion possibilities are usually linked to additional coursework. But provisions for training within school systems and teacher organizations are on a considerably smaller scale—and have a more intermittent schedule—than prevails in many business corporations and in the armed services. In school systems, "in-service" efforts tend to be measured in days, and even hours, rather than in weeks or months.

Our review of schooling, mediated entry, and learning-while-doing in teaching reveals that the total induction system is not highly developed. Teaching does not require as much preparation as some professions, crafts, or other skilled fields. Teaching is relatively high on general schooling and somewhat low on specialized schooling. Mediated entry is limited; the few weeks of practice teaching are outmatched in lower-ranked occupations. Induction after work has begun generally takes the form of continued college study; provisions for additional training within school systems are sparse. One is struck both by the heavy reliance upon formal classroom instruction and by the protracted subordination of the teacher to persons who, properly speaking, are not members of the occupation. The earnest teacher begins as a student in a college classroom and may continue (part-time) in that status for many years.

Teacher Perceptions of the Induction Process

Socialization is a subjective process—it is something that happens to people as they move through a series of structured experiences and internalize the subculture of the group. Although it is helpful to compare the sequence in teaching with that in other occupations, more germane data lie in the experiences of those who have undergone the process. We turn now to testimony from classroom teachers who have been asked to reflect on their induction experiences. I will follow the outline provided by the categories I have used in the previous section. But I will be looking for answers to some general questions. How do teachers weigh the various stages of their induction experience? Do their comments identify informal processes which are not immediately apparent? To what extent, if any, do classroom teachers see themselves as sharing a common technical culture?

General Schooling and the Apprenticeship of Observation

My mother was a teacher, her sisters were teachers—it's a family occupation. I always wanted to go into teaching. I can't remember when I didn't want to....I remember as a little girl sometimes seeing teachers have a hard time. I thought, well, I will be careful because some day I'll be on the other side of the desk. [#60 F-59-6th]

One often overlooks the ways general schooling prepares people for work. Such an oversight is especially serious with public school teachers, for participation in school has special occupational effect on those who do move to the other side of the desk. There are ways in which being a student is like serving an apprenticeship in teaching; students have protracted face-to-face and consequential interactions with established teachers.

Those who teach have normally had sixteen continuous years of contact with teachers and professors. American young people, in fact, see teachers at work much more than they see any other occupational group; we can estimate that the average student has spent 13,000 hours in direct contact with classroom teachers by the time he graduates from high school.[3] That contact takes place in a small space; students are rarely more than a few yards away from their teacher. The interaction, moreover, is not passive observation—it is usually a relationship which has consequences for the student and thus is invested with affect. Teachers possess power over their charges; for those who aspire merely to "survive" school, the teacher must at least be placated. But for persons with higher aspirations (e.g., the hope to attend college), the stakes are higher; they learn the significance of good grades and the value of teacher favor. In the terminology of symbolic interaction theory, the student learns to "take the role" of the classroom teacher, to engage in at least enough empathy to anticipate the teacher's probable reaction to his behavior. This requires that the student project himself into the teacher's position and imagine how he feels about various student actions. As our opening quotation suggests, the motivation to engage in such role-taking is especially great when students have already decided to become teachers. But it is likely that taking the role of the teacher is general among students whatever their occupational intentions. It may be that the widespread idea that "anyone can teach" (a notion built into society's historical reluctance to invest heavily in pedagogical research and instruction) originates from this; what child cannot, after all, do a reasonably accurate portrayal of a classroom teacher's actions?

But there are important limits on the extent to which being a student is like serving an apprenticeship for teaching. There are two major restrictions. First, the student sees the teacher from a specific vantage point; second, the student's participation is usually imaginary rather than real. The student is the "target" of teacher efforts and sees the teacher front stage and center like an audience viewing a play. Students do not receive invitations to watch the teacher's performance from the wings; they are not privy to the teacher's private intentions and personal reflections on classroom events. Students rarely participate in selecting goals, making preparations, or postmortem analyses. Thus they are not pressed to place the teacher's actions in a pedagogically oriented framework. They are witnesses from their own student-oriented perspectives. They assess teachers on a wide variety of personal and student-oriented bases, but only partially in terms of criteria shared with their teacher and with teachers in general.

It is improbable that many students learn to see teaching in an ends-means frame or that they normally take an analytic stance toward it. Students are undoubtedly impressed by some teacher actions and not by others, but one would not expect them to view the differences in a pedagogical, explanatory way. What students learn about teaching, then, is intuitive and imitative rather than explicit and analytical; it is based on individual personalities rather than pedagogical principles.

Imagining how the teacher feels and playing the role of a teacher are different experiences; the difference is intensified, moreover, because children have not yet acquired sufficient emotional experience to make accurate empathic attributions. Students have no reliable basis for assessing the difficulty or demands of various teaching acts and thus may attribute teachers' actions to differences in personality or mood. It is hard to see how the idea of technique would arise in their experience or what situational factors would reinforce it if it did. Lacking a sense of the problematics and a sure concept of technical performance, they are not likely to make useful linkages between teaching objectives and teacher actions; they will not perceive the teacher as someone making choices among teaching strategies. There is ample indication of affective responses of liking and disliking, identifying with or rejecting, but there seems relatively little basis for assuming that students make cognitive differentiations and thoughtful assessments of the quality of teaching performances.

The student's learning about teaching, gained from a limited vantage point and relying heavily on imagination, is not like that of an apprentice and does not represent acquisition of the occupation's technical knowledge. It is more a matter of imitation, which, being generalized across individuals, becomes tradition. It is a potentially powerful influence which transcends generations, but the conditions of transfer do not favor informed criticism, attention to specifics, or explicit rules of assessment.

It would take complex research to confirm this analysis. Data gathered in Five Towns, however, lend it support; it is a fruitful line of thought. We turn to data on the influence of former teachers and on the transition from student to teacher.

Although Five Towns teachers were not asked about the influence of former teachers, it is evident that many consider it important (question 29, App. B-1). A large proportion of respondents *volunteered* information about how their current work is affected by the teaching they received. The information was elicited by a question asking respondents to describe an outstanding teacher they had; 42 percent of the respondents went out of their way to connect their own teaching practices with his. An additional 16 percent described a teacher whose role was similar to their own. Since they also linked that striking teacher with their decision to enter the occupation, the presumption is high that the remembered teacher is a strong model for the respondent.

Teachers of both sexes and at both elementary and secondary levels connect their current practices with their mentors. Excerpts from five interviews illustrate the wide range of attributed effects.

The teacher I had in sixth grade was good, interesting. There are a few things I used this year that I remember having done in her room. [#6 M-24-5th]

There was one particular teacher in my 8th and 9th grades. She was very hard, very strict, and used to say "I know some of you don't like me since I'm so strict but when you get out of school and think back, a lot of you will probably think of me as being the best teacher." She really was. She probably taught me how important classroom discipline was. [#23 F-42-3d]

My second grade teacher was kind. She knew it was a terrific change for me to come all the way from Iowa and she'd take the time to talk to me, to take away some of the fright. I never forgot that and when new youngsters come into my room I always try to team them up with someone. I have a special word for them. [#27 F-59-5th]

I had one college professor.... This is the man who had more to do with my techniques than any other person. [#40 M-46-Eng., Hist.]

I had her in U.S. history and she whetted my appetite for history....I may be one of her products. I think I am. [#10 M-38-Soc. Stud.]

The data at my disposal suggest that the continuing influence of former teachers is present in more than half of the Five Towns cases; since the information was volunteered, a considerably higher proportion might have been ready to admit to such influence had they been asked. There is another reason, however, to suspect that the phenomenon is more important than these data disclose. Social psychologists have noted that some kinds of learning (e.g., the acquisition of a dialect) occur through a slow, unwitting process involving imitation; the individual takes on the ways of others without realizing he is doing so. My information is limited to instances where teachers realize that their current behavior reflects former teachers; when we recall that students have protracted and consequential face-to-face interaction with many teachers, and that some young people identify strongly with their teachers, it is likely that many are influenced in ways they do not even perceive. Some respondents, in fact, said as much:

I would say that I probably have at times [used former teachers as models]. Not actually knowing, not meaning to, but I think there are times I have. [#52 F-47-3d]

The only way I've tried to teach is just by teaching by probably using a little psychology, a little judgment and, I suppose, as a result of my own experience as a child. The teachers I had made me subconsciously. What you do in class, you listen to their work, and tests, and so on. I don't think there is any great science to teaching.... If you want to teach, you can teach. [#64 M-60-Bookkeeping]

The second respondent connects influence from former teachers with the idea that teaching is not an arcane or scientific undertaking; in short, those who have been students are equipped to be teachers.

I argued above that the apprenticeship-of-observation is not likely to instill a sense of the problematics of teaching—that students, because of the limits of their vantage point and empathic capacity, will see it simplistically. Five Towns data are consistent with this argument. Asked how their expectations of teaching differed from reality, nine times as many resondents said that teaching was more difficult than expected as said the opposite (question 12, App. B-1). Teaching made more demands on their time and energies than they expected: some said that their training was unrealistic, that responsibility made the work different, or that it was harder to achieve discipline than they thought it would be. Others thought that students had "changed for the worse" or that they were misled about students' eagerness to learn. Generally, teachers were not surprised at the nature of their tasks; with the one exception of clerical tasks (students apparently do not fully perceive this aspect of the teacher's work), teachers ended up doing things they had expected to do. But they found those tasks harder and more taxing than anticipated—the subjective reality was misperceived. It seems that neither the apprenticeship-of-observation nor their formal training prepared them for the inner world of teaching.

Teaching is unusual in that those who decide to enter it have had exceptional opportunity to observe members of the occupation at work; unlike most occupations today, the activities of teachers are not shielded from youngsters. Teachers-to-be underestimate the difficulties involved, but this supports the contention that those planning to teach form definite ideas about the nature of the role. People entering other occupations are more likely to sense that their information is limited. The meaning of teacher training is likely to differ as a result of this special feature of the occupation. The latter statement is warranted by previous analyses and by data gathered in Five Towns.

Hughes has described professional socialization as a turning point in the entrant's perceptions of the role and of himself; prior conceptions are reversed as the learning individual looks back on his former self from inside (Hughes 1958). It is remarkable that the talk of Five Towns teachers does not fit this description; they place events which preceded their formal preparation for teaching within a *continuous* rather than a discontinuous framework. Thus when they describe their former teachers they do not contrast their "student" perceptions with a later, more sophisticated viewpoint. They talk about assessments they made as youngsters as currently viable, as stable judgments of quality. What constituted good teaching then constitutes good teaching now; there is no great divide between preentry and postentry evaluations. Training (and even subsequent experience) is not a dramatic watershed separating the perceptions of naive laymen from later judgments by knowing professionals. The lack of dramatic change in outlook we have been discussing supports the allegation that education training has low impact on students, and we shall return to this later. It also provokes questions about their receptivity to instruction in pedagogy. One thinks, for example, of the engineering student's relationship to his professors. Given the complexity and low visibility of engineering tasks and specialties, it is an unusual student who rejects, or even screens, professorial dicta on the basis of personally formulated judgments about engineering practice. But education students have spent years assessing teachers and many enter training with strong preconceptions based upon firm identifications. Students in education may simply classify education professors as new members of a category (teachers) with which they are already most familiar. The mind of the education student is not a blank awaiting inscription.

Education students have undergone diverse prior experiences and their assessments will presumably reflect personality differences, varieties of social experience, and the different contexts within which their assessments were made. There is little reason to expect that any group of teachers-to-be will share common images or proclivities; the descriptions Five Towns respondents gave of remembered teachers point to variety rather than similarity (question 29, App. B-1). Those providing instruction to teachers, therefore, confront classes composed of students who possess varying definitions of good teaching and cathect diverse models of the occupation. Professors will not find it easy to develop consensual standards of practice, and in such circumstances instruction can easily move to a superficial level of discourse. Unless students in training can experience at least some sense of genuine collegiality—some sharing of technical problems and alternative solutions—they will be ill-prepared for such efforts when they work alongside one another.

Teacher training is increasingly influenced by ideas drawn from behavioral science. Those trained in behavioral disciplines are inclined to conceptualize teaching in instrumental terms—to talk of "treatments" and "options" and to assess outcomes in terms of measurable and discrete objectives. One wonders how effectively such professors communicate with the many students who, it appears, see teaching as the "living out" of prior conceptions of good teaching. Students who conceive of teaching (consciously or not) as expressing qualities associated with revered models will be less attuned to the pragmatic and rationalistic conceptions of teaching found in behavioral science. The two groups—students and professors—may talk past one another. Research on teacher training programs ought, in any event, to test for problems which may lie in divergent predispositions and perspectives.

In summary, the apprenticeship-of-observation undergone by all who enter teaching begins the process of socialization in a particular way; it acquaints students with the tasks of the teacher and fosters the development of identifications with teachers. It does not, however, lay the basis for informed assessment of teaching technique or encourage the development of analytic orientations toward the work. Unless beginning teachers undergo training experiences which offset their individualistic and traditional experiences, the occupation will be staffed by people who have little concern with building a shared technical culture. In the absence of such a culture, the diverse histories of teachers will play a cardinal role in their day-to-day activity. In that respect, the apprenticeship-of-observation is an ally of continuity rather than of change.

The Special Schooling of Teachers

Teacher education has been one of the stormier sectors of higher education for decades (Tyack 1967, p. 412). The subordinate status of classroom teachers is vividly symbolized by the roster of participants in these recurring academic brawls; the amplified voices have belonged to university presidents, freelance writers, eminent scholars, professors of education, leading citizens, and even an admiral of the United States Navy. But who recalls hearing the opinions of a classroom teacher? Even though the continued confrontations have had serious effects on the standing of teachers (e.g., the quality of their training is a frequent issue in considerations of professional status), the views of teachers have been muted. In this section, I shall turn to those who have undergone teacher training for their assessments of the process and its effects on them. My concern is less with the intermittent battles about the topic than with the question of how influential teachers' training is in shaping their occupational socialization. Since professional preparation is a major capital resource of teachers, we would expect them to protect it by avoiding adverse criticism. Any readiness to discount or minimize the effectiveness and potency of their training must therefore be accorded serious attention.

My information on teachers' evaluations of their preparation programs indicates that they do not belong to either of the major camps arguing the matter of teacher education. They agree with those who feel that mastery of subject matter is important, but they are not prepared to say that specific preparation for pedagogical tasks is futile. They believe that their work is complicated and difficult and requires more than subject matter knowledge, but they are not strong defenders of the current level or kinds of pedagogical instruction being offered. They are, in fact, critical of the preparation they received.

These points are exemplified in a national study conducted by the National Education Association (NEA 1967, pp. 72-73). Few respondents complained about the amount of time spent on substantive study; 82 percent said that they spent "about the right amount of time" on general studies, and 76 percent said the same about their area of substantive specialization. Smaller percentages (but still the majority) expressed similar approval of time spent on studies which are related to teaching but not specifically to technique. These include "psychology of learning and teaching" (69 percent), "human growth and development" (73 percent), and "history and philosophy of education" (68 percent). Teachers were considerably less approving, however, of the practical instruction they received. More than half (52 percent) said they had too little preparation in "classroom management, routines, and discipline," and 57 percent said the same about "the use of audiovisual equipment and materials." And 36 percent complained that they did not have sufficient instruction in "teaching methods."

The judgment that they did not have enough instruction in the practical aspects of teaching is *not* coupled with universally favorable assessment of the training they did get. For although respondents gave high ratings to their substantive courses, smaller percentages approved their pedagogical instruction. The former kind of study got votes of 90 percent to 82 percent approval; the latter received favorable votes of 69 percent (teaching methods), 58 percent (classroom management, routines, and discipline), and 47 percent (use of audiovisual equipment and supplies).[4] Data gathered from a sample of beginning teachers yield higher percentages expressing disapproval of their practical courses (Hermanowicz 1966). Respondents criticize the more practical courses on two grounds—they did not have enough, and what they had, important numbers say, was not good enough. As we shall shortly see, respondents were much readier to praise practice teaching than practical courses in education.

What lies behind the lack of enthusiasm for practical courses in education? Two negative themes crop up: instruction is, teachers say, "too theoretical," and the intellectual content is thin—the courses are repetitive and boring (Hermanowicz 1966). The rhetoric is initially confusing: teachers seem to be saying that their least theoretical courses (method courses) are "too theoretical" whereas they praise courses in disciplines which are usually more theoretical. But the confusion is apparently semantic; when teachers criticize education courses for being "too theoretical," they do not mean that the content is too abstract or general. They are not saying that methods courses contain too many concepts or too complex an ordering of ideas; such meanings would not fit with the accompanying charge that the intellectual content is sparse. "Too theoretical" means that the aims held out in such courses are excessively exalted, that they proffer impractical expectations and a utopian conception of classroom reality. The professors who teach such courses are said to be too remote from classroom exigencies; they proclaim goals which are unattainable and advocate behavior which is not feasible. The twin allegations "too theoretical" and "scant intellectual substance" seem to mean that professors of education inculcate high and difficult goals in students without providing the means for their achievement (Ladd 1966). The outcome is evidently frustrating; unable to reach the horizons pointed out to them, students must choose between seeing themselves as incompetent and seeing their prophets as false. They apparently lean toward the latter.

How are we to account for this pattern of grand ideals and scant strategy in teacher education? It may be related to ideology and to fads and fashions within the field. The stable ideological component is the egalitarian optimism of public education—the belief that educational attainment is possible and desirable for all. (We shall see other consequences of this ideology in chapter 5.) But that persistent theme has been supplemented by a series of fads and fashions in pedagogical thought over the last few decades—witness the sequence only partially described by such terms as "Life Adjustment," "Basic Education," "Scientific Manpower," and "Relevance." Ideologies like these are normally advanced by discrediting former practices and outlooks; Progressivism, for example, was often upheld by picturing earlier schools as cruel and repressive.

This repetitive discrediting of the past has contributed to the gap I mentioned earlier—the lack of systematic codification of practical experience. Teaching has not been subjected to the sustained, empirical, and practice-oriented inquiry into problems and alternatives which we find in other university-based professions. It has been permitted to remain evanescent; there is no equivalent to the recording found in surgical cases, law cases, and physical models of engineering and architectural achievement. Such records, coupled with the commentaries and critiques of highly trained professors, allow new generations to pick up where earlier ones finished. Research in education—until very recently a small-scale affair—has concentrated on learning rather than on teaching and has generally employed models and techniques at some distance from the realities of the classroom (Smith and Geoffrey 1968). The result is that to an astonishing degree the beginner in teaching must start afresh, largely uninformed about prior solutions and alternative approaches to recurring practical problems.

For example, beginning teachers face genuine dilemmas in resolving the conflict between appropriate treatment of individual children and the demands of equity.[5] In matters of discipline they must match their response to the personality of a student with the classroom rules they themselves have set up. Teachers act in fishbowls; each child normally can see how the others are treated. Teachers also learn that they must create a system of rules early in the year and must behave consistently in terms of these rules (Smith and Geoffrey 1968). It is evident in their talk about this dilemma that they have had little or no preparation for it; they possess no special concepts (legal, philosophical, or sociological) for describing their plight or analyzing alternatives. Their professional training, in short, has not linked recurrent dilemmas to available knowledge or to condensations of reality (e.g., cases, simulations) where such issues are deliberated. The repudiation of past experience conjoins with intellectual isolation (a historical feature of teacher training) to produce curricula which extoll the highest virtues but fail to cope with routine tactical and strategic problems. It is small wonder, then, that teachers are not inclined to see themselves as sharing in a common "memory" or technical subculture. Since they have not received such instruction, they are forced to fall back upon individual recollections, which in turn are not displaced by new perspectives. Such a pattern encourages a conception of teaching as an individualistic rather than a collegial enterprise. We shall see later how teachers' attitudes conform to such a pattern.

The Mini-Apprenticeship of Practice Teaching

The closest thing to a genuine apprenticeship for teachers is the practice teaching they normally experience as undergraduates or as part of a postbachelor's program. I have noted that it is a short and relatively simple affair in which a student works alongside an established teacher and teaches classes under his watchful eye. But it is interesting that Mason's national study of beginning teachers shows that despite its limited duration, most teachers rank practice teaching ahead of courses in education in usefulness. After analyzing his data, Mason concludes that "practice teaching was valued by all types of beginning teachers," and "in all subgroups, practice teaching was more valued than education courses" (Mason 1961, p. 45). Hermanowicz (1966) found a similar pattern.

Understanding the dissatisfaction teachers feel about their courses helps us to understand their preference for practice teaching. Practice teaching has the texture of reality; it gives the student the distinct sense of movement toward his goal—teaching. The supervising teacher is concentrating not on an ideal state of affairs but on the how of teaching; and his suggestions can be demonstrated. Actual teaching gives the student teacher valuable reassurance. In a review I made of beginning teachers' diaries, it was manifest that their principal anxiety concerned whether they could actually conduct instruction.[6] Practice teaching helps to allay such doubts; even modest success affirms the choice of occupation. There are indications that teachers (at least in Five Towns) remember those who supervised their practice teaching with special warmth.

It would be unwise, however, to credit practice teaching with more impact than its form permits. Practice teachers normally work with one teacher (or sometimes a small number) and thus get a limited view of teaching techniques. The restricted contact reduces the probability that the student teacher will be matched up with a truly sympathetic, congenial mentor; because of the varying conceptions people bring to teaching, mismatches may lessen influence. Supervising teachers do not usually receive any important reduction in workload or any significant compensation for their extra work. And there is no assurance that the supervisors are selected for ability to explain underlying rationales for decision-making. Because of its casualness and narrow scope, therefore, the usual practice teaching arrangement does not offset the unreflective nature of prior socialization; the student teacher is not forced to compare, analyze, and select from diverse possibilities. The risk is, of course, that practice teaching may simply expose the student to one more teacher's style of work. The value of practice teaching is attested to by many who have participated in it, but there is little indication that it is a powerful force away from traditionalism and individualism. It may be earthy and realistic when compared with education courses; but it is also short and parochial.

The Primacy of Personal Experience and Informal Exchange

Sink or Swim. The special quality of the teacher's early work experience is highlighted when we contrast it to classical arrangements for apprenticeship. Formal apprenticeship has important cognitive characteristics; the neophyte is ushered through a series of tasks of ascending difficulty and assumes greater responsibility as his technical competence increases. Apprenticeship illustrates the learning principle of "simple to complex sequence." When sequences are well timed (either through schedules which work well for many or through flexible provisions for advancement), apprentices are unlikely to accumulate enough anxiety to impede their learning. The classical forms of apprenticeship, moreover, support the beginner in two important ways; he receives personal assistance from co-workers and he gains mastery of the group's technical vocabulary and the knowledge nested in it. There are ancient crafts where prior general schooling is relatively unimportant and the novice can move from ignorance to mastery within the format of formal apprenticeship. In modern professions based on science and scholarship, the beginning worker may bring theoretical knowledge with him, as does the medical school graduate "up on the research" or the law clerk who has just studied the latest court decisions. There is an element of exchange in such instances; the tyro brings "book knowledge" to his masters, and they provide the skills of practice and the wisdom of experience.[7]

The circumstances of the beginning teacher differ. Fully responsible for the instruction of his students from his first working day, the beginning teacher performs the same tasks as the twenty-five-year veteran. Tasks are not added sequentially to allow for gradual increase in skill and knowledge; the beginner learns while performing the full complement of teaching duties. The anxiety so induced is exacerbated by his probationary status; Jersild found widespread anxiety among beginning teachers (Jersild 1966). If it is true that too much anxiety retards learning, some beginning teachers will have difficulty making accurate perceptions and thoughtful decisions as they learn the job.

Anxiety is increased by the limited support teachers receive in the demanding early months. As we shall see a little later, they turn to others for help, preferring the informal exchange of opinions and experience to reliance upon the hierarchy. But the cellular organization of schools constrains the amount and type of interchange possible; beginning teachers spend most of their time physically apart from colleagues. Beginners receive more supervisory attention from principals and others, but even where the school system can afford the best of such assistance, it rarely amounts to more than a few hours a month. Since the beginner spends so much of his time away from other adults, it falls upon him to discern problems, consider alternative solutions, make a selection, and, after acting, assess the outcome. Jackson's observations convinced him that classroom teachers make hundreds of decisions daily; the probability is low that an experienced colleague will be present during anything but a small fraction of the beginner's decision-making (Jackson 1968). Edgar and Warren (1969) have shown, however, that beginners do tend to move toward the values of the supervisors who evaluate them. But it is unlikely that such influence can match that exercised by senior colleagues who work closely with them. One thinks of a shop where beginners and experienced mechanics jointly observe common problems, collectively consider alternative solutions, and as a group witness the success or failure of attempts to solve the problem.

Because of his isolation the beginning teacher frequently works things out as best he can before asking for assistance; Blau has documented the resistance workers feel to indiscriminate advice-seeking (Blau 1955). When his untutored eye identifies a difficulty, he may request help. But there is a secondhand quality to such assistance: if the advisor is not someone who regularly visits the classroom, the teacher must describe the situation. The advisor may offer suggestions, but the beginner must attempt a solution and decide on his own whether it has sufficed. The beginner's perceptions and interpersonal skills mediate between external advice and classroom events; his learning is limited by his personal resources—the acuity of his observation and his capacity to take effective action.

The gaps in interpersonal support are matched by weaknesses in the subculture of classroom teachers; although there are indications that peers influence newcomers, there is little to suggest that this amounts to a significant sharing of common understanding and techniques. Haller analyzed my interview tapes from Five Towns and found a very low proportion of words which are not commonly used; since the interview dealt with teaching, it should have elicited a technical vocabulary shared by teachers (Haller 1966). Teaching is not like crafts and professions, whose members talk in a language specific to them and their work. Thus the absence of a common technical vocabulary limits a beginner's ability to "tap into" a preexisting body of practical knowledge. Without such a framework, the neophyte is less able to order the flux and color of daily events and can miss crucial transactions which might otherwise be encoded in the categories of a developed discourse. Each teacher must laboriously construct ways of perceiving and interpreting what is significant. That is one of the costs of the mutual isolation which attends the absence of a common technical culture.

The beginning months of teaching, therefore, can be something of an ordeal, as the comments of Five Towns teachers indicate. It is important to observe, however, that the ordeal is private—it is not an experience shared by a cadre of teachers. I have explored the ramifications of the lack of a shared ordeal elsewhere; we can say here that that shared ordeal seems to contribute to the solidarity and collegial feeling found in established professions (Lortie 1968). Courses in education are not "tough" enough to lead to collective strategies and deep sharing among students; the entry to work is person by person, each working largely in isolation from others.[8] Whatever the effects of private ordeal may be, it is not likely that they build the common bonds which help construct a common occupational subculture. Its privateness reinforces the individualism we have already encountered.

The Limited Influence of the School Hierarchy. The structure of public schooling which emerged from the nineteenth century had two major mechanisms for improving teacher performance. One was a modified principle of professionalization based upon faith in increased general and special schooling. The second was the principle of bureaucratic control wherein administrative superiors would raise performance levels by supervising teachers. We have seen that the first principle has not produced a powerful technical culture to guide teachers in their pedagogical behavior. But the second remains: Is there evidence to suggest that a technical culture of teaching resides in the supervisory arrangements in public schools?

Whatever knowledge may be possessed by those charged with supervisory duties, that knowledge cannot be said to control teacher behavior if teachers themselves choose to pay little heed. We shall not concentrate, then, on the enormous task of assessing the knowledge of those in positions of school leadership; we shall, rather, examine teachers' perceptions of the role supervisors play in their daily work. Do teachers think of themselves as responding to the initiations of superiors? Do they see superordinates as major sources of technical help? We shall rely on data from Dade County and a national NEA survey to answer these questions.

Teachers in Dade County were asked how "good teachers" gauge the effectiveness of their teaching. They were given a choice between the reactions of students, teachers familiar with their work, the principal, other supervisors, test and examination results, and the teacher's "general observation of students in light of the teacher's conception of what should be learned" (question T1, App. B-2). The question produced a heavily modal response; 59.1 percent selected the last alternative, the essentially individualistic position. That response exceeded by 45.6 percent the next most frequent choice, the results of tests and examinations. (Since many tests and examinations are composed and graded by teachers, some of those responses also point to reliance upon self rather than others.) The modal selection is an even greater challenge to the assumptions of hierarchical control when we note that "good teachers" not only monitor their own progress but do so in terms of *teacher conceptions of instructional goals.* Nor was this the view solely of experienced teachers who are presumably more sure of their command over classroom exigencies; 64 percent of the younger teachers (those in their twenties) chose that alternative. These teachers give assent to norms which reflect dependence on self rather than others and personally held rather than "vertically authoritative" opinions. There are several implications to this viewpoint; one is that teachers who hold to it (and they constitute a large majority in an important sample) put themselves in the "gatekeeper" position over activity in their classrooms. They picture themselves as standing between the students and "external" influence; it is incumbent upon them to assess classroom events in light of their personal judgment.

It is important to observe, however, that teachers do *not* say that they work without assistance from others. But it is interesting that they accord secondary position to officially designated sources of help. This pattern is observable in Hermanowicz's study and in Dade County. Hermanowicz reports that the beginning teachers he studied were lukewarm or negative about the help they got from those officially designated as their sources of supervision and assistance (Hermanowicz 1966). Dade County teachers included administrators among those assisting them, but less frequently than they included classroom teachers (question 39, App. B-2). They clearly preferred the help they obtained from those closest to them in rank; they mentioned teachers (including department and grade chairmen) 53 percent of the time and full-time administrators 43 percent of the time, and most of their administrative choices (28 percent) were the lower-ranked assistant principals. and curriculum assistants. Younger teachers (again those in their twenties) were even more inclined to turn to peers; they mentioned other teachers 58 percent of the time and full-time administrators 37 percent.

The secondary position of administrators is reflected in another set of responses obtained in Dade County. Respondents were asked to select the most important source of "ideas and insight on my work," from a list including in-service courses, reading, college courses, meetings in the system and elsewhere, their immediate superior, and "informal conversations with colleagues and friends" (question 37, App. B-2). The last was clearly the modal choice from this mixed list; informal interactions with peers were chosen by 37 percent of the total sample and by 47 percent of teachers in their twenties. Informal channels are preferred to the institutionalized means, and the peer group rather than administrative superiors (or, indeed, college professors) is seen as the most salient source of classroom ideas.

That teachers do not depend greatly on the school hierarchy for technical assistance is supported by responses to a national survey conducted by the NEA (1967). When questioned about activities which might "contribute to professional growth," respondents showed limited enthusiasm for school-based programs. In-school activities received modal ratings as "some contribution" or "little or no contribution," whereas external activities (usually college-based) were evaluated more positively; in three instances they were modally ranked as making a "great contribution" (p. 85). It is noteworthy that respondents indicate greater enthusiasm for continuing university study than for their pre-service instruction. It may be true, as some suggest, that pedagogical instruction makes more sense *after* one has taught awhile. There may be another factor as well; summer and part-time courses for teachers often provide a forum for the exchange of information among experienced teachers and may thereby benefit from the preference for exchanges with peers. Teachers, in any event, do not seem unduly impressed with the supervisory resources available within school districts. Elsbree argues that such systems were created to improve the quality of teaching; he states that this objective was the major rationale, in fact, for creating the administrative hierarchy (1939, p. 164). If the testimony of teachers is a reliable indicator of the influence of supervisors, that rationale is not an overpowering one today.

The data at our disposal, therefore, underscore the individualistic convictions of classroom teachers; they see themselves as the key figures in monitoring classroom affairs. They do not deny the utility of help from other sources, but they clearly rate informal peer exchanges above official systems of supervision. It would be foolhardy to say that the officials who supervise teachers have no influence over their daily work, but it would be risky, in my view, to think that supervisory arrangements constitute a potent repository of technical knowledge.

The Terms of Informal Exchange. We arrive at a difficult question. Teachers, we see, work largely alone; there is little indication that they share a common technical culture. Yet we have observed that they turn to one another for assistance and consider such peer help their most important source of assistance. The observations seem somewhat discordant, some suggesting individualism and others mutuality of influence. How are we to resolve this apparent contradiction?

The interviews gathered in Five Towns are most helpful, for they point to beliefs and practices which make individualism and mutual assistance compatible. After reviewing the responses teachers gave to a question on how they learned to teach, we will examine the themes which permeate their talk about mutual influence.

Five Towns teachers said experience was their major means of learning how to teach (question 51, App. B-1). Two-thirds emphasized classroom experience, with 44 percent indicating employment as teachers and 23 percent practice teaching. More than a third (38 percent) said other teachers taught them their craft: 20 percent alluded to peers and 18 percent to former teachers. The same smaller percentage of teachers mentioned courses in education and experiences entirely *outside* school matters; in this sample, formal pedagogical instruction had no greater valence than experiences in recreational work or motherhood (15 percent in both instances). Smaller numbers credited in-service programs, school officials, and professional reading. The pattern is similar to the data we have already discussed; personal experience is supplemented by collegial influence, and formal agencies of socialization are secondary to informal ones.

The richness of interview data permits analysis which cannot be undertaken with self-administered questionnaires. I reviewed the protocols to uncover what role respondents accorded to influences from other teachers and how such influence was connected with personal experience. One central theme stood out: time and again, Five Towns teachers insisted that they adopted the ideas of peers on a highly *selective* basis. They qualified statements on what they had learned from other teachers and were clearly reluctant to present themselves as imitating colleagues. Their talk underlines the idea of *adapting* others' practices to their personal styles and situations. They do not refer to learning general principles of instruction from colleagues; when they do refer to peer influences, they talk about specific kinds of classroom activity. They describe the "tricks of the trade" they picked up—not broader conceptions which underlie classroom practice.

The respondents qualified the flow of interpersonal influence in two ways. First, to be adopted a practice must be seen as consistent with the receiver's personality and "way of doing things." They portray the diffusion of classroom practices as passing through the screen of the teacher's self-concept—of the way he visualizes his peculiar style of work. Thus the individualism and gatekeeping we saw earlier are reaffirmed:

the teacher mediates between ideas and their use in terms of the kind of teacher he is. The assumption associated with such screening is particular rather than general; techniques are not efficacious for everyone, since their value depends on the personal context.

The second major qualifier is closely linked to the first. The value of any collegial practice is unknown until the receiving teacher has tried it in the classroom and decided that "it works." The criterion of suitabliity to self is supplemented by a pragmatism of a highly personal sort. The practice must work "for me," and the teacher is the judge of what works.

> This is the only valid way of learning how to teach—by getting in and doing it. You can observe and watch to see what someone else is doing but it doesn't mean it is going to work for you. [#38 F-35-3d]

> Really, trial and error...and then asking others and talking and listening to them. I like to listen because they are so completely different and I try to take what I think will help me from each of them. [#9 F-23-2d]

> I don't think there's any way around trial and error...not that you do it any old way....But you have to experiment and find a way to teach which is best for you so that you're not under strain and that's easiest for the children....No one can give you a lesson plan and say go to it this way because what works for one may be poor for another. [#47 F-32-1st]

> Thinking of some of the successful teachers, teachers who appeal to me and who also fit my personality or at least I think fit my personality. Observing methods that other teachers use and my own application of them, fitting them to my personality. [#11 M-41-Science]

The criteria used for screening remind one of artistic rather than scientific conceptions of work; practices which suit the person of the teacher become candidates for admission to his kit of regular behaviors and are then tried out. The personal nature of such selections is even more manifest when teachers justify their practices on the basis of their individual experience as students. What worked on me, they say, despite its possible uniqueness, will work on others:

> I think the good teachers that I've had. The ones that have impressed me with the knowledge they have and the discipline they keep. [#20 F-54-1st]

> I think perhaps you might tend to look back on your own education and pick individuals whom you thought were successful and perhaps try to copy their style. [#14 M-33-6th]

I remember how I would feel. I remember why I would like someone . . . or why I did not like a teacher. I think just remembering these things can give you a general idea of what you want to do, what you want to be and what you want your children to think of you. [#67 F-24-3d]

Five Towns teachers, therefore, seem to balance individualism with some degree of mutual influence, primarily by reserving the right to assess any possible addition to their repertoires in strictly personal terms. The conceptions voiced by Five Towns teachers (conceptions which are consistent with other data) are not those of colleagues who see themselves as sharing a viable, generalizable body of knowledge and practice. There is little idea of a "state of the art." Such a viewpoint presumes that there are identifiable principles and solutions which are possessed by all those within the colleague group. The image projected is more individualistic; teachers are portrayed as an aggregate of persons each assembling practices consistent with his experience and peculiar personality. It is not what "we, the colleagues" know and share which is paramount, but rather what *I* have learned through experience. From this perspective, socialization into teaching is largely *self-socialization;* one's personal predispositions are not only relevant but, in fact, stand at the core of becoming a teacher.

Summary and Implications

Socialization, as found in teaching, places the occupation between those marked by casual entry and those in which protracted and difficult demands are made on would-be members. College attendance and some specialized schooling are required; members of the occupation, however, depreciate the latter. Mediated entry is part of preservice training and is at most a minor apprenticeship: the transition from college student to responsible teacher is abrupt. Years of unformulated experience as a student precede formal socialization; teachers themselves emphasize the importance of the private experiences they have as beginning teachers.

This kind of socialization sequence leaves room for the emergence and reinforcement of idiosyncratic experience and personal synthesis. In neither structure not content is it well suited to inculcating commonly held, empirically derived, and rigorously grounded practices and principles of pedagogy. The lessons taught by early yet persisting models rest on chance and personal preference; training in pedagogy does not seem to fundamentally alter earlier ideas about teaching. Teachers say that their principal teacher has been experience; they learned to teach through trial and error in the classroom. They portray the process as the acquisition of personally tested practices, not as the refinement and application of generally valid principles of instruction. They insist that influences from others are screened through personal conceptions and subjected to pragmatic trial. The connotations of the term "socialization" seem somewhat askew when applied to this kind of induction, since they imply greater receptivity to a preexisting culture than seems to prevail. Teachers are largely "self-made"; the internalization of common knowledge plays only a limited part in their movement to work responsibility.

Socialization patterns in teaching affect many aspects of the occupation, and I will refer to such consequences at various points throughout the book. I should like to mention three specific effects here: (1) the constraints socialization places on the status of the group; (2) the subjective costs it imposes on teachers; and (3) the relationship between socialization and the occupational conservatism discussed in previous chapters.

Teachers' doubts about possessing a common technical culture affect their collective status in two ways: they make them less ready to assert their authority on educational matters and less able to respond to demands from society. An occupation is recognized as a profession in part because people believe that its members jointly possess arcane knowledge on matters of vital public concern; when that belief is held by key decision-makers like legislators, judges, and state officials, they take action to avoid whatever dangers may lie in permitting noninitiates to practice the trade. Leiberman (1956) shows that teachers have less control over such matters than do members of established professions; those charged with surveillance of the occupation's affairs do not believe that they require teacher participation. What part have teachers themselves played in perpetuating this point of view?

Professional recognition calls for delegating state powers to a group of practitioners; it is presumed that the group possesses collective knowledge not available to "laymen." Yet teachers do not hold the beliefs necessary to assuming such responsibility; they do not claim to be common partakers in a shared body of specialized knowledge or common contributors to "the state of the art." Their depreciation of their special schooling and their individualistic conception of practice run counter to a view of the art as the common (and exclusive) property of initiates; their individualism, I believe, underlies their reluctance to press their case.

There is a tendency today to make greater demands on teachers as members of a common occupation. A case in point is the current emphasis on "accountability." Such demands are in all likelihood a response to teachers' assertiveness in collective bargaining, which I shall discuss at greater length in chapter 9. One perceives a dilemma for teachers here: not knowing how to think about productivity as a collective matter, they are forced back to individualistic responses which belie their resistance to individualized reward patterns. Since their conception of performance is individualistic, they find it difficult to develop strategies to raise the performance level of the group; they do not know how to plan increases in the potency of the technical culture. This incapacity to respond to demands *as a group* poses a threat to the status of the occupation.

The individualism of teacher socialization also creates subjective problems for members of the occupation. People in other lines of work also have occasion to doubt their personal efficacy and the value of the services they offer. But in fields where people perceive their knowledge (and their ignorance) as jointly shared, the individual burden is reduced. A person can take comfort from his compliance with normal expectations within the occupation; he can feel that he did everything possible within "the state of the art." (Physicians so argue when they are charged with malpractice.) Thus the individual can cope with unpleasant outcomes by sharing the weight of his failure and guilt; his inadequacy is part of the larger inadequacy of the field. Teachers derive little consolation from this source; an individualistic conception of practice exacerbates the burden of failure.

In conclusion, we note that individualistic socialization supports the conservatism we observed in the record of the occupation and the recruitment system. There is some direct effect; we saw that the "apprenticeship-of-observation" laid the basis for traditional, intuitive approaches to teaching. Teachers seem to emerge from their induction experiences with a strongly biographical orientation to pedagogical decision-making.

But perhaps the most important conservative influences are indirect. The lack of potency in the formal socialization system means that earlier conservative influences (such as those described in chapter 2) are not systematically offset in the course of induction. Teachers do not, apparently, acquire new standards to correct and reverse earlier impressions, ideas, and orientations. Nor does later work experience supplement low impact training with a general conception of teaching as a shared intellectual possession. Science, for example, would probably not change too much even if it recruited more conservative persons; once engaged in scientific work, scientists participate in a reward system which generates and reinforces novel ideas and proofs. As we shall see in the next chapter, the career lines of teachers do little to encourage sustained concern with the technical resources of the occupation.

4

Career and Work Rewards

Discussion of occupational rewards frequently focuses on average earnings. Although this is important, other aspects of the reward system also have significant consequences. The distribution of income over the working career is one. Nor should we ignore the nonmonetary rewards people derive from their work. In this chapter, therefore, we will consider (1) the income profile of teachers over time and (2) the balance between monetary rewards and other kinds of rewards in teaching. Analyzing these aspects of the rewards found in teaching will help us understand the ethos of the occupation.

The term "income profile" refers to the typical flow of earnings over the working life of an individual (Hall 1944). In entrepreneurial work, such profiles vary greatly; but where careers unfold in organizational contexts it is possible to identify characteristic types of income profile. Our special interest lies in the distinction between "staged" and "unstaged" profiles. In some fields the beginner may start at a relatively low income but, with success, move into a series of significantly higher earning positions (e.g., law firm practice). Other occupations may offer relatively little staging; income gains may be steady but small. In fields where income rises sharply from one stage to the next, we usually find a corresponding shift in status; in occupations where increments are modest, it may be difficult to find clear status differences between practitioners. Classroom teaching is notably unstaged. The first part of this chapter explores how this affects the occupation.

The balance of monetary rewards and other rewards differs from occupation to occupation. Building janitors, for example, earn high incomes relative to their low status position (Gold, n.d.). The personal publicity and acclaim sought by the television performer may be anathema to the financier. There are politicians who covet power and eschew financial gain: and serious artists may sacrifice money and power to win the approval of a small circle. What about teachers? What rewards do they emphasize?

This examination of teaching careers and rewards brings together two strands in the occupation. The first is structural—we will see how the structure favors a particular kind of time orientation among teachers. Studying the balance of rewards, however, requires attention to the daily tasks of teachers and the meanings they attach to them. This chapter therefore serves as a bridge between the two major emphases of this book; the first part stresses the kind of analysis found in the chapters 2 and 3, and the second part anticipates the phenomenological emphasis of later chapters.

Unstaged Careers and Disjunctive Rewards

Teaching was initiated as contractual, salaried work in early colonial times; thus some features of the reward system have centuries of tradition behind them. Other characteristics, however, result from conditions which prevailed during the Common School Crusade and the subsequent bureaucratization of public schools.

The burgeoning schools of the nineteenth century faced the problem of recruiting thousands of teachers each year—they developed a system of remuneration that would attract new members and paid little attention to those who already taught. I suspect they did not have to worry about losing women who did not marry—they had few alternatives. A pattern was established: teachers with long service earned relatively little more than beginners. Subsequent efforts by teachers to raise salaries relied on a standardization strategy; the resulting salary schedules incorporated limited increases through time, usually at a ratio of two (for highly experienced teachers) to one (for beginners). High turnover within teaching continued well into the twentieth century, and teacher organizations consequently had many members with limited experience. The strategies of teacher organizations have reflected this influence; they have pressed for higher beginning salaries rather than for more income for experienced teachers.

The cellular pattern of organization developed during the nineteenth century also affected payment arrangements. Although teachers might teach in different grades and specialize in different subjects, they were largely generalists; each had many tasks in common with other teachers. The logic of the organization favored teachers when they pressed for single salary schedules which equalized payments across grades; how could one argue that particular grades were "more important" than others? Standard schedules also spared school boards the embarassment of having to assign some students to highly paid teachers and others to low-paid teachers; in a system of common schools, such inequities would have aroused objections.

The result is that income profiles of teachers today are predictable, comparatively unstaged, and "front-loaded." A beginning teacher knows what he will earn and can see that long service brings limited reward. Those who persist in teaching experience the drop-off in percentage gains associated with fixed dollar increments: each pay increase is a smaller percentage of the salary base than the previous one. Earnings are "front-loaded" in the sense that one begins at a high level relative to one's ultimate earning potential.[1]

Compared with most other kinds of middle-class work, teaching is relatively "career-less." There is less opportunity for the movement upward which is the essence of career.[2] People who work in highly established bureaucracies, for example, can move up a hierarchy of statuses, each movement involving a significant gain in income, and they can frequently do so without endangering their occupational identities. (A soldier is still a soldier when he is promoted.) White-collar work is often highly stratified; secretaries' career lines may be attached to the fates of their bosses. Even ostensibly nonorganizational professionals who work for fees have powerful interpersonal networks which produce career stages involving income, prestige, and control over one's tasks and clientele (Hall 1948).

The potential upward steps in teaching are fewer and hold less significance than one normally finds in middle-class work. Becoming an administrator or specialist (e.g., a counselor) blurs one's identity as a teacher and means abrupt discontinuity in tasks. High-school teachers may assume part-time administrative duties as department chairmen; such promotion normally entails modest financial and prestige gains (Maguire 1970). A teacher may make a lateral move to another school within the same system, which may offer advantages of clientele and so forth (Becker 1951). Some teachers increase their earnings by moving to more prosperous school systems (Pedersen 1973). Seniority may bring certain informal benefits (e.g., more options in students and facilities).

But in contrast to the larger packages of money, prestige, and power usually found in other careers, the typical career line of the classroom teacher is a gentle incline rather than a steep ascent. The status of the young tenured teacher is not appreciably different from that of the highly experienced old-timer. Does the lack of staging in teaching careers make any appreciable difference in the work of teachers? That is obviously a difficult question, but there is a way to attack it. We can identify the functions performed by stages in other kinds of careers and inquire into the state of such functions within teaching. We can, for example, state that one function of staging in careers is to institutionalize the delay of gratification; stages force younger people to expend effort in the hope of ultimate gain. Beginners in staged fields may have to accept considerable deprivation in the early years—the professions offer good examples. A brilliant law student may go from the high estate of law review editor to service alongside a judge of the Supreme Court; but his next position may be as a lowly clerk in a large law factory (Lortie 1958). The beginning physician finds himself, after twenty years of continuous schooling, putting in months and perhaps years as a low-paid, low-ranked, and sleep-deprived intern and junior resident (Doctor X 1965). Young professors may wait years before they can teach courses which reflect their specialized interests. Career lines of this nature orient people to the future; personal ambition is successively whetted and satisfied as the individual moves from one stage to the next. The law student strives for good grades so he can get a good position in a law firm; if he succeeds, he finds himself confronted with new challenges and strivings—this time, to get a partnership. Staged careers produce cycles of effort, attainment, and renewed ambition. In tying the individual to the occupation they give him a stake in its future. Staging gives reality and force to the idea of the future; it generates effort, ambition, and identification with the occupation.

Career staging may also serve another function; it may balance the relationships among effort, capacity, and reward. Not all who begin staged careers go the full route, but where the reward system is seen as legitimate, people believe that the largest rewards go to those who earn them through effort and talent. Supporting beliefs emerge to buttress the contention that reapers deserve the harvest; it is interesting how rarely Sumner's "aleatory element" (sheer luck) is mentioned in journalistic accounts of outstanding success (1906, p. 6). There are mechanisms which give credibility to the beliefs; people who fail to get the scarcer rewards (e.g., promotion) may "confirm" the negative judgment made about them by reducing their effort. In short, there seems to be a strain toward consistency in reward systems which justifies their outcomes.

If stages perform the functions I have attributed to them, we should find that their absence has consequences for teaching. We would expect that teachers would be less future-oriented than people in staged career systems and that disjuctions would appear between effort and reward. Since a high proportion of the available rewards are quickly received—and subsequent rewards are less impressive—it makes little sense to sacrifice present earnings for future prospects. The delay of gratification becomes irrelevant. Since benefits are not highly differentiated within the teaching group, and since extra effort brings scant reward, those who do exert extra effort are likely to feel underrewarded. People who work long hours and commit more of their life energies to work will realize that others who give less get similar rewards. I will hypothesize, then, that the lack of stages in the teaching career results in (1) the dominance of present versus future orientation among teachers and (2) a sense of relative deprivation among those who persist in teaching and work at above-average levels of effort.

The balance between effort and reward in teaching is complicated by the presence of members of both sexes in similar roles and the divergent life contingencies experienced by men and women. We will have to take account of these complications as we examine data on time perspective among teachers and the issue of disjunction between effort and reward.

The Tentativeness of Future Commitments

Although teachers tend to serve for more years now than they did in the past, available data indicate that a minority of beginners expect to teach continuously until retirement. In his survey of beginning teachers, Mason (1961, chap. 10) found that only 29 percent of the men and 16 percent of the women projected uninterrupted futures in the classroom. Men and women have different prospects and emphasize divergent contingencies in thinking about the future. Although most women expect their careers to be interrupted, the vast majority think of teaching as a terminal status. Most men reject teaching as an ultimate goal; they see teaching as a means toward another end—as an interim engagement. We will discuss women and men separately since the patterns differ by sex.

Beginning women teachers do not hide their intention to put family matters first; 65 percent of Mason's respondents planned to leave the classroom within five years and 84 percent expected to leave it before they reached retirement age. When asked what circumstances would induce them to leave, 80 percent of the young women mentioned family-related events. The teaching futures they project are contingent on relationships outside work. Seventy-eight percent of the single teachers said that marriage would cause them to leave; 60 percent of the married women cited childbirth as the key contingency. Married teachers also mentioned occurrences in their husband's lives, such as completion of schooling (24 percent), changes in employment (27 percent), and increases in income (31 percent). Fifty-eight percent of the beginning women teachers thought they would return to the classroom after they had raised their children. In sum, more than half looked ahead to teaching as an "in-and-out" engagement hinging on marital and maternal commitments. Few women expected to work outside classrooms; only 9 percent expressed interest in administrative or specialized positions. Mason's respondents were ready to commit themselves to teaching as long as they worked, but work itself was a secondary commitment.

Marital status influences the amount women invest in preparing for their careers. Single women begin to teach with more schooling than married teachers; 73 percent of the single women versus 68 percent of the married fell into the highest preparation category in Mason's sample (1961, chap. 4). The contingent schooling pattern I mentioned in chapter 1 widens the gap with time. Single women continue to teach while married women may drop out, and so unmarried women accumulate more course credits. An NEA survey conducted in 1966 disclosed that 22 percent of the single teachers had master's degrees, compared with 14 percent of the married ones (NEA 1967, p. 71). Single women invest more in their education; we shall see that this is not the only respect in which their investments exceed those of married women teachers.

The majority of beginning male teachers have no intention of ending their work careers as classroom teachers; that is a major finding in Mason's study. Seventy-one percent said they intended to leave the classroom; 51 percent hoped for higher-ranked positions within education, and the rest (20 percent) anticipated working outside education altogether. Asked what would influence them to leave, they answered "pay, salary, and standard of living." Sixty-three percent said they were concerned about "being able to support a family on a teacher's salary." Married men were more likely to express economic apprehensions; 71 percent of them, versus 51 percent of the single men, mentioned financial worries. The major projection of male beginners is temporary engagement in teaching but continued involvement in education; they hoped for positions which would yield greater income than classroom work. But one out of five showed no persisting interest in education as a field of work.

The higher aspirations of men and the knowledge that they will work throughout their lifetimes probably underlie their readiness to invest more heavily in education. For though men typically decide to enter teaching later than women, they acquire more schooling; the difference holds up when differences due to level are taken into account. It seems that men tend to concentrate their postgraduate study on subjects required for certification as administrators (Mitchell 1972, p. 35). They usually work without interruption and accumulate study credits which raise their incomes and may increase their chances for promotion. They hope for full-time administrative work; few intend to stay with teaching. Classroom teaching, therefore, is not their major point of identification; their psychological bonds to teaching are loosened by their mobility aspirations.

Several characteristics of teaching join to reduce future orientation among members of the occupation. Since access is not particularly difficult, people with low commitment can enter, and many begin teaching without plans to persist. Women may enter expecting to work for a short period before marriage or childbearing; they may or may not plan to return later. Twenty percent of beginning men expect to leave education altogether; most of the others are hoping for jobs other than teaching. The career line has little appeal for most entrants.

Men and women react differently to the nature of the career line. The steps upward within teaching are too small to satisfy the ambitions of most male entrants; they want the greater rewards associated with administrative positions. But the gentle incline of teaching fits the aspirations most women bring with them; it facilitates their "in-and-out" plans. Absence would be costlier if teaching careers were staged; the reentering teacher would have lost more in comparison with those who stayed on and moved into higher statuses. Under the present system, the major cost is the loss of incremental earnings, and for married women this is probably not perceived as serious. (Married women might be expected, therefore, to resist moves to stratify teaching careers.) We also note that "in-and-out" rests on the assumption that no major technical changes are likely to take place while one is absent; so married women may also (consciously or not) have a stake in slow rather than rapid change in teaching technique.[3]

Most young teachers do not consider a lifetime of classroom teaching "enough." Men want to move through teaching to other work; women see it as supplementary to marriage and motherhood. But not all who make plans on these grounds will be able to attain them. Many male teachers will not be promoted into administrative work; some women who plan to marry will not do so. We expect, therefore, that men who are not promoted and women who do not marry will have to adjust to these realities. To persist in teaching is, in a sense, to be "passed over" for higher position or marriage. Do such experiences affect the person's satisfaction with teaching? Do other obligations influence commitment to the occupation? It is to questions of this kind that we turn next.

The Disjunction between Engagement and Work Satisfaction

People differ in their readiness to involve themselves in work; to some it is a major engagement; to others, something less.[4] It is also obvious that people vary in the amount of satisfaction they get from work. All else being equal, we expect higher engagement to be associated with higher satisfaction, as in the adage that one gets out of life what one puts into it. Our social norms uphold this principle; rewards should stand in relation to the amount of personal engagement (and effort) people put into their work.

Questions of this sort are subtle and difficult to measure; at best, we get rough indicators of the degree of personal involvement and the level of overall satisfaction. This section examines the relationships between involvement in teaching and the level of satisfaction reported by teachers; that level of satisfaction is thought of as summarizing the person's assessment of his total rewards in teaching. We will review national data first, then undertake an intensive review of Five Towns data—those data provoke questions for future research. The analysis should help us to answer the question implied in earlier pages: "Are contributions and rewards misaligned in teaching?"

One way to define "involvement" is as the individual's readiness to allocate scarce personal resources to his work. Time and money are personal resources with general value which can be allocated in any number of ways; those who choose to channel such resources to their teaching can be said to be more involved than those who do not. An NEA national survey provides us with some information on the patterns of time and money expenditures by teachers; we can learn from the reported distributions even where the range is not great. (Time put in, for example, is constrained at the lower end; teachers must work a minimum number of hours.)

Respondents in the NEA survey reported that they worked a mean of 47.4 hours weekly and a median of 46.5 hours on all duties connected with their teaching (1967, p. 83). Elementary teachers reported somewhat lower averages than secondary teachers; their median was 45.5 and their mean 46.5, while the corresponding figures for secondary teachers were 47.2 and 48.3. Although men appeared to work longer hours than women, the difference did not hold up when level was controlled; with level held constant, in fact, women proved to work slightly longer weeks. (The median and mean hours of female secondary teachers were 47.3 and 48.8 compared with 47.2 and 47.9 for men.) The ''average male teacher'' works a little longer than the ''average female teacher'' only in the sense that he is more likely to work in a secondary school.

Unmarried women work slightly longer hours than their married colleagues; the median difference is one-half hour and the mean difference is 1.2 hours. Slightly more single women put in extremely long hours; 15.3 percent of single women compared with 11.3 percent of the married women report that they work sixty hours or more a week. There are teachers who spend great amounts of time on their work, and it is interesting that some married women are among them (14.3 percent of the men fell in this group). But the edge is to single women.

These teachers also varied in their willingness to invest personal funds in ''professional growth activities'' such as courses and workshops (NEA 1967, p. 87). Overall, 61.8 percent reported some such expenditure and, again, secondary teachers contributed more than elementary teachers; the mean expense of the former was $147.40 and of the latter, $93.50. Men in general spent more ($165.50 to $98.10), and this also applied specifically to the secondary level, where men spent $176.10 and women $113.10. Single women outspent married women $112.00 to $91.20. If we assume that money expenditures of this type indicate involvement, men make greater efforts than women and single women greater than married women.

Taking the two indicators together, single women invest more than married women, although not greatly more. Comparing men with all women, men have the edge primarily because they are more often secondary teachers and work longer hours; they spend more, however, on professional matters. If people's involvements matched their reported satisfactions, single women would report greater satisfaction than married women. Men would approach parity with women or be somewhat more satisfied.

Those reporting higher involvement, however, do not report higher satisfaction with teaching. Using the frequently employed index of readiness to repeat one's occupational decision, married women are clearly the most satisfied group of teachers. Men, moreover, do not approach parity with women; they are considerably less certain that they would again select teaching (table 1).[5] This difference holds up when we compare men and women on the secondary level (table 2).

The involvement represented by time and money expenditures does not balance with satisfaction as measured by readiness to teach again. Those who contribute least—the married women—are most eager to teach again; if anything, they are the apparent "gainers" in the occupation. Single women come next in their willingness to repeat the decision to teach, although their contributions exceed those of married women. Men put the largest number of their scarce resources into teaching; yet they report the lowest yield of satisfaction. If any group seems to lose, it is male teachers. We observed in chapter 2 that many men entered teaching reluctantly; it seems that an appreciable proportion remain unenthusiastic after they have taught.

The system of effort-involvement and net satisfaction, then, is not in balance; there is, in fact, a tendency for satisfactions and contributions to be negatively related. We will look into the factors which lie behind this imbalance by reviewing the interviews collected in Five Towns.

Probing the Disjunction in Five Towns

It was possible to develop overall measures of involvement and satisfaction using the questions asked in the Five Towns interview.

TABLE 1. TEACHERS' WILLINGNESS TO TEACH AGAIN

Response	Total Sample	Total Men	Total Women*	Single Women	Married Women
Certainly would become a teacher	52.6%	38.0%	59.2%	51.1%	61.6%
Probably would become a teacher	25.4	25.3	25.5	26.6	25.9
Chances are about even for and against	12.9	20.0	9.6	14.1	7.6
Probably would not become a teacher	7.1	12.6	4.6	6.5	4.1
Certainly would not become a teacher	2.0	4.1	1.1	1.6	0.9
Total	100.0%	100.0%	100.0%	99.9%	100.1%
Number reporting	2,331	724	1,607	368	1,043

Source: NEA 1967, p. 99.
*The NEA tables do not include data on women who are widowed, separated, or divorced. That omission accounts for the discrepancy between the total for this column and the totals for single and married women.

TABLE 2. SECONDARY TEACHERS' WILLINGNESS TO TEACH AGAIN

Response	Total	Men	Women
Certainly would become a teacher	44.9%	35.8%	55.6%
Probably would become a teacher	26.5	26.3	26.6
Chances are about even for and against	16.1	20.5	10.8
Probably would not become a teacher	9.7	13.0	5.7
Certainly would not become a teacher	2.9	4.3	1.2
Total	100.1%	99.9%	99.9%
Number reporting	1,107	600	507

Source: NEA 1967, p. 100.

Effort-involvement was based on three questions: (1) total hours put in during an average work week; (2) number of professional associations to which the teacher belonged and the level of activity within them; and (3) proportion of "life space" the teacher allocated to teaching work (questions 27, 80, 82, App. B-1). Three items were used to indicate the level of satisfaction: (1) a direct question asking respondents to select their level of satisfaction with teaching; (2) readiness to repeat the choice of teaching as one's occupation; and (3) citing (or not citing) specific costs when asked about losses attendant upon being a member of the teaching occupation (questions 44, 47, 83, App. B-1). A simple score of satisfaction was developed, with the higher score indicating greater satisfaction. [6]

Because of the sample size, it would not be wise to attach great weight to these distributions, but it is interesting that the pattern found is similar to the national sample just discussed; cross-tabulation of levels of satisfaction and involvement disclosed no positive association. The patterns involving men and women and single and married women, however, were similar to those in the national sample study. We turn to these now, discussing first the women and then the men.

Single women in Five Towns report somewhat higher involvement in work than their married colleagues. They put in slightly more time (one-half hour per week on the average) and join slightly more associations (.6 more). They are more active in the associations they join; 53 percent report active levels compared with 22 percent of the married teachers. Thirty-seven percent of the single teachers, compared with 6 percent of the married, engage in the highest levels of activity. It seems that differences in the involvement of time between single and married teachers occur primarily *outside* regular school activities. It is highly probable that married women allocate outside time to their families rather than to their work.

There is also an interesting difference in responses to the life space question; married women report a mean of 3.9, and single women a mean of 5.4. Married women group their responses around the midpoint of 4, probably circumventing the pan of underinvolvement and the fire of overinvolvement. Their remarks suggest that according teaching too small a place in their lives would imply inconveniencing husbands and children frivolously; some teachers said they would not feel justified in being away from home for work which was not truly important. But to accord teaching more than half of their life space is also problematic—it subordinates husband and children to work. These responses, in short, are a paradigm for the situation of the married woman who works;

occupancy of two sets of demanding roles requires careful and diplomatic balancing of their claims. The responses of single women, on the other hand, show great variation, reflecting their comparative freedom to allocate their resources as they see fit. Where single women are so inclined, they can express all-encompassing commitments to work without normative restraint.

The age of women teachers in Five Towns is also related to their level of involvement; in general, women over forty are more involved than those under forty. The main difference lies in the number of weekly hours they report (four hours more) and the proportion of life space they allocate to teaching; older women typically assign five-eighths, young women four-eighths. Inspection of the distributions reveals that few women, single or married, become deeply involved during their twenties; they seem to be hedging their bets if single and if married awaiting the arrival of a child or a change in their husband's status (e.g., completion of training). Married women who have returned to work are those who typically choose the carefully split (four-eighths) response; the truly high allocations of life space to teaching occur among the older single women. It seems that commitment to work expands when women conclude that they will remain single (Peterson 1956).

Reading an entire interview at one time provides an overall impression of the quality of a respondent's involvement. The cumulative impression gained is that women vary their definition of teaching work according to their life stage and what is happening at the time; Hughes's observations about phases and facets are germane.[7] In some interviews (especially when the interviewer was a sympathetic woman), respondents talked of adjusting work plans to marriage prospects; some single women, for example, moved in order to keep a promising relationship going. Young married women placed their work futures in the context of their husbands' careers. Older married teachers tended to be serious about their work and frequently mentioned the difficulties they encountered in convincing their husbands that household rearrangements were worth it. The strongest commitments came from some older single teachers; it was in this group that one heard statements like "teaching is my life." Such teachers connected travel and other activities to their classroom work; teaching was definitely the master role which organized other aspects of their life. (But of course there were exceptions.)[8]

Charters (1970), a serious student of "teacher survival," concludes that women's participation in teaching is a function of the life cycle; such considerations outweigh specific working conditions in school districts. The Five Towns data support this view; age and marital status, rather than grade level or socioeconomic conditions, show the larger associations. The energies and interests of women teachers flow back and forth between family and work claims in discernible, regular rhythms. Those who marry follow different courses than those who do not. Further research could profitably focus on these processes, for the evidence suggests that they are more important than the incentives provided by school systems. My findings underscore the relative weakness of organizational resources in mobilizing the involvement of women; the capacity of school officials to influence the engagements of female subordinates is sharply constrained.

As in the case of the national data, men in Five Towns (without disentangling differences due to level) are slightly more involved than women teachers. They work a little longer each week (one and one-half hours), belong to slightly more associations (.8 on the average), and are somewhat more active in their associational life—55 percent report active levels compared with 42 percent of the women. When we control for level, their edge in involvement becomes too thin to warrant attention. The position of men falls between single women and married women.

The small number of cases makes internal comparisons statistically risky, but differences observed in Five Towns are suggestive for further research. Involvement apparently varies with age for men as it does for women, but the bases for variation are probably different. Younger men (under forty) put in longer hours (three and one-half hours more), but older men accord teaching a higher proportion of their life space (5.2 to 4.5). There is more variation in the life-space scores of the younger men: two groups, elementary teachers and those planning to leave education altogether, report low scores. But men high school teachers under forty who hope for promotion have the highest scores among the younger teachers; their involvement probably reflects the wish to create the impression needed for promotion. The older men, on the other hand, cluster around a similar life-space allotment, roughly five-eighths. Their involvement pattern suggests stabilization. Teaching occupies a definite niche within their life, but they normally have strong outside interests.

Impressions drawn from reading the total interviews support inferences we can draw from the involvement data. The modal young male teacher is a man "on the way up," eager for promotion and ready to show his capacity through hard work; Griffiths (1965, p. 137) has described this orientation among New York City teachers. But two subgroups differ. The first consists of the few male elementary teachers in the sample who from all appearances are relatively passive, with low commitment. They so described themselves, saying their interest in work was low. Ironically, each hoped for promotion to principal within five years. The second subgroup consisted of young men using teaching as a temporary haven while preparing for work elsewhere. The presence of these two subgroups reflects one of the consequences of the eased entry syndrome: people with limited commitment can get into and stay in teaching. The Five Towns pattern is similar to that described by Mason; only a small proportion of the men intend to stay in teaching for a lifetime. Most hope for promotion into administrative work or for other positions outside the classroom.

One feature in the life involvement of male teachers over forty is especially interesting; almost every such man in Five Towns had either a strong avocational interest outside teaching or an additional source of employment income. One of the high schools had a very complicated administrative structure in which many teachers occupied minor positions. Teachers in that school emphasized such semiadministrative duties. Most talked about engagements outside education, however, such as ancillary careers in business and athletics or hobbies which consumed much of their interest. Sometimes the other positions they held seemed more important to them than their teaching. I could not tell whether these outside interests had always been important or had become more so after chances for promotion waned; the respondents did not seem eager to talk about earlier aspirations that had not been realized. But it is interesting that low salaries favor lower involvement for men; they may take on outside work primarily for the income and gradually become more involved in it. Although these respondents did not say they had hoped for promotion, several went out of their way to allege that promotions in their school system were based on political connections, not on merit. To the extent that patterns in Five Towns reflect those within the occupation, men may temper their involvement in teaching by developing strong outside interests. It may be that one of the major mechanisms men use to adjust to lack of promotion is partial disengagement from their roles as teachers.

The relationship between reported satisfactions and involvement among Five Towns teachers matches that found in the national survey discussed earlier. We find a similar pattern of imbalance between effort and satisfaction.

Married women report higher satisfaction levels than their more heavily involved single colleagues; the mean score of the married teachers is 7.5 and that for single teachers is 6.2. Despite the fact that they put more of themselves into their work, single women are less satisfied with teaching. The difference between married and single teachers apparently increases with age, with a 1.0 edge in satisfaction among marrieds under forty but a difference of 2.2 points in the older group. We recall that although married women over forty reported steady, balanced involvements, the highest scores were obtained by single women in that age category. The spinster teachers who have historically symbolized high commitment to teaching (e.g., the Miss Dove ideal) describe themselves as less satisfied with their work than married teachers who dedicate less of themselves to it.

Men in Five Towns, taken together, are somewhat more involved than women in toto; the mean satisfaction score of the men, however, is lower by 1.1 points (5.8 versus 6.9). Younger men—most of whom are striving for promotion—report lower scores than older men: 5.5 compared with 6.3. The lowest satisfaction scores in all subgroups occurred among young men who did not yet know whether they would be promoted. One is reminded of Stouffer's soldiers awaiting word on their disposition. Those with the lowest morale—even lower than those who knew they were getting undesirable assignments—were men uncertain of their fates. It seems that a process of reconciliation occurs as older men realize they will not be promoted.[9] But this does not occur rapidly enough to prevent considerable anxiety among male teachers under forty.

Two subgroups, therefore, show a negative balance between involvement and satisfaction—young men and older single women. Married women are most likely to show a positive balance. We can get further insight into the reasons for these differences by examining data on the "costs" associated with being a member of the teaching occupation. Responses to a question about what it cost to be a teacher correlated with the categories we have been examining (question 47, App. B-1).

More than a quarter of the teachers (28 percent) denied the premise of the question, saying that teaching had *not* entailed costs for them; this response, however, was given by twice as many women as men—36 percent versus 16 percent. More than half the married women, however, gave such an affirmative assessment of teaching; 53 percent of them, compared with 26 percent of the single women, denied that they had lost anything by choosing to teach. When men and women cited costs, they differed in their selections; 59 percent of the men said "inadequate money income," but only 4 percent of the women referred to low salaries. Women who cited costs were much likelier to say "teaching is isolated work"; they said that in 42 percent of the cases while men did so in 22 percent. Since the teaching roles of men and women are largely similar, the differences point to divergent perspectives and concerns. Three times as many single as married women mentioned the isolation

96

involved in teaching (59 percent versus 18 percent). *Every* single woman under forty citing costs mentioned isolation; the modal response of married women, on the other hand, was "no costs." The specific meanings attached to isolation were not always made explicit, but some variations could be identified. The young single women stressed that teaching is a poor base from which to meet people (including eligible males) and that the social life of the teacher is normatively constrained.

One of the things you lose is personal contact with other people. You're not meeting new people all the time....I think if you were outside the school, if you were in an office or some other kind of job, you would be meeting more people, adults. [#67 F-24-3d]

That Waller's descriptions of special moral controls over teachers are not completely outmoded is also evident (Waller 1961, p. 45):

Teaching is confining, emotionally and socially. I mean a teacher has to be a Caesar's wife, beyond reproach, particularly in the eyes of the community. You think twice about doing things. [#7 F-34-5th]

Teaching is too confining....You find that you're always watching who is around who might know you from school, and how you have to behave and who shouldn't I be seen with here and all this and that. [#9 F-32-2d]

Schools are "guarded" sites; adults in the community do not casually move in and out of them. Many schools (particularly elementary) have few males on the staff. The young woman who teaches encounters obstacles in her movements outside school; some said that they were not free to frequent places where singles meet one another (e.g., bars) since "everyone is watching." (Such moral controls may produce different results in different eras; in earlier times, they permitted young girls to work away from home and meet people they would not otherwise get to know. Today the reverse is true.)[10]

Other meanings were attached to the term "isolation," and these were alluded to by both married women and men. Teaching controls one's daily interactions so that most take place with children; some teachers expressed concern about the effects of protracted contact with children.

I think in other occupations you may meet more people with different interests. I think you are limited as to the interests of the people you meet. It gets to be "Well, Johnny..." or "In my school, they do so and so." That's about all you can talk about. [#73 F-57-3d]

I think you lose an opportunity to meet a certain group of interesting people. Many teachers are not too broad-minded about things; they lead a somewhat narrow existence." [#34 F-45-4th]

Some teachers worried aloud about how constant interaction with children might reduce their degree of adulthood and injure their intellectual functioning (Haller 1966).

If you stay with the students too long, you get to talk like them sometimes. You don't come in contact with too many adults, and your students, you are supposed to talk down to their level so that they can get it. [#25 F-28-Business]

I just think you sort of stagnate in a way. You could stagnate more if you wanted to let it happen, if you did not read, etc., but I would just like to give and take with adults once in a while. Just to be able to be in [a large office building complex] once in a while and be talking to someone in my same age bracket. [#42 F-31-1st]

Isolation can be perceived as a cost by both men and women and by both single and married teachers. Yet we can see why it is mentioned most often by single women; isolation makes it harder for them to meet potential mates. (Some unmarried teachers blame the occupation for their difficulties.) But older single women are also affected; modern family life makes the position of the single person socially marginal; single teachers are thrown back upon each other's company to a considerable degree. Relying upon other teachers to prevent loneliness intensifies the role of teaching in one's life; cultural isolation follows personal isolation. Waller (1961, p. 420) was much concerned with the narrow social range of teachers, arguing that it restricted their outlook. It is difficult to see how it could be otherwise given the life circumstances of unmarried women in modern society.

We can understand the preoccupation young men (particularly in their thirties) show with promotion and additional income. As I noted in chapter one, this is typically a period of life in which their obligations expand rapidly and their income increases slowly. There is, moreover, the discomfort involved in feeling that one is not succeeding; when others are being offered· administrative positions, the sense of being "passed over" can become painful. It seems likely that many men who leave teaching do so at this point; unfortunately, the studies of teacher dropouts do not pay close attention to these issues. Yet we must also observe that people who persist in teaching often come to terms with their situation. Wives may work outside the home to ease the economic load, and male teachers may redistribute their involvements so that teaching plays a smaller part in their lives. A small promotion in school may help, as may the informal benefits associated with seniority. Data gathered in Dade County suggest that by the time they reach their fifties, most men in teaching have made peace with their status; in fact, many no longer find the possibility of administrative rank attractive.

Summary and Implications

Teaching presents a relatively unstaged career. The main opportunity for making major status gains rests in leaving classroom work for full-time administration. The primary benefits earned by persistence in teaching (annual increases in pay) are the outcome of seniority and course-taking; the incentive system is not organized to respond to variations in effort and talent among classroom teachers.

My data support the expectations with which we began this chapter. Few beginning teachers project long futures in the classroom; men expect, in the main, to leave, and women see their participation as contingent. Entrants project a somewhat hazy picture of the future; the system does not require them to sacrifice current gratifications for long-range goals once tenure has been gained.

We expected that the lack of stages would be associated with lower rewards for those who invest much of themselves in teaching. This seems to be true; persisters are relatively disadvantaged. Men who are not promoted and women who do not marry are not defined as having made voluntary commitments. Most men work for promotion; if they fail and continue to teach, they must resign themselves to classroom teaching as a terminal status. Young single women hold off their work commitments, increasing them when they conclude that they will not marry; those who throw themselves into their work do not, it seems, earn extra benefits of satisfaction. Married women are comparatively satisfied; a flat career line permits them to come and go without serious loss of status. The system of career rewards, in sum, works most satisfactorily for those who give teaching less than full commitment; "gainers" are teachers who plan on short-term or less than full-time engagement. We are witnessing consequences of a historical pattern; the career system in teaching continues to favor recruitment rather than retention and low rather than high involvement.

There are other implications associated with this kind of reward system. It subtly depreciates the status of classroom teaching; it is not enough to be "merely" a teacher, for one must also be on the way to higher rank or, if a woman, married. This pattern of depreciation probably gives a certain fragility to relationships between younger and older teachers. Young men do not see older male teachers as models for emulation—their models are likely to be administrators. Young women probably show respect for older married teachers and qualify their admiration for those who have not married. Such discontinuities weaken the solidarity of the occupation and should receive independent research and analysis; they may be major obstacles to more effective collegial relationships among teachers. Tensions between older and younger teachers may complicate the problem of collegial leadership: a "natural" elite of highly experienced practitioners is missing. Patterns of deference and tension among members of different generations and marriage groups could provide a useful perspective for the study of organizational affairs. We might speculate that age and marital cleavages within teaching reduce the collective power of the teacher group and thereby contribute to its subordination within the system.

There is another side to this system of weak career incentives, however, which enhances teacher autonomy: it works to reduce the capacity of officials to exert influence over *individual* teachers. Although young male teachers must be sensitive to the evaluations of superordinates (they play a large part in the distribution of promotions), most other teachers have less stake in superordinate assessments. Experienced teachers, moreover, are protected by tenure and automatic pay increases; the sanctions superordinates possess have limited impact. This leverage allows married women to vary their involvement (to some extent) depending on family demands and allows men to engage themselves in activities outside teaching. Older single women can quietly define themselves as the teachers who "really care" and probably acquire moral authority as a consequence; such moral authority may provide them with considerable freedom from superordinate intervention. The system of rewards, therefore, contributes to teacher individualism by permitting variations in involvement.

Career arrangements seem to be integrated with other aspects of the occupation. Like recruitment and socialization, they foster private rather than shared orientations. Career rewards complicate vigorous collegiality among teachers. Their joint status is depreciated, few consider it "enough" for a lifetime, and those who persist occupy ambiguous positions. The peer group has no effective control over the distribution of rewards, and its most experienced members may encounter resistance when they attempt to assume leadership. On the other hand, most teachers are not greatly constrained by the set of career incentives, since money rewards do not depend on the individual decisions of superordinate officials.[11] The system permits teachers a significant degree of personal autonomy.

The Primacy of Psychic Rewards

The organization of career rewards in teaching fosters a present-oriented rather than future-oriented point of view; those who intend to stay in the classroom have limited need to delay gratification in the hope of future gain. Few beginning teachers intend to stay very long, and the majority of teachers are women who have little interest in leaving the classroom for other work. Most teachers will therefore emphasize rewards they can earn in the present; this propensity affects the *kinds* of rewards which will matter to them.

The thesis of this section is that cultural and structural aspects of the occupation influence teachers to emphasize psychic rewards in their work. The cultural influences stem from a long tradition of teaching as service; that tradition, as we saw in chapter 2, affects recruitment into the occupation and the outlook of those who are drawn in. Structural considerations affect the differential responsiveness of various rewards to teacher effort; teachers consequently tend to concentrate their energies at points where effort may make a difference (Lortie 1969).

We can classify rewards into three types: extrinsic rewards, ancillary rewards, and psychic or intrinsic rewards. The first includes what we usually think of as the "earnings" attached to a role and involves money income, a level of prestige, and power over others. These earnings are "extrinsic" in the sense that they exist independently of the individual who occupies the role; since they are experienced by all incumbents, they have an "objective" quality. Ancillary rewards are simultaneously objective and subjective; they refer to objective characteristics of the work which may be perceived as rewards by some (e.g., married women might consider the work schedules of teaching to be rewarding while men might not). Ancillary rewards tend to be stable through time, and to be "taken for granted" rather than specified in contracts; for example, people expect teaching to be cleaner than factory work. Psychic rewards consist entirely of subjective valuations made in the course of work engagement; their subjectivity means that they can vary from person to person. But they are also constrained by the nature of the occupation and its tasks; we would not expect lighthouse keepers to list sociability as a work reward or street cleaners to rejoice in opportunities for creative expression. It is an empirical task to find recurrent patterns in such subjective, psychic rewards; the goal is to uncover rewards which cut across the preferences of individuals.

The culture and surrounding structure of an occupation are likely to influence the emphasis on some kinds of rewards rather than others. We get the types of variations I mentioned at the beginning of the chapter; in one occupation, achievement will be defined essentially in money terms; in another it will be measured by rank attained or power acquired. The values of the occupation work together with the core tasks to produce a characteristic reward structure among the membership. For example, deference and approval flow to the wealthiest financiers, the most powerful politicians, and the highest-ranked bureaucrats.

The culture of teachers and the structure of rewards do not emphasize the acquisition of extrinsic rewards. The traditions of teaching make people who seek money, prestige, or power somewhat suspect; the characteristic style in public education is to mute personal ambition. The service ideal has extolled the virtue of giving more than one receives; the model teacher has been ''dedicated.'' (I suspect these values are linked to the sacred connotations of teaching in early American history.) Some will assert that teachers abandon this tradition when they organize and strike; this is probably so in some respects. But we cannot conclude that collective aggressiveness legitimates *individual* ambition; group activity to raise salaries is not the same as individualistic attempts to raise one's standing. Nor can we infer that it will produce a normative change in which teachers channel deference and approval to those who make idiosyncratic gains. There may be instances, in fact, where the opposite is true and group mobility reduces support for individualistic ambitions; if the group is successful in getting more money and other rewards, the individual's claims may be weakened. Teachers continue to oppose internal differentiation in rewards on grounds other than seniority or education; their behavior has been consistently egalitarian.

The way extrinsic rewards are distributed makes it difficult for individual teachers to influence their flow in the short run. Salary payments are fixed annually; one's income goes up primarily as one acquires seniority and takes courses. The formal standing of teachers within a given system tends toward equality; the major distinction is between beginners (probationary teachers without tenure) and others. (Some teachers, of course, develop informal reputations as outstanding or ineffective, but these are not reflected in formal status.) Important research could be done on the issue of power and teachers; officially, however, teacher power is limited to specified authority over students; teachers are not supposed to *enjoy* exercising power per se. Extrinsic rewards tend to be comparatively undifferentiated.

Opportunities to increase extrinsic rewards are also limited in the long run. Some teachers improve their lot by moving to more prosperous school systems; we recall, however, that many teachers are place-bound, particularly women with family responsibilities. Teachers who accept intermediate positions of responsibility (e.g., department chairmen) are likely to complain that the obligations exceed their authority and that money rewards are inadequate for the effort required. Fame and fortune are rarely the lot of the classroom teacher.

Ancillary rewards affect entry to a given line of work more than the effort of those in it; organizational theorists make the distinction between incentives which affect membership and incentives which affect participation (March and Simon 1958). People may be attracted to teaching partly because it offers economic security or has a schedule perforated by frequent holidays and vacations; but once they are in teaching, they probably take such advantages for granted (for one thing, they are also enjoyed by everyone else around). Ancillary rewards are present whether one makes high or limited effort on the job. The significance of ancillary rewards, in sum, lies in the contrast with other kinds of employment; they may restrain a person from leaving the occupation, but they are unlikely to affect the effort he exerts on a day-to-day basis.

Unlike extrinsic and ancillary rewards, the psychic rewards of teachers fluctuate; the teacher's enjoyment of his work can vary. Effort will not make much difference in the flow of extrinsic and ancillary rewards, at least in the short run. Effort, on the other hand, might increase task-related satisfactions. Nor are teachers so constrained that they feel their decisions make little difference in their work; they are not assembly line workers whose every move is paced by externally controlled systems of production. (Jackson [1968] reports that teachers make well over two hundred decisions hourly.) One would expect teachers, then, to concentrate on psychic rewards; energy directed toward their realization can affect total rewards. The structure of teaching rewards, in short, favors emphasis on psychic rewards. When we recall that the culture emphasizes service, we should not be surprised if the data underscore the significance of psychic rewards in the work life of classroom teachers. We turn next to such data.

The marked tendency for teachers to connect their major rewards with classroom events was first noticed in the Five Towns interviews. Respondents fused the idea of work gratification and the idea of work goals; they made little distinction between deriving satisfaction from their work and reaching classroom objectives. In answering questions which asked specifically about the satisfactions they received from teaching, they overwhelmingly cited task-related outcomes. On one question, for example, 125 mentions were coded as psychic reward references, while 11 dealt with ancillary rewards and 9 with extrinsic; on a follow-up question, all but 4 of the responses were connected with work outcomes (question 40, App. B-1). The major emphasis in answers to both questions was that satisfaction accompanied desirable results with students; respondents experienced gratification when they felt they had influenced students.

Similar data are found in a national survey conducted by the National Education Association (NEA 1963, p. 69). Twenty percent of respondents were asked an open-ended question in which they were requested to identify "sources of professional satisfaction and encouragement." "Students" was selected by 78.9 percent of the respondents, and 18.3 percent said "teaching in general." All other sources mentioned received fewer mentions; they included administrators, working conditions, teachers, parents, facilities, and the community. The typical quotations presented in the text reveal that concern with classroom results dominates the modal replies; teaching is satisfying and encouraging when positive things happen in the classroom.

The most detailed and relevant data were those I gathered in Dade County, Florida. Respondents were asked a series of four questions; the first listed alternative extrinsic rewards and asked respondents to select the one which provided them the greatest satisfaction. A similar procedure was used in two additional questions which asked about psychic and ancillary rewards. The fourth question asked respondents to select from the three clusters of extrinsic, ancillary, and psychic rewards (questions T8, T9, T10, T11, App. B-2). The data are presented in table 3.

The answers to the last question indicate that these teachers consider psychic rewards their major source of work satisfaction; 76.5 percent chose psychic rewards compared with 11.9 percent selecting extrinsic rewards and 11.7 percent ancillary rewards. The modal response is *six times* as frequent as the closest contender. It is also noteworthy that the psychic income responses "piled up" under one of the alternatives listed; the modal answer got 86.1 percent of the choices. That alternative was "the times I know I have 'reached' a student or group of students and they have learned." The next most frequent response also dealt with students, but the emphasis was on association with them rather than discernible results. Fewer than 1 percent said none of the psychic rewards was important; 13.3 percent selected that response for extrinsic rewards, and 15.3 percent did the same for ancillary rewards. Since the vast majority of responses to this question dealt directly with classroom and student events, it is clear that these teachers consider the classroom the major arena for the receipt of psychic rewards. Thousands of teachers in Dade County report the same "joys of teaching" which Jackson and

TABLE 3. TYPES OF REWARDS, DADE COUNTY TEACHERS

Extrinsic Rewards	(N)	(%)	Psychic Rewards	(N)	(%)	Ancillary Rewards	(N)	(%)	All Combined	(N)	(%)
Salary	835	14.4	Chance to study, read, and plan for classes	200	3.4	Security of income and position	1,302	22.4	Extrinsic	693	11.9
Respect from others	2,127	36.6	Discipline and class-room management	69	1.2	Time (esp. summers) for travel, etc.	1,348	23.2	Psychic	4,463	76.5
Chance to use influence	2,083	35.8	Knowing that I have "reached" students and they have learned	5,067	86.1	Freedom from competition, rivalry	288	5.0	Ancillary	681	11.7
No satisfaction from these	773	13.3	Chance to associate with children or young people	470	8.0	Appropriateness for people like me	1,977	34.1			
Total	5,818	100.1	Chance to associate with other teachers	63	1.1	No satisfaction from these	890	15.3	Total	5,837	100.1
			No satisfaction from these	17	0.3	Total	5,805	100.0			
			Total	5,886	100.1						

Belford (1965) found among teachers who were rated as especially competent.

It is of great importance to teachers to feel they have "reached" their students—their core rewards are tied to that perception. Other sources of satisfaction (e.g., private scholarly activities, relationships with adults) pale in comparison with teachers' exchanges with students and the feeling that students have learned. We would therefore expect that much of a teacher's work motivation will rotate around the conduct of daily tasks—the actual instruction of students. In that regard, the exertion of effort and the earning of important rewards are congruent; they are not in the position of those who must trade away psychic rewards in order to make a living (Becker 1951). Teachers face different problems.

The nature of teacher rewards makes it important for us to understand what we can about the content of teacher goals. What do they mean by "reaching students"? Such knowledge will help us to get a better grasp of how schools work and how teachers define their tasks. We will examine teacher goals in the next chapter. First, however, I will make a few comments on the direction being taken by this analysis of teaching as an occupation.

The first four chapters of this book have dealt with the development and perpetuation of the structure of teaching as an occupation; we have focused specifically on recruitment, socialization, and the system of work rewards. We find that these processes give rise to characteristic outlooks among teachers; the recurrent themes are conservatism, individualism, and presentism. A circle is completed as the structure produces orientations which reinforce it; historians who have described schools as self-perpetuating institutions get support from this analysis (Tyack 1967, p. 314).

The perspective in the following chapters is somewhat different. I will talk less about structure and more about meanings; the approach will be more phenomenological as we examine the tasks teachers perform and the ways they define them. I will pay particular attention to "cathected attitudes"—to the work sentiments found among classroom teachers. I am not leaving my interest in the ethos of the occupation but rather am coming at it from a different direction; the center of attention is now on tasks rather than on occupational perpetuation.

Nor am I leaving my interest in system; sentiments, no less than orientations, are likely to interlock in mutually supporting ways. We may find, in fact, that the sentiments teachers hold toward their everyday tasks reflect the orientations we have explored so far. The ethos of an occupation—if it is integrated—probably reflects various realities confronting those who work within it.

We think of work as activity directed toward achieving goals. It is how people earn their living. But it is usually something more; the story of work is largely a matter of elaboration beyond economic necessity. From preliterate mythology to modern ideology, man has "made more" of his daily routine, investing it with special feeling and broader meanings. This is in part what Everett Hughes means by alluding to "the drama of work."[12]

But it is no simple thing to find out what meanings people attach to their work. Occupational groups are likely to fill the air with rhetoric which purports to explain the intentions of their members. Some such talk reflects concern with recognition as a "profession"; members of many occupations are preoccupied with persuading others that their work deserves that designation. There are defenses built against attack from the outside; occupations have members who recall past insults and mount symbolic counterattacks. In occupations like teaching which rely on public support, there is pressure to justify the group's disposal of tax resources, to show that public expectations are being fulfilled. It is easier to state than to resolve the social scientist's problem. To gain and give an accurate picture, he must penetrate the rhetoric of prestige-seeking, defense, and public justification to identify the genuine sentiments of people within the occupation.

The following chapters represent serious efforts to solve that methodological problem. We will, for example, test various kinds of statements against each other, particularly in chapters 5 and 7. Greater reliance will be placed on data which are personal, concrete, specific, and cathected, a strategy I will discuss in chapter 5. The issues explored in the next few chapters require intensive interview materials which are usually too expensive (in terms of time as well as money) to gather and process in large numbers. This means that I will not be able to support as many patterns with national data as I would like, but limits imposed by sample size will be respected; most of the analysis will examine themes without major reliance on quantitative distributions. The data employed have an enormous advantage; they were gathered in interviews which encouraged respondents to talk at length in terms of their conceptualization of the teacher's world. If we succeed in understanding the language used, we can be assured that our observations arise directly from firsthand experience with the realities of classroom teaching.

The next chapter will deal with the personal goals of Five Towns teachers, using three perspectives. That discussion will introduce us to the complexity of achievement and reward realization in teaching. In chapter 6 we will examine the problematics of the teaching craft in some detail. Chapters 7 and 8 will reveal that the way teachers define their tasks underlies the sentiments they hold toward their daily work and the interactions which flow from it.

5

Perspectives on Purpose

Psychic rewards are an important part of the total rewards received by classroom teachers. Since psychic rewards apparently revolve around classroom achievement, understanding their nature requires familiarity with how teachers define achievement. The way teachers see achievement will influence the level of psychic reward they achieve in their daily work. If they perceive achievement as easy and regular, their psychic rewards will be high and assured; but if they believe achievement is difficult and unpredictable, they will experience psychic rewards as scarce and uncertain. As we shall have occasion to see later, the flow of rewards in teaching has consequences for other aspects of occupational life.

To find connections among psychic rewards, the definition of achievement, and other features of teaching, we must delve into the meanings teachers attach to accomplishment. The term *achievement* denotes "the act of accomplishing or finishing something." To grasp the substance of teacher achievement, therefore, we must be able to specify that "something."[1] This brings up the question of goals. What do teachers seek to attain in their classroom work?

This chapter focuses on the substance of teacher purposes; in the next chapter, we will examine the processes of assessing and operationalizing achievement. Yet identifying teacher goals is not a simple task. Some organizational theorists leave the impression that we can infer the goals of members by reviewing the formal purposes of the organization. We saw in chapter 4, however, that such inference is dangerous in the case of schools; official statements of school objectives and the daily reality of classroom teaching are not the same thing. Empirical inquiry is needed to establish what goals are meaningful to classroom teachers and, as we also observed in chapter 4, we must find ways to penetrate abstract and ambiguous language. The sentiments of teachers, in short, can be hidden behind opaque language. We will explore three perspectives on teacher goals and analyze what each yields. Each perspective produces useful information, but they seem to be of unequal value in penetrating to teacher sentiments. I favor four criteria in assessing different kinds of data on sentiments: (1) indirect versus direct questions, (2) personal versus impersonal referents, (3) concrete versus abstract referents, and (4) cathected versus low-affect issues. If the respondent is asked overtly to discuss his objectives, the question is direct—and likely to evoke an ideological response. But if a question stimulates evaluative comments which indirectly reveal the respondent's objectives, the chances of evoking ideological statements are reduced.[2] Respondents are better able to provide details on personal experiences and, if well interviewed, will be more spontaneous than in discussing general matters. The more concrete the events elicited, the freer the analyst is to develop his categories of analysis; concreteness permits him to compare responses which might otherwise be rendered incomparable by divergent and abstract rhetorics. Finally, questions which tie attitudes to strong feelings (e.g., pride and shame) come closest, in my view, to expressing the core idea of the term *sentiment*.[3]

The first perspective elicits teacher hopes and ideals—a direct, personal question provoked talk about the ways Five Towns teachers elaborate curricular objectives. The second perspective connects with classroom events; it reveals the standards respondents use in assessing colleagues. The questions are indirect and concrete. The third perspective meets all four of the favored criteria; a question about what occasions generate pride is indirect, personal, concrete, and cathected. After reviewing the three perspectives in separate sections, I will conclude the chapter with a general summary.

Phenomenological analysis of the kind undertaken in this chapter requires open-ended, detailed, and intensive data; the categories and findings which emerge reflect analysis of how teachers see their world. Since few researchers have addressed themselves to the issues considered here, we will not be able to rely on comparative data to support or qualify interpretations. The approach is thematic and only lightly quantitative; few comparisons will be made within the sample itself. It should be possible, however, for others to inquire into the generality of the findings, for the exploratory functions performed by this chpater should allow researchers to develop economical ways of studying other samples. They can do so in the knowledge that the analysis is grounded in close contact with teachers' definitions of their work reality.

Beyond the Curriculum

People at work are inclined to dignify and elaborate the significance of the tasks they perform to earn a living; that proclivity has been observed from one end of the occupational spectrum to the other, from building janitors to medical specialists (Gold, undated; Lortie 1949). Classroom teachers are no exception. It should prove helpful, therefore, to examine the forms their elaborations take. High ideals are not, after all, without significance in the affairs of men and women.

Much of the teacher's role is defined by his position in the division of labor established by the school curriculum. There is little to suggest that classroom teachers struggle against the specifications included in such curricula; they do not seem to share the sentiments of university professors who believe they are exclusively equipped to control instruction. Yet the available data indicate that many teachers want to add something personal (by way of emphasis) to their curricular responsibilities. In Dade County, for example, most of the teachers selected a response which, while granting the legitimacy of the prescribed curriculum, permitted them some degree of individual freedom.[4] Five Towns teachers showed the same propensity when they were asked about their ultimate objectives (question 34, App. B-1). In the modal response (77 percent), the teacher described curricular responsibilities but went on to talk about special, personal concerns.

The "extras" alluded to by Five Towns teachers were coded into three major categories. These are (1) the moral aspects of teaching, (2) the "connecting" function of the teacher who instills love of school or a particular subject, and (3) the theme of inclusiveness—of reaching *all* the students in one's charge. I will describe each in turn, citing quotations which convey the tone. The responses may surprise some readers who are familiar with educational ideologies.

The Teacher as Moral Agent

The ideal goals of some teachers are consistent with the moral roots of American schooling. About half of the Five Towns teachers emphasized moral outcomes they hoped would result from their work. Although secularized, the talk of some respondents reminds one of the basic tenets

111

of the colonial founders and of the linkage they perceived between reading and goodness. A first grade teacher comments:

> What am I trying to do most of all? Well, in the first grade, trying to teach the child to read and want to read, but what I suppose I'm really doing is trying to get that child ready to live in society, to take care of himself and become the proper kind of member of that society. [#70 F-65-1st]

De Tocqueville (1954) was impressed by the preoccupation of nineteenth-century Americans with the public consequences of schooling. Several generations later, one hears the same motif:

> I'm trying to make them good citizens in the community. Not only as far as subject matter, but as far as what their obligations are....We have special elections in class....They know what is expected of them by the time they are out of sixth grade, the difference between right and wrong. [#55 F-25-6th]

> Every spare minute I try to stress good citizenship, and if anything comes up in the classroom, the subjects are dropped and I go into that particular thing. Even if you just took someone's pencil, I would say, "Do you realize, etc."...I think that's the most important thing, more than subject matter. Some of them don't get it at home. [#1 F-28-4th]

There has been much talk about the effects of educational movements such as Progressivism and Life Adjustment. But the rhetoric of teachers suggests that ideas generated by such movements can be absorbed into more traditional conceptions of the teacher's role:

> You have to prepare them for life. I don't care if they don't know how to typewrite, they have to be individuals first. They have to be respectful...honest and respectful...good citizens and so forth. [#25 F-28-Business]

> To develop pupils who will become wholesome individuals in society ...who will recognize that I am fair and that is the way they should be in their dealings with other people. They will respect not only the teacher but have respect for others. [#54 M-43-History]

Cotton Mather and Benjamin Franklin would have been comfortable with such goals as independence, knowledge of right and wrong, respect for property, honesty, and respect for those in authority.

Teachers are charged with maintaining good order and discipline in their classrooms. It is highly probable, in my view, that elaborations along moral lines, in addition to demonstrating continuities within teaching, give additional meaning to these disciplinary activities.

If you're a good child, you'll grow up to be a good, useful citizen. [#20 F-54-1st]

Now discipline problems are either emotional or moral. In other words, he does not obey.... In other words, I look upon it as morality. [#17 M-37-English]

Although some respondents stressed the desirability of independence of mind, most allusions to moral outcomes and citizenship emphasized compliance and obedience. Connecting compliance with classroom norms to future citizenship authenticates the teacher's control efforts. Thus discipline becomes more than mere forbidding and ordering; the dross of classroom management is transformed into the gold of dependable citizenship. Whereas some critics of schools cry "oppression" at teacher dominance of classrooms, these respondents see it as preparing citizens for the Republic.

Various sociologists have commented on the tendency of teachers to instill "middle-class" attitudes in children from lower-class families (Havighurst and Neugarten 1957). It is questionable whether all the values implied in the responses are exclusively middle class—honesty, decent treatment of one's fellows, industry, and so forth are not the sole property of one class. But some teachers working with lower-class students allude to issues of social class and the presentation of self:

I'd say a background of workable English. They give themselves away when they speak. While they make themselves understood, they all classify themselves when they say "Do you want me to put them letters in the post box?" You know what they mean but they won't be as comfortable among different kinds of people if they are not familiar with their native language. [#5 F-68-English]

To see moral training as an ideal outcome from one's teaching is to assume, consciously or not, that schools should supplement the moral influence of the family. These teachers put themselves in a countervailing role vis-à-vis their students' homes; they see school as doing work the family has failed to do. There is some suggestion in the Five Towns data that this orientation is more frequent when teachers teach students from lower-status homes; and the point merits further inquiry. (Some of the difficulties which arise in the instruction of urban black children may reflect teachers' preoccupation with moral rather than strictly instructional concerns.) Those who see teaching as offsetting the moral deficien-

113

cies of family rearing obviously define teaching as a general socialization function. That the viewpoint is widespread in Five Towns (and I suspect elsewhere) is not surprising when we recall that for many decades one of the major functions of the public school system was to "Americanize" the children of foreign-born parents.

Connecting Children to School and Learning

Other respondents elaborated their answers in quite a different way— they hoped for outcomes specifically related to the intellectual functions of schooling. But their hopes are not strictly cognitive in nature; what they find exciting is the prospect of inducing positive attitudes among their students toward school or toward a particular branch of learning. They hope their teaching will produce affective changes. Their aspirations are to "solder" the student to school or to a particular subject, and the emphasis, unsurprisingly, varies by level:

Superficially, I'm trying to put across my subject matter. Basically, I want them to learn to be eager to want to learn things. [#15 F-54-1st]

I like to think I try to make them like school. I know some of them don't. I don't think it's normal...I think a laugh here and there is good; in fact, you have to have it. [#6 M-24-5th]

Instill a love of learning from within. Not learning for the sake of bettering one's economic status but the love of education for the sake of education. The enrichment of the individual's life. [#6 M-24-5th]

Trying to make them think on their own, be independent. To me, fine if they learn chemistry, but in examinations I want to see if they can take it down and think it out clearly...cause and effect is the main thing. [#51 M-26-Science]

The assumptions underlying the hopes of these respondents are not those of "romantics" who believe that children are naturally eager to learn. They believe it takes a teacher to stimulate intellectual curiosity and interest in school. These respondents differ from their colleagues who express objectives of a moral sort, and they define their roles in more strictly intellectual terms. One wonders, Are these elaborations related to other orientations such as favoring or rejecting the image of school as a general socialization agency? (Research might be conducted on this question.) In any event, the fact that these different elaborations occur suggests that some degree of value pluralism obtains among classroom teachers.

Inclusive Teaching: The Concern with Universalism

The ideals of American public schools include two principles: the importance of equity in treatment and the assumption that all children can benefit from schooling. The structure makes it difficult (though not impossible) to openly favor particular children or to argue that some children cannot be taught; compulsory schooling would be undermined if the possibility were granted that not all children profit from schooling. Whatever the reality may be, public schools are *supposed* to be fair in their treatment of children and, as instruments of mass education, are expected to provide educational services for all who attend.[5]

It seems curious, therefore, that some Five Towns teachers cite effective work with all students as something "extra," as beyond the mere fulfillment of their duties. One can only presume that they do so in the conviction that attention to all is *not* the rule, that students can and do slip through school without close attention from some teachers. But there are Five Towns teachers who are particularly concerned with this issue:

> I'm trying to get every kid to read as well as he can. Until every kid that I touch can read what he's supposed to, I'm not happy. [#21 F-56-Reading]

> I would like to be able to get every child to read and enjoy reading and be able to think because if a child can read he's way ahead of everybody else. [#31 M-26-6th]

> If I have thirty students, I want to get across to all thirty of them, after school, during recess or something like that. [#24 M-33-Business]

The three kinds of elaboration found in Five Towns point to a modest yet real degree of value pluralism within the occupation.[6] It should be borne in mind, however, that these are elaborations around a common curricular base; respondents largely accept the rule of the curriculum and are subject to controls which foster its implementation (e.g., some systems use standardized tests to check on student progress in terms of the curriculum; teachers who "receive" another's students may be critical if there are gaps in their prescribed knowledge). It would be rash to assume that subtle differences in emphasis produce highly divergent behavior by teachers in the same subject or grade. Whatever the effects of these differences in emphasis may be, I suspect they are subtle and require sensitive inquiry. Yet it may be that these differences in elaboration reveal value differences which retard occupational solidarity.

It is interesting, moreover, that the range of ideals expressed by these

115

respondents is neither as broad nor as modern as we might expect from knowledge of educational philosophy. The three themes stressed do not exhaust the range of educational objectives, nor do they point to sharp discontinuity with the beliefs of earlier generations of teachers. I get the impression that much pedagogical discourse has either been rejected by these teachers or absorbed into earlier viewpoints. Today's teachers probably show greater concern for affective and egalitarian aspects of their work than did their ferule-wielding predecessors. But in the moral aspects of teaching continuity rather than change seems to prevail. The individualism enhanced by the structure has had the result we might expect; teachers select different values for personal emphasis.

The types of elaboration found in Five Towns are not likely to produce an easy sense of classroom achievement or a lavish yield of psychic rewards. The ideals presume a high level of interpersonal impact on the part of the teacher; he must change moral or emotional attitudes or permeate the consciousness of every student. If the desired outcomes are to be reinforced by personal precept, the teacher must conduct himself in a morally blameless, intellectually alert, or extremely conscientious manner. The most obvious test of one's achievement—student behavior —is also stringent when one uses these standards; noncompliant behavior, lack of enthusiasm for study, or failure to learn remind the teacher that his work is not accomplished. The structure of school organization is sufficiently loose to give teachers some say in the allocation of their psychic rewards. To the degree that they employ the standards involved in these elaborations, they cannot be accused of dealing themselves "fixed hands."

Collegial Performances: Criteria for Respect

Occupational insiders do not assess the performance of co-workers in quite the same way as outsiders; knowing the true difficulties in the work, they distinguish between the showy, easy maneuver and the subtle, difficult feat. If we can explicate the criteria insiders use in assessing one another's work, we learn much about the standards of the occupational group. If we can identify the outcomes insiders associate with superior performances, we can locate the working goals of members of the group.

How do teachers describe someone they consider to be an outstanding teacher? What results do they link with such persons? We can answer these questions for Five Towns teachers, since they gave full descriptions of their own outstanding teachers and discussed outstanding contemporaries (questions 29, 30; App. B-1). In analyzing the content, I paid particular attention to the outcomes the respondents associated with such teachers—the interview called for probing on that point. These data have the advantages of indirection and concreteness we discussed in the introductory comments.

It did not require much probing for Five Towns teachers to talk about the outstanding teachers they had in school and college. The teachers they described were not all alike; they were male and female, young and old, warm and cold, attractive and repulsive, exciting and methodical. It is also noteworthy that the same teacher frequently described strikingly diverse persons; this happened in more than half the cases where a respondent described more than one former teacher. We can illustrate the diversity with a few examples:

And in college, the one I disliked the most. . .I now realize gave me all I have today. She was excellent, if you could survive. . . . She was like a witch. . .cynical and sarcastic. . .she didn't seem to have a heart. . .but you could not beat her for not wasting time. . . .It was just clear-cut, cold informtion. . . .I realized in later years she really was good. [#42 F-31-1st]

I have still very, very vivid remembrance of a school teacher I had in third grade in the little country school. She was one of the most loving types of people with youngsters and made every one of us feel that she had a great deal of thought for all of us. She was peppy and full of fun, we learned, we worked harder than we probably realized we were working but we loved it. [#73 F-57-3d]

The finest teacher I ever had was Mr. ——— at ——— State College. He taught a course in Dickens and his age and he inspired me to do a good deal more in this field of Dickens. He made me want to work more than any other person I had. . . .He was a teacher. It is intangible. He loved his work and he spread that love to his students. [#11 M-41-Science]

The outcomes respondents mentioned in describing the teachers were classified into two major categories: ultimate, instructional results and proximate, relational conditions. The first, hereafter abbreviated to "instructional" outcomes, are the conventional kinds of educational objectives we find in curriculum outlines, educational specifications, and books and articles on teaching goals. The second, however, can more properly be seen as "means" which contribute to such instructional ends; they consist of interpersonal transactions and states which teachers realize with their students. The latter are usually portrayed not as ends in themselves but as conditions for effective teaching; we do not normally

117

think of schools as existing so that students can be disciplined, work hard, or have a warm relationship with a teacher. I will subsequently refer to the second kind of outcomes as "relational."

Five Towns teachers mentioned more instructional than relational outcomes in describing their outstanding mentors.[7] Instructional outcomes included references to cognitive effectiveness and to affective outcomes linked to learning.[8] Cognitive effectiveness was coded when respondents made statements such as "she got it across to me" or "he made algebra make sense to me." Affective outcomes meant that the respondent's feelings were influenced; examples are "I came to love poetry" or "I wanted to read more." Instructional references were usually personal in nature—the respondent commented on the teacher's ability to promote his learning and to change his attitudes.

Three kinds of relational outcomes were found in the testimonials of these teachers: (1) the teacher produced affection and respect from students; (2) the teacher got work out of the students; and (3) the teacher was effective in winning student compliance and discipline.[9] The outstanding teacher generated affection or respect or both: "I liked her"; or "she had everyone's respect." The high-performance teacher elicited effort—the speaker and his classmates worked hard: "we were afraid of her but we worked hard"; and "he worked hard and expected you to." Some respondents commented on the firmness of the recalled teacher's discipline with remarks such as "her discipline was strict and she wouldn't put up with anything," or "you learned from her, or else." Teachers are remembered for their leadership capacity as well as their instructional effectiveness. Loved or feared, they got students to work.

It should be pointed out that the distinction between instructional and relational outcomes was not made explicit by respondents; it was superimposed for analytic reasons. Respondents did not separate and label the strands implied by the distinction between ends and means; their comments flowed back and forth between instructional outcomes and descriptions of the honored teacher's methods or approach. The way they talked suggests that they do not have a differentiated view of the outcomes associated with outstanding teaching; it seems, rather, to be a unity of effective action and desirable results. (This fits, I believe, with the nonanalytic bent I identified in chapter 3.) The outstanding remembered teacher, then, induced learning and love of learning and elicited positive feelings and high effort while maintaining discipline. The specific configuration of the unity differs from instance to instance, but whether the recalled teachers were martinets or madonnas, their interpersonal capacities are perceived as an integral part of their memorable results. The mastery of interpersonal processes, then, can be seen as close

118

to the heart of the respondents' definitions of high performance in their craft.

It is probably easier for most of us to be generous with our mentors than our contemporaries; as Hughes points out, colleagues are competitors as well as cooperators.[10] Five Town teachers, in the main, were willing to nominate peers as outstanding. A few, however, demurred, saying that they had too little occasion to observe other teachers at work. The explanation for their reluctance suggests that they consider direct evaluation of classroom technique an indispensable ingredient of any assessment. The same categories (with one addition) were used to classify the outcomes associated with outstanding contemporaries as were used with outstanding past teachers; the addition consisted of a subcategory under instructional outcomes for instances where respondents saw the admired colleague "rescue" a child who was considered an "impossible case."

Although the talk about contemporaries is similar to that we discussed for past teachers, there is one interesting difference. In describing peers, Five Town teachers emphasized relational outcomes.[11] One could interpret this by observing that teachers have little opportunity to assess each other's results, but the same limitation presumably applies to assessing the quality of the teacher's relationships with students. My interpretation of this difference is that teachers assess their peers largely by how they handle relationships with students. They do so, I believe, because they have a particular stake in the methods used by colleagues.

Teachers at different levels (i.e., elementary versus secondary) tend to use different rhetoric in describing the feelings students demonstrate toward their outstanding colleagues. Elementary teachers tend to use affectively hot terms such as "students adore her" or "students love her." High school teachers, on the other hand, employ more restrained language, substituting words like "respect" and "esteem." Both kinds of teachers, however, link the evocation of such positive feelings with the capacity to establish and maintain control. When they select a peer as outstanding, they make it clear that his popularity is *not* purchased by pandering to student wishes for an easy time:

> In many classrooms, when the 3 o'clock bell rings the kiddoes are anxious to leave the building. In her classroom, they are not. They like to hang around after school. . . . She is reaching them and doing a good job of it. They certainly like her and she's not lax and I don't mean to say that she lets them get away with murder. She's very frank. She has good discipline. [#18 M-36-4th]

> She lays the cards before them. They know she is a dedicated sincere teacher who knows her business and won't stand for any monkey busi-

ness. . . . The children really just adore her. They come back year after year thanking her. [#37 F-29-4th]

It happens to be a man I personally dislike as a person. . . but he has a magnificent ability to inspire youngsters. . . . He has strong discipline and yet the kids adore him for his knowledge and his background and they will work for him. [#22 F-55-English]

Why do Five Towns teachers stress interpersonal relationships in describing outstanding peers, and what lies behind the connection between eliciting student affection or regard while maintaining discipline? My own view is that two factors are at work. I agree with Waller that teachers have an interest in maintaining faculty solidarity vis-à-vis students; the "easy" teacher lets the side down (Waller 1961, p. 428). But there is another reason, if one pays attention to the quest for psychic rewards. In assessing whether they are attaining their objectives, teachers observe student behavior and use indexes to interpret it; students who show enthusiasm for the teacher may, after all, be showing that they are learning and enjoying that learning. Such student affection and regard are also intrinsically rewarding; people normally enjoy being the object of affection and esteem. In trying to elicit favorable feelings from students (whatever the motivation), teachers are willy-nilly placed in competition with each other; some will obviously succeed better than others. Thus they nominate for honors only those who they feel have earned respect through "fair means"—that is, not by reducing the demands they make on the students. (In chapter 6 we will go into more detail on the problem of balancing demands from students with response from them.)

In summary, then, we have obtained additional information about teacher purposes by examining the criteria they use when describing others they consider outstanding. The elaborations elicited by direct questions concentrated on the ultimate outcomes of instruction, on learning changes in students. But when we ask teachers to describe the outcomes achieved by outstanding colleagues, they emphasize results of a proximate and relational nature. The outstanding teacher not only produces learning and the love of learning but evokes respect and affection, high effort from students, and compliance with classroom rules. The outstanding teacher, past or present, manifests classroom leadership; the qualities cited suggest a degree of personal charisma.

When we compare teacher criteria for outstanding performance with the announced objectives of school systems, we find that what formal statements are likely to assume, teachers do not. School systems often advertise their goals as including, for example, "the full realization of each child's potential." It is clear that the aims of classroom teachers are less exalted; they are ready to consider a teacher outstanding if he gets observable results and exercises firm leadership. Since these outcomes are labeled "outstanding," the inference is that most teaching falls short of those standards. The implication is clear; teaching is inherently problematic and its psychic rewards are not automatic.

Craft Pride as Realized Purpose

People experience craft pride when they succeed in reaching work goals which are important to them. Knowing what occasions generate such feelings can help us to understand the objectives of members of a particular occupation. It tells us what insiders consider the more challenging aspects of their work; one is not likely to feel pride at attaining something relatively easy. When do teachers feel the glow of high achievement?

Respondents answered a question about prideful occasions with colorful and specific comments (question 32, App. B-1). These data warrant close attention, and we shall consider them in detail. The elementary teachers' answers were marked by a large modal response; the answers of high school teachers were more varied. I will mention, but not emphasize, statistical distributions; my aim is to identify significant themes and their characteristics.

The Spectacular Case

Well over half (64 percent) of the elementary teachers in Five Towns organized their discussion of craft pride around striking success with one student.[12] They told how the student in question was seriously problematic—in many instances others thought the student was beyond help by classroom teachers. The student was usually a boy and somehow stigmatized; he suffered from severe personal difficulties, ill health, or depreciated social position. The plot in these stories features a dismal beginning, the teacher's persistence in the face of unfavorable prospects, and a happy ending in which the student is restored to normal functioning. Thus the unruly child learns to comply, the child with a reading problem learns to read, or the withdrawn child begins to participate, and academic improvement follows. It would be nearly impossible to paraphrase the stories without distorting them in some way; I present four which have been only slightly edited:

> I had a child who came in from California and he had just had an emotional shock. His mother had been killed. . .he was the most unhappy

child you ever want to see. He did nothing. He couldn't read his name, he couldn't write, he couldn't spell, and he couldn't do a thing. As the year went on he came out of his shell and he began to respond and work with the group and not off by himself. He came up above grade level and went on for a full promotion which I didn't expect even at the middle of the year. This was a sense of accomplishment because if I didn't get through to thirty-four others at least here was one who accomplished something. [#38 F-35-3d]

I had a little boy and I had been told he was a problem. It was awfully hard to make him concentrate on anything at the beginning of the year. . . .He seemed to be picking up in his work and I had a conference with his mother and she said, "You know, Miss ———, I just want to let you know that this is the first year that Eddy has enjoyed school." Things like that make you feel awful good. . . .If you can make an individual child, I think more than a class—you don't notice it as much—but with an individual child, I think it really makes you feel awfully good. [#67 F-24-3d]

I had a mulatto boy who was a real terror. He was overage for his class, 12 in the fourth grade. . . . I remember the principal telling me "If he's too much for you, I'll take him." I worked with him for a while. . . .I started to make progress with him and finally found out how to reach him. A colored athlete in ——— was his cousin. . .a respected man in the city. I told him he had something to live up to. I told him I watched him in the schoolyard and the children respected him. . . .I wondered what became of him because of a colored father and white mother. . . .This boy was living with a big colored family with 12 children. The colored woman loved him but he was a handful even for her. I can remember at Christmas time getting a little note on old tissue paper in poor English and poor spelling and with it the 25¢ box of chocolates in it and a note from this woman thanking me for all I had done for her boy, and how much he had changed, improved, tried. I practically cried when I got it. It really meant an awful lot. [#28 F-26-5th]

I think when you have one or two children in a class who might not have the advantages at home that some children have, you might lean a little bit toward that child. . .or make some inward excuses for him. Then when you see that child has really grasped something, it's worth its weight in gold. . . .Two years ago I had a boy who came from another school and a supervisor said, "Oh, you've got him in your room." I never had any trouble with him, I praised him. Now he's in high school and comes back to see me. . . . To know that you were really instrumental in helping him and straightening him out. . . . That boy was quite a problem before he came to our school. He's getting ready for college now. [#35 F-60-4th]

It is ironic that teachers may consider the special attention they gave such students to be counternormative; as the comment "you might lean a little bit toward that child" suggests, the concern shown for one child may be at the expense of others. Given the organizational structure of schools and norms of universalism, teachers have little justification for making differential allocations of affection and effort; they are expected to treat all students equitably. But these values of universalism are not central for the many teachers in elementary grades who cite as their highest moment of pride successful work with one child. Perhaps the fact that the special object of their attention is stigmatized makes it easier for them to justify elation when one is helped; they can, after all, feel that they are righting social wrongs. But the respondents did not generally seem to worry about the limited nature of success with one child; some consciously used such success to overcome feelings of depression about lack of success with other students (note the first quotation). The spectacular case gets much of its potency from the visibility of the teacher's impact.

The stories also manifest purposes we have encountered earlier in this chapter. Cognitive gains are made and the formerly alienated child comes to enjoy school. The teacher's relational skills are demonstrated by her succeeding where others had failed. When we add such outcomes to the definiteness of the accomplishment and the obvious need of the child, we can understand why such events generate strong feelings of self-approval.

Gratifying Graduates

Although secondary teachers were less likely to concentrate their responses into one major category, nearly half (49 percent) alluded to two closely related themes which can be considered together. Some (31 percent) spoke of the pride they take in their former students' success in education and work. An additional 16 percent told of the pride they feel when students return and express appreciation for past assistance. The two kinds of responses tend, in fact, to merge; students return, presumably, when things are going well and tell teachers about it. In any event, it is abundantly clear that former students can be a key source of pride to secondary teachers.

One reason teachers place particular value on the grateful comments

of former students is the conviction that such testimony is trustworthy—
that the time for calculated flattery is past:

> When they come back and tell you, they have nothing to gain, there is
> no handshaking involved and consequently when they tell you that you
> have been a great influence and want to thank you, I think this is a
> great moment in any teacher's life.... They may tell me that when
> they have me in class and I know I've been working on them so I take
> that with a grain of salt... but I have had many, many happy moments
> and I have seen many of them go a long way. They probably might
> have never gone anywhere if it hadn't been for the little I had to con-
> tribute in their life along the line. Now you asked the question, I am
> not boasting, you asked the question. [#65 M-63-Science, P.E.]

The reluctance of teachers to trust the current gratitude of students (at
least in high school) leads to an interesting side thought; heavy emphasis
on grades, and thus on teacher evaluations, reduces the psychic rewards
teachers experience. To the extent that teachers have allocative powers,
they must mistrust the response of students who may simply be "making
out." It is also interesting that older teachers have more deposits in the
"bank" of favorable past sentiment, suggesting that it may be one source
of gratification offsetting the losses in career rewards we discussed
earlier.[13]

The achievements of former students which brought pride to respondents included admission to high-prestige colleges, awards for academic
excellence, success in college, high quality job performance, and attainment of professional status. The comments indicate that student achievement reassures teachers about *their* achievement.

> Ordinarily, I get the greatest satisfaction from the people who come
> back after they're in college and they may say that they didn't realize
> how much the teaching could help them. A student may say that he's
> been better prepared than the average. That's the proof of the
> pudding, that's the most pleasing thing. [#89 M-59-Soc. Stud.]

> This year I had the pleasure of seeing two of my pupils that I had in
> seventh grade receive awards for outstanding citizenship and scholastic
> achievement.... When you see a youngster successful, because right
> now you don't. I mean, being constantly with seventh and eighth
> grades you don't see that much growth happening... when a young-
> ster comes into the first grade, he doesn't know an A from a Z and in
> June he does... in the other levels it's more difficult to see any kind of
> achievement on the part of the youngsters, you know? [#17 M-37-
> English]

There is, moreover, the pleasure of feeling that one's influence has endured:

> I went to the theater one night in my choice second-balcony seat and this young man and woman came over and spoke and said that when I had them in school I had required everyone to see a professional performance (I still do) and they said I had started them going to the theater and they had never missed a performance since. I mean that's the type of thing that gives me great happiness. I taught them something. [#22 F-55-English]

> Of course you have many others who are outstanding in the less academic fields and who also come back to you although you perhaps feel that academically you have not affected their lives too much. At least they remember you and it gives some teachers satisfaction to know that you are remembered. Therefore, since we all have an ego, we like to feel that they are carrying part of our teaching with them, if not in the subject matter, perhaps in being a guide to their life. [#11 F-52-Homemaking]

Like the individual student whose sensational improvement affirms the elementary teacher's competence, former students who credit their high school teachers with beneficial effects, or who go on to better things, produce pride in their teachers. Universalistic considerations are put aside; one takes pleasure from good outcomes and does not look for the bad. These teachers were apparently eager to accept such events as authentication of their effectiveness in pursuing cognitive and affective goals. The quality of their relationships with students is affirmed by appreciation, and they get the bonus of knowing they are remembered. In that regard, those who identified closely with their own teachers (chapters 2 and 3) can feel pleasure in emulating them.

We turn to prideful occasions which were not modal in elementary or secondary teaching ranks. There was no sharp variation in the frequency of the following themes by grade level—they occurred more or less equally at all grade levels.

Successful Displays

Because of the cellular organization of schools, it is easy to imagine that teachers stay behind their closed doors with no one but their students to witness and (possibly) applaud their performances. But occasions arise when the doors are flung open and the class moves to a public arena or visitors are asked in for a special show; the audience may involve others within the school and, on special occasions, parents and other community members. Such opportunities allow the teacher to give a public demonstration of his accomplishments; one is reminded of the visitations and public recitations by which the teacher was assessed in colonial times (Elsbree 1939, chapter 3). The list of such events is long. It includes assemblies, plays, science fairs, art shows, athletic contests, fashion shows, concerts, panel presentations, field trips, public speaking competitions, industrial arts exhibitions, and so forth. That teachers can experience such displays as emotionally charged is illustrated by the following quotations:

I felt very proud when I was in [school system]. They had an art contest and it was in the whole elementary school. . . . It was my second year in teaching and each room went all out for different things and subjects. . . . I won that and felt very proud of that. Another achievement was the first year I came here. Each grade had to give an assembly to be presented to parents and the other fourth, fifth, and sixth grades. We worked about a month or so. . . many parents said it was the nicest thing they had seen. . . the children loved it. . . . There was a writeup in in the paper. . . . It really paid off. . . . The children were learning stage manners and were doing everything on their own by heart. They were performing and were confident about it. It was written up in the paper. I felt very pleased with my accomplishments at that time. [#37 F-29-4th]

One year I put on an auditorium program and the participants were some boys and girls and some of them were quite difficult problems in the school. . . . I spent a great deal of time training them. . .and I must say there were many comments with some of the individuals I used in that program that were truly amazing, what I accomplished with some of the boys who were problem boys and they have become very good friends of mine, they frequently come back to see me. [#72 M-37 Math]

We had a fashion show. I had my eighth-graders make all the refreshments. We served over three hundred people. They told me it couldn't be done. We did it. We were very pleased with ourselves and I was very pleased that they did so well. [#12 F-52-Homemaking]

Displays dramatize the teacher's achievements, giving high visibility to efforts which generally take place in private. The narcissistic benefits are obvious; favorable feedback, moreover, is immediate—this kind of teaching performance has a distinct beginning, middle, and ending. Success which is witnessed, applauded, and remembered by others (including adults) has greater psychological substance than the evanescent flow of everyday teaching. People can recall the event and refer back to it. Learning and involvement are demonstrated; and since rapport is often high on such occasions, the visibly loyal conduct of the students testifies to the teacher's relational skills.

One should observe, however, that displays have their critics within teaching—some teachers doubt they are suitable occasions for teacher pride.[14] The displayed learning may be only a fraction of the intended curriculum. More capable students may be featured at the expense of the rest. Some teachers reported that colleagues have been known to "pass off" their own work as students' in art shows, woodworking, science fairs, and so on. Perhaps the central point is that displays are overtly competitive events between teachers; one's gain is implicitly another's loss. The zero-sum quality of displays can lead to feelings of envy and ill-will within faculties.

Objective Group Results

If teacher pride were ordered in strict adherence to organizational, formal goals, we would expect to find heavy emphasis on results attained with entire classes; school systems present themselves as concerned with the learning of all students. It is provocative, therefore, that fewer than one-third (29 percent) of the Five Towns teachers mentioned generalized outcomes with entire classes, and that most of these did so in an offhand manner. Such responses seemed to occur with teachers working in particular subjects and grades—the more tangible and visible the learning they were seeking to promote, the likelier they were to emphasize general gains with students. Examples are initial reading, physical education skills, typing, and skill subjects in home economics. A few elementary teachers linked pride to favorable outcomes on achievement tests, but they seemed hesitant to do so. These themes are illustrated in the following excerpts:

> I feel proud at the end of the year when every one of my youngsters can read. That's about the only time. The rest of the year I'm wondering. [#20 F-54-1st]

> If I work all year and there is a good median at the end of the year in my reading, I feel rather proud. I really shouldn't. But the children give you a nice feeling of accomplishment. But I really think the most satisfying thing is to do it with an individual—one who needs help or who isn't the average or normal child. [#15 F-54-1st]

> Of course, at achievement testing time if they do come out well, you

127

feel, well I helped, you know. We've covered the work and so forth. [#7 F-34-5th]

We in coaching have a great many opportunities for pride, or many different kinds of pride. What I mean is the pride that comes from what we've accomplished with the kids, and what the kids have done on their own. I've had my share of champion teams, but I think the most pride of all I've had is from the gym team this year. We began under very poor conditions...a problem on practicing...we started out with practically nothing; we won 5 and lost 6. The achievement in the year, when you know our schedule and situation, means that the kids' progress and hard work is phenomenal. I'm proud of them for doing it and I guess of myself for keeping them together and needling them to do it. [#93 M-30-P.E.]

These responses emphasize tangibility, as in references to visible reading gains and athletic records. In that respect, they are similar to such responses as spectacular cases, gratifying graduates, and successful displays. Teachers in Five Towns mention visible results with all their students. But they discuss achievement test performance in a subtly different fashion; it is as if they are uncertain of the tangibility of measured gains or the rightfulness of their claiming credit for them. One wonders why this is so. Do they think that testing results reflect innate rather than learned capacities? Has their training, with its emphasis on the individual child, left them unprepared to think about measurements for *groups* of children? Such questions are becoming more important today as schemes for "accountability" are developed which tie teaching to specified outcomes and, in some cases, reward teachers for measured gains in cognitive areas. Special research should be instituted into the perceptions and values of teachers in this area.

Evidence of Student Interest

One of the hoped-for outcomes mentioned in the first section of this chapter is the subjective attachment of students to school and to their studies. There is a wistful quality in the responses of those Five Towns teachers who cited evidence of student interest—special interest—as the basis for pride; one gets the impression that it is not a daily occurrence.[15]

And if a child on his own initiative did some outside research, was interested enough in the subject to do a little more studying himself. At least you would know that you were stimulating a child. I think that would be a feeling of achievement, too. [#75 F-29-4th]

When I made someone really like Shakespeare—you have to work to do that! The kids start off convinced that they're going to hate it. [#22 F-55-English]

When students exert more than usual effort or show special enthusiasm, some teachers feel self-approval and pride in their craft capacities. One can conceptualize such student behavior—as perceived by the teacher—as "voluntary contributions" to their joint enterprise. To have meaning to the teacher, such contributions should constitute a surplus beyond what he normally expects of students. As is indicated by the quotations, such special interest need not be shown by all to gratify the teacher.

Special Projects

Much teaching work is routine; Jackson (1968) talks of the "daily grind." Teaching requires regularity and repetition, but there are occasions when the teacher can, on his own initiative, undertake something special, usually with a group of volunteers or specially selected students. When things go well, the teacher feels pride:

I tried an experiment. Maybe it was a little too stiff for fifth graders. I broke them into groups for the purpose of writing term papers. . . .I left it on a voluntary basis. . . .I kept them after school a few nights and they seemed very interested in it, they thought it was real big time. I taught them all the fundamentals. . .only one group did wind up finishing it but they did finish it, and I thought that was an accomplishment for fifth graders. . . .And one of the little girls came up to me and said, "Well, it was worth it, Mr.——," which made me feel a little good. [#6 M-24-5th]

It was exciting. We were down at the U.N., we went to the Russian mission. . .for a briefing. I was moderator. So he [the press attaché] of the Soviet Union was giving a little talk. . .and threw it open for questions. And of course my students, we were ready. . .asked many, many significant questions. In fact, some of the questions, shall we say, this press attaché became quite upset over. [#10 M-38-Soc. Stud.]

I had some kids present an in-class panel on values in American life. I was proud of the way the kids presented different points of view and conducted an adult discussion. They weren't snowed under by patriotism, they could see the faults as well as the good things. I talked with them about it and helped them plan it. . . .It's when you see some John Bircher being broadened. [#77 M-44-Soc. Stud.]

129

The specifics of such projects—and, as we have seen, the values expressed—differ from teacher to teacher. But outcomes need not be dramatic, nor need all students be involved, for them to produce self-approval. Their potency for pride probably lies in their idiosyncratic nature. They bear the marks of personal authorship.

Recognition and Response

We observed in chapter 4 that the career line in teaching lacks opportunities for recognition based on upward progression; it is also true that in the normal course of events, teachers rarely receive overt honors for their achievements. (A question aimed at uncovering such honors had to be dropped from the questionnaire because it embarrassed respondents.) Some respondents, however, alluded to events which brought recognition; they mentioned compliments from superordinates, mentions in the local newspaper, appointments to special committees, receiving a fellowship, or being invited to teach on closed-circuit television. The list impresses one with the paucity of honorifics available to classroom teachers.

My final illustrations deal with the pride a few teachers experienced when they received special appreciation from students or their parents. As the last quotation indicates, imitation can be experienced as the sincerest form of flattery.

I took my youngsters on a trip, and you get some teachers who say, "Oh, how can you?" You know, they would never cope with that. . . . And I did come home exhausted. . . . But a few days later the youngsters had a surprise party for me which they planned themselves. They brought in money, and they had a little gift for me. It was appreciation, naturally. [#23 F-42-3d]

I felt proud when parents would come in and they would say to me, "What can I do to get my youngest in your room?" They felt I was doing a good job, or why would they want their children in my room? [#29 F-26-3d]

Or after I discourage students from going into teaching. On a percentage basis it's not as rewarding for boys as other fields, but I do get a tremendous kick when a kid tells me he's considering it seriously. I had four one year. Or afterward when they write me and tell me they're going into teaching. [#81 M-39-Soc. Stud.]

Summary Comments on Craft Pride

I place special reliance on the responses to the pride question because the purposes implied are personal, connected with real events, indirect, and demonstrably affect-laden. It is instructive, therefore, to compare them with responses in the earlier sections. There are similarities and dissimilarities. I will begin with the similarities.

The activities which generate pride among respondents are *teaching duties*; as with hoped-for outcomes and the effects of outstanding colleagues, craft pride is centered on instructional outcomes and relationships with students. Scant attention is paid to other aspects of the teacher's role; pride is not evoked by participation in schoolwide affairs. The classroom is the cathected forum—not the principal's office or the professional association. That goals focus on teaching per se underscores the fusion we discussed in chapter 4; psychic rewards associated with achievement center on the instructional tasks of the classroom teacher.

The specifics of craft pride are permeated by themes of instructional impact and effective relationships with students. We can see both of those preoccupations in the modal responses—the spectacular case and gratifying graduates. Instructional influence on students is evident in displays, group results, student interest, and projects, and less so in recognition and response. Relational qualities are stressed in displays, student interest, projects, and recognition and response. We find the same interweaving of instructional outcomes and relational issues we observed in teachers' talk about outstanding colleagues.

The pride responses differ from those elicited by other questions in four ways. First, the emphasis on moral training is less prominent. Interpretation is difficult, but I suspect that respondents see moral outcomes as long-range and therefore beyond the reach of immediate assessment; another possibility, however, is that compliance itself is taken as evidence of moral growth. Second, most of the specific sources of pride involve relatively visible events. Major change is discernible in the spectacular case. Visibility marks the acknowledged success of the graduate, the display before an audience, clear signs of student interest and project achievement, recognition and response, and the demonstration (for some) of measured change in a group of students. Teachers cathect outcomes which are tangible and indisputable; this feature of prideful occasions fits well with the analysis of assessment problems we will undertake in the next chapter.

The most provocative difference between responses to the pride question and responses to other questions lies in the *scope* of outcomes claimed by the teacher. In speaking about their ideals, respondents emphasized reaching *all* students; some teachers, in fact, made such universality the focus of their answers. But the occasions associated with pride, *in all but one instance*, involved a single student or a small number of students. (The exception is group results.) Pride, in short, is generated by "elitist" outcomes, which are overtly rejected. Although their stated ideals are universalistic, Five Towns teachers feel pride at results which fall below universalistic standards. They reveal a real but unintended "elitism."

How do we interpret this gap between the stated ideal and the prideful acceptance of considerably less? I believe that it is associated with a characteristic of teaching which will become evident as we move deeper into the psychological world of teachers. That characteristic is the widespread feeling of *uncertainty*; teachers are not sure they can make all their students learn. They hope for widespread or even universal effectiveness, but such aspirations receive too little reinforcement to yield assurance. Thus they are ready to accept indications of partial effectiveness as the basis for pride.

The fourth difference is a generalization of the third. Occasions for pride are more modest than expressed ideals and less impressive than some of the outcomes attributed to outstanding colleagues. They are assuredly more modest than the assumptions made by those who write statements of school objectives. It is not likely that teachers would feel pride in the visible accomplishment of a minority of their students if schooling had surefire effects. Teaching, from these appearances, is a hit-or-miss affair.

Chapter Summary

We can analyze the personal purposes of teachers on two levels. Such purposes obviously have instructional importance; since authority structures in schools are loose and students spend most of their time with classroom teachers, the goals to which teachers are committed are particularly influential. In assessing the impact of schooling, therefore, it is wise to take account of the beliefs, goals, and actions of teachers. They are the ones who instruct students. The data in this chapter suggest that despite generations of philosophical ferment and ideological controversy, teachers favor outcomes for students which are not arcane. Their purposes, in fact, seem to be relatively traditional; they want to produce "good" people—students who like learning—and they hope they will attain such goals with all their students.

There is another way of viewing these purposes, a social psychological approach which asks about their implications for teaching as work. At the risk of repetition, let us review teacher goals in this light before going on to chapter six. We find that the goals sought by teachers cannot be routinely realized. Their ideals are difficult and demanding: exerting moral influence, "soldering" students to learning, and achieving general impact presume great capacity to penetrate and alter the consciousness of students. Although our knowledge of interpersonal influence leaves much to be desired, we do know that it is extremely difficult to alter the outlook and behavior of others. When such change must be effected with people whose participation is at least in part involuntary, the difficulty increases. From this point of view, it must be reassuring to have curricular objectives and outlines to lean on; that may partially explain teachers' reluctance to assert hegemony over curricular affairs.

Five Towns teachers obviously think they are engaged in a complex craft; that belief emerges clearly in their descriptions of outstanding members of the occupation. In discussing such exemplars, they emphasize interpersonal and leadership skills; they believe that such skills play a major part in the conduct of instruction. Respondents do not seem to define subject knowledge as particularly problematic; perhaps they take it for granted among outstanding teachers. But it is evident that they are impressed by teachers who establish and sustain cordial, disciplined, and work-eliciting relationships with students. Such abilities, it seems, can be held by persons of various personalities and teaching styles; respondents do not express doctrinaire or simplistic conceptions of oustanding teachers. There is some suggestion of charisma—of the outstanding teacher as possessing the "gift of grace." They lavish no praise on the "crowd pleasers" in their midst—they reserve their esteem for teachers who get results in the context of superordinate status and demands on students. Their image of good teaching combines demonstrable effects on students with high interpersonal capacity.

We need not tarry longer with the pride findings. But the theme of craft complexity is also evident in those responses; the modesty of the occasions which produce prideful feelings underscores the difficulty teachers see in attaining worthwhile results.

Historians have pointed out that Americans have expected much from their schools (Hofstadter 1963, p. 299). Optimistic rhetoric accompanied the birth of the mass system of public schools and burgeoned with its development; compulsory attendance laws put state power behind mandatory participation. Today we are constantly exposed to messages upholding the benefits of schooling. Yet that hope, legitimation, and clamor can induce us to forget that education is a tenuous, uncertain affair. It is necessary to keep such uncertainty in mind if we are to understand the psychic world of classroom teachers, for uncertainty is the lot of those who teach. In the chapter which follows, we shall discuss the characteristics of teaching which make it so.

6

Endemic Uncertainties

Impressive as its accomplishments may be, the division of labor in our society has not attained perfection. Misalignments occur, for example, between the work assigned to particular occupations and the technical capacity of their members. In some cases too little is asked, in others too much. People may be capable of more than they are routinely asked or permitted to do; such complaints are heard from members of a variety of occupations.[1] On the other hand, society may expect those in a given line of work to achieve results beyond their capacity, and those within the occupation may demand more of themselves than is readily possible. Although members of occupations at opposite ends of this continuum probably express different concerns, we would expect some degree of discontent in both instances.

Where do teachers stand? We have observed that our society asks much of those who staff our public schools; official ideologies tend to support high expectations. We have also concluded (in chapter 3) that the technical culture of teaching is not highly developed. And we found that teachers take pride in outcomes which fall below their professed ideals; they do not find that they can routinely meet the high expectations held out for schools. If there is a gap between social expectations and technical capacity in teaching, therefore, it is probably toward overdemand rather than underdemand. If this is so, what makes school goals so difficult to reach? We will tackle that question here.

In searching for an answer I will compare teaching with other occupations, inquire into how teachers monitor their work and what problems they meet in doing so, and consider interpersonal dilemmas and troublesome emotions. In the final section I will discuss additional complications which come from the structure of teaching. By the end of the chapter we should better understand why teachers consider psychic rewards less than assured.

Some Analytic Considerations

People outside a particular occupation can examine the tasks performed by those within it and, taking role issues into account, identify the difficulties which are likely to confront practitioners. I shall undertake such an analysis, paying particular attention to the two aspects of teaching which respondents emphasized—the attainment of instructional goals, and appropriate relationships with students. Reflection suggests that teachers confront a unique set of difficulties. By itself, however, analysis is insufficient; we need empirical data to support it. Teachers, like members of some other occupations, may have developed a subculture which "solves" the recurrent problems which face them. I will test for that possibility.

In thinking about teachers it is useful to conceive of members of the occupation as engaged in a craft; we can then compare conditions affecting the practice of this craft with those in other crafts.[2] All craftsmen must adjust and readjust their actions in line with hoped-for outcomes; they must monitor their steps and make corrections as they proceed. Monitoring of this kind is particularly important when the outcome is remote in time; mistaken assessments can deflect movement toward the goal and prove extremely costly when the proof comes in. Teachers' goals tend toward the remote; although there are shorter schedules of effort (e.g., lesson plans, marking periods), the basic unit of work assessment is the academic year—a period of nine or ten months. Monitoring one's efforts and effectiveness is extremely important when the productive sequence is long. Yet the monitoring of teaching effectiveness, defined as achieving instructional goals, is fraught with complications.

Compared with other crafts, the work processes in teaching, and the products sought by teachers, are difficult to measure by several assessment criteria. We speak of teaching goals as "intangible" and thus underline their insubstantial qualities. Persons who make tangible products may use a fixed and reliable model as a guide for comparing intermediate outcomes with the goal; craftsmen in tangible fields use working models, blueprints, plans, and detailed specifications. Teachers possess no physical standards of this kind; they may find the very idea inconsistent with respect for the individuality of children and young people. Craftsmen in tangible fields, moreover, usually work within clear boundaries; they know what part of a particular product they are responsible for and normally have control over the steps within that stage. Such demarcation of responsibility means that they can identify their contribution to the overall effort and assess its quality. The classroom teacher, however, is normally only one of the significant adults who has influenced a child; assessment of his impact requires a difficult judgment about the relative influence of self and others.

In some crafts, the service or product offered can be assessed in light of a single, major purpose—the standard of assessment is unitary. The lawyer wins or loses his case; the engineer's bridge bears the specified weight or does not. But teaching acts are normally assessed in terms of multiple criteria applied simultaneously. The teacher who holds the class spellbound may be faulted for inaccuracies of content; reprimanding a particular child may calm the rest of the students but provoke allegations of inequity from the accused. Few people seem to define schooling as purely intellectual in intent—the general tendency is to include a variety of socialization goals. Breadth of purpose means that teaching performances will be judged in terms of moral, aesthetic, and scientific values all at once: But what *is* good or beautiful or true? General socialization can be free of controversy only in societies which are marked by an extremely high degree of value consensus (Dahlke 1958).

An airline pilot knows immediately whether his landing meets expected standards; feedback is immediate and definite and the timing is unambiguous. But the appropriate time to assess teaching outcomes is ambiguous—it varies, moreover, from one goal to the next. It is widely thought that it is appropriate to measure cognitive learning soon after instruction; but those concerned with moral learning (e.g., citizenship goals in social studies) may argue that years elapse before the relevant evidence is in. People in many crafts can count on the stability of their efforts: the novelist or mason need not worry that his imprint will soon vanish. But teachers work with inherently changeful materials; the objects of their efforts—maturing children—are supposed to keep changing after they have been taught.

The teacher's craft, then, is marked by the absence of concrete models for emulation, unclear lines of influence, multiple and controversial criteria, ambiguity about assessment timing, and instability in the product. These circumstances do not favor monitoring and self-assessment: What do teachers report? Has their subculture come to grips with these problems?

Teachers do "people work," but they do it under somewhat special conditions. Three peculiarities are evident: the low degree of voluntarism in the teacher-student relationship, the problem of extracting work from immature workers, and the grouped context of teacher endeavors. Each characteristic influences the relational issues faced by classroom teachers.

The clients of teachers, unlike those in most interpersonal kinds of work, exercise no choice about attending school until the age of sixteen (in most states) and have practically no say about what teacher they will have. Children legally must attend some school; those who are not sent to private schools must normally attend a particular school and be taught by whatever staff member is assigned by school officials. The obligatory nature of the arrangement means that the student's interest (or lack of it) plays no part in his disposition; any class will include at least some students who would rather be elsewhere. There is also considerable compulsion on the other side of the relationship. Teachers choose the school district in which they will work but are then assigned by administrators to a particular school and to particular classes within it. Teachers have no formal right to select their clients.[3]

The absence of voluntarism in the teacher-student relationship means that neither party brings preexisting bonds to the relationship. It is the role obligation of the teacher to forge bonds which will not merely ensure compliance but, it is hoped, generate effort and interest in "learning jobs." (Thus, it is said, the teacher "must motivate the students.") The responsibility of the teacher can be likened to that of the foreman, but there are interesting differences: not only are the teacher's workers conscripts, but they are in the process of learning how to work. Students go to school, in part, to learn how to sustain work performances and to internalize other norms of adult society (Dreeben 1968). Teacher leadership is more than supervisory in function; the teacher compensates for deficits in work capacity among sociologically "immature" workers.

There is a third, critical feature in the interpersonal situation of the classroom teacher—goals must be met and relationships managed in a group context. This feature is so obvious that it is often overlooked; in fact, those who train teachers are not always sensitive to its implications. The teacher's attempts to shape children are continually constrained by the fact of "classness." Teachers do not establish entirely distinct and separate working contracts with each student—they establish general rules for class conduct and find it necessary to discipline deviation from those rules.

Actions taken with or for one child are generally visible to other children, and like subordinates in other settings, students are quick to resent treatment they see as inequitable. Action with one, therefore, can become precedent for all; the claims of "individualized instruction" must be seen in light of these fundamental constraints.

The people work of teaching, then, is carried on under special circumstances: the relationship is involuntary, the workers are less than fully socialized, and the teacher's actions are constrained by dealing with groups rather than individual students. These are among the reasons that teachers, as we shall see, find it difficult to take relationships with students for granted. We will discuss data on teachers' assessment problems and the relational complexities of their work. But first, it should help if we examine the ways teachers monitor their day-to-day efforts.

Monitoring Outcomes: Variation within Constraint

We have already learned that teachers are committed to the idea that the good teacher informs his practice with personal observations of classroom events (chapter 3). But we have not yet examined the approaches teachers use in such monitoring. How do they tell when things are going well—or badly? We turn to Five Towns data for our answer (Question 37, App. B-1).

The monitoring techniques available to teachers are limited in number and precision; essentially, they must rely on various tests of student knowledge and on observations of how students behave in the classroom. Tests include teacher-prepared examinations, verbal quizzes, student workbooks, and standardized tests. Observing student behavior includes judging student interest, watching work effort, checking compliance, and noting the degree of responsiveness to the teacher. In Five Towns, most respondents (47 percent) said they used both tests and observation to monitor their teaching; some, however, reported relying on tests alone (18 percent) or observation alone (24 percent). Tests figure, therefore, in 65 percent of the responses.

The range of indicators, then, is limited; it is interesting, however, that there are subtle but significant differences in how respondents go about using the forms of assessment. The variety is evident in the following quotations:

> Of course I test a great deal. In arithmetic, I test very often. I see each child work at the board every single day and then we have a test, if not every day, every other day so that I know what they can do. [#60 F-59-6th]

If I give an examination and I find 40 or 50 percent of my class didn't get it, I know I should do more teaching. [#40 M-46-Eng., Hist.]

I test, see if they're making improvement....I'm never satisfied with normal improvement. I'd like it a little more because if you teach it right, they will do better than normal. [#21 F-56-Reading]

How well they respond, when they do their work papers and I ask questions and they answer them intelligently—then I know—well, I guess I'm getting it across....We compare notes with other teachers, what they're doing, how well advanced they are, what their first group is doing and so on and so forth. [#20 F-54-1st]

The response of the students in discussion or any type of achievement test...it's very difficult to measure. In history, you're dealing with attitudes. You can't say if you failed with a kid....You're dealing with concepts of responsibilities, citizenship, relationship with other individuals. What I really try to get across is that love is the key to life....As the year goes on, class rapport should improve, the class should be more cooperative, capable of doing more independent work, closer to you. [#81 M-39-Soc. Stud.]

One way, of course, is tests. Almost any questions the students ask. If they volunteer to come in after school. A lot of little things. [24 M-33-Business]

If the class is not attentive I feel that I'm not doing a good job... perhaps I am not making it as interesting as it could be. [#87 F-52-English]

I think if I have a quiet, busy roomful of children. I think if they're happy in their work and everybody is really accomplishing something then I feel that I have had a good day and I've really accomplished something...the fact that children can settle down and work by themselves and...be happy in their work and their room. [#59 F-58-1st]

Scrutiny of the excerpts discloses subtle differences in the specifics of test and observational practice. Tests may be daily or intermittent, central or peripheral; acceptable performance ranges from evidence that more than half the class has learned to demands that performance exceed the norm. Observational criteria are similarly diverse, including class rapport, progress compared with other classes, indications of student interest, the nature of questions asked by students, attentiveness, and "a quiet, busy roomful of children." These differences point to the significance of

cellular structure and the teacher discretion which accompanies it—
curricular objectives are "operationalized" differently as teachers bring
particular criteria to bear on classroom events. Seen from the outside, the
mechanisms of assessment seem sparse, but teachers' reports reveal
important variations in emphasis and teacher behavior.

The mechanisms available to teachers for monitoring classroom events
make it easier to implement some values than others. The ideal outcomes
discussed in the previous chapter, for example, are not readily tested in
everyday classroom affairs. One can test and retest in arithmetic and feel
confident that one is determining the level of learning. But one of the
respondents just quoted asks how one tells whether "concepts of responsibilities, citizenship, relationship with other individuals" are being
internalized. Such goals must be translated into indirect and sporadic
cues—there are no reliable, systematic ways to test or to observe such
learning. The demands of monitoring make it hard for teachers to deviate
from the more specific and concrete features of the curriculum. Thus we see
that limits are placed on teacher discretion; severe departure from
curricular objectives is forestalled by problems of monitoring and assessment. The classroom behavior of teachers blends idiosyncratic preference
and evaluative constraint; they can exercise some choice in how they
evaluate events, but the boundaries are real.

Questions on monitoring produced interesting sidelights on variations
in teacher behavior. Elementary teachers usually have peers whose work is
formally similar to theirs; as is evident above, they sometimes compare the
progress of their classes with that of others. It develops, however, that
students may force such comparisons on the teacher:

> You can tell. . .if you haven't got across what you're supposed to put
> across. You know where the other teachers are and what their children
> are doing and whether or not your children are ready for it. [Do you
> discuss this with other teachers?] Not too much. We don't get together
> and discuss it, but things come up in conversation and, of course, the
> children know too. "Miss So-and-so is doing such-and-such. Why aren't
> we?" Or, "We know this and they don't"; and the children will tell
> you. [#67 F-24-3d]

In these circumstances, important sociological forces play on the implementation of the curriculum. It is likely that those teachers whose classes
move rapidly or who (for other reasons) command the special respect of
their colleagues set the pace within a grade. If this is so, such "leading
teachers" may have a disproportionate influence on the specification of
curriculum—their decisions influence those of others. The point merits
research.

A few teachers were exceedingly explicit in telling how they consciously look for evidence that they have had some effect on their students. One put it this way:

> You wonder at the end of a day or sometimes at the end of a lesson. I think if you can occasionally—at the end of a lesson or a monthly marking period—pick out one or two or hopefully more individuals and see the change, whether it is something they had difficulty with and now they understand. Even if it is only one child, I think you can get some accomplishment. [#14 M-33-6th]

One suspects that most teachers would scorn such transparent efforts to cope with uncertainty about one's personal effectiveness. But the question arises: How often do teachers unconsciously act in ways which, unknown to them, are directed toward getting reassurance? Holt (1964) tells, for example, of teachers who anticipate the answers to questions they have posed for students; they "tip off" the student on the right answer before he has had the chance to think through the problem. Tipping off may be motivated by the wish to believe that the students are doing better than they are; sensitive social psychological research might prove useful on this question.

The monitoring of student progress stands at the heart of effective instruction. But since teachers equate achievement and psychic earnings, the favorable judgments they make are *also* allocations of psychic rewards to themselves. Although there are obvious limits on this process (teachers will not take satisfaction in wildly disobedient classes) latitude which permits self-allocation means that teacher personality plays a part in the amount of psychic reward they receive. The demanding perfectionist will feel depressed by outcomes which cheer a more easy-going colleague. We need psychological inquiries which examine the variations in standards among teachers as they allocate psychic earnings to themselves.

It seems likely that teachers will have a vested interest in cellular arrangements which permit them latitude in getting rewards. Discretion permits an elementary teacher, for example, to concentrate on her high skill in teaching arithmetic rather than on her indifferent performance in teaching reading. The high school teacher can increase his total rewards by focusing on classes which pay off while slighting those which do not. The lack of close organizational control permits teachers to use the techniques they think productive and to eschew those they dislike. Given the linkage between cellular isolation and opportunities to optimize psychic rewards, it is not surprising that many teachers resist alternative instructional arrangements.

There is another side to this issue. Freedom carries burdens; the opportunity to assess one's own progress is also the obligation to do so. The rule of conscience is not always benign; in the pages that follow we will see that a high proportion of classroom teachers experience recurrent doubts about the value of their work with students.

Intangibility and Assessment

The analysis presented earlier indicated that there are a priori reasons for expecting teachers to encounter serious difficulties in assessing their work performance; the view from outside is one of complexity and ambiguity. How does it look from within the occupation? Do teachers experience uncertainty as they try to judge their effectiveness? Are there indications that problems of this sort reduce their psychic rewards? The data gathered in Five Towns and Dade County reveal that many teachers find it difficult to rate their performance; and there are indications that doubts about one's effectiveness can spoil the pleasures of teaching.

Dade County teachers were asked how much difficulty they had in assessing "how their teaching is going" (question T5, App. B-2). Of the approximately six thousand teachers who answered the question, 49 percent chose the response "I believe it is possible to know one's effectiveness *at times.*" Six percent said, "I believe it is relatively difficult to know when one is really teaching effectively." The rest (45 percent) selected "It is relatively easy to know when one is really teaching effectively." The modal tendency is to admit some difficulty, but the distribution is close to bimodal. Although we lack information on why teachers differ in this perception, we can explore the kinds of difficulties encountered by those who are not certain they can readily assess their work.[4] The fact that over half indicate some difficulty in knowing how well their work is going merits attention. It is especially important in an occupation where psychic rewards loom large.

Respondents in Five Towns had opportunity to discuss the problem of assessment (question 36, App. B-1). Sixty-four percent said they encountered problems in assessing their work, and of those two-thirds said the problem was serious. We will review the testimony of Five Towns teachers by identifying the themes in their responses without emphasizing distributions; by close examination of the themes associated with assessment difficulties, we should get insight into how the intangible nature of teaching complicates reward-getting for some who are engaged in this kind of work.

It is safe to say that no aspect of the teacher's work evoked as much emotion as this issue of assessing outcomes. That teachers found such inquiry trying was apparent in the earliest pilot interviews: early attempts to probe deeply into the subject had to be revised lest respondents break off the interview.[5] I settled on a final version which was worded gently and used general probes. Despite these adjustments, the responses continued to show affective influence, as we shall shortly see. Among the questions asked, only this was subject to a kind of emotional "flooding" in which respondents slid off the central question into broader anxieties about their work effectiveness. In the strictest sense, this produced a number of "illogical" answers, answers whose significance is probably greater on that account. We turn now to the major themes.

Is Anything Happening?—Assessment and Diffuse Anxiety

I feel very inadequate and hopeless at times. [#21, F-56-Reading]

A noteworthy proportion of Five Towns teachers (about 25 percent) chose to talk about their problems in identifying changes in students and the discouragement they felt when they were unable to see beneficial change. Some linked such difficulties to limitations in available ways of testing students; others asserted that the quality of teaching cannot be measured. Their talk sometimes veered toward a frightening possibility—perhaps they have *no* discernible effect on their students.

The connection between assessment difficulties and frustration at the intangibility of teaching is illustrated by one junior high school teacher:

It's most difficult to assess the work you're doing—especially this thinking business. I've looked around for a test I could give the advanced placement children to measure their thinking...to give a posttest later on and see if I've done them any good. And I've only come up with this Watson-Glazer critical thinking appraisal which is all right, but it doesn't have an alternative form, so I can't assess. I'm looking for something concrete and I'm afraid that it's most difficult to achieve....
There is no science to this. One just plods along, hoping for the best.
I do wonder, at the end of every single year, how much good have I done? And it's hard to see....For me to tinker with my car, the little I know about it, and fix it is great satisfaction. I often say to my colleagues, honestly, that brings pleasure to me and I just wish I could see more of it in teaching. But it's one of those things...you're dealing with the human mind. It's so complex that you can't expect to see any great changes. [#26 M-34-Reading]

Similar themes are echoed in the responses of other teachers; assessment problems and fears of failure apparently produce a generalization effect:

Sometimes I feel like chucking it all—at times it all means nothing to me. I do what I feel I ought to. No one can ever know how it affects the students, no one can know what they're thinking, or how my teaching affects them now or in the future. I simply teach what I believe I should. I give the usual tests, etc. You can assess only the insignificant things. [#48 M-30-English]

I always feel that if I'm not succeeding with some child it's my fault, that I should be able to find some way to appeal to him and make him want tò do. You get a little discouraged. You think, well, I'm no good as a teacher and then you have some children who do get it and you think, well, it can't be *all* my fault. [#70 F-65-1st]

Oh, yes. You can go on and think endlessly that you might be doing a good job or maybe you could do so much better but you don't really know and it's only every once in a while when you do see progress.... You can go on for an eternity with nothing. They seem to be regressing. [#2 F-25-2d]

Yes, I think it's hard for me and I've been told I'm very hard on myself and I think I am....I've been teaching fifteen years....I sometimes think I'm awful in teaching....I mean I haven't done anything, I don't teach anything...papers come back and you wonder what you've done for the whole week, I mean there's nothing. You've taught them absolutely nothing....After teaching fifteen years you ought to begin to appraise yourself...there are some things you can do and some things you can't do. You can't put brains in them....I've gone home and worried about my work and worried about students and I wish that I could walk out of my office and just close the door or something.... [#62 F-43-Science]

Thus a seemingly simple question on problems of evaluating progress unleashed a torrent of feeling and frustration; one finds self-blame, a sense of inadequacy, the bitter taste of failure, anger at the students, despair, and other dark emotions. The freedom to assess one's own work is no occasion for joy; the conscience remains unsatisfied as ambiguity, uncertainty, and little apparent change impede the flow of reassurance. Teaching demands, it seems, the capacity to work for protracted periods without sure knowledge that one is having any positive effect on students. Some find it difficult to maintain their self-esteem.

On Setting Goals

It falls to the teacher to decide how general curricular objectives are to be specified with a particular group of students. To test and experience accomplishment, the teacher needs specific standards which are relevant to his peculiar situation. Some Five Towns teachers (a dozen mentioned this) stressed this problem; they talked about such questions as the ultimate aims of instruction, differences among teachers, and concepts like "student potential."

The issue of ultimate goals was raised by a social studies teacher who, asked whether he had trouble assessing his work, replied, "Who doesn't?" and then went on to say:

My chief problem is what should be my principal aim? Take history—what is the responsibility of man in a God-centered world? What are all the values? I've fiddled with the Cornell studies of attitudes and values, but it's hard to know whether they're useful. Are you really out to sell a kid on the essentials of the American way of life?... Subject matter is not hard... if that is all we do as teachers, we're overpaid. [#81 M-39-Soc. Stud.]

Groups of students can differ and pose special problems for the teacher:

I am not always sure that I am asking too much or too little. I set up a program as I see it, and sometimes I think maybe I require too much because I don't know exactly what's expected of the top group. All those things they give you [all the materials]—are you expected to use them?... I would just like to know just how much of everything you do... whether or not I am asking too much. [#27 F-39-5th]

Statements of educational objectives are likely to list the desirability of students' reaching their "full potential." But what is it, and how does one discover it?

It's a very nebulous thing. It's more a question of evaluating potential ability and present performance. As in the grading, you sometimes doubt your ability to evaluate potential. You may see flashes of ability and say, well, if they can do it sometimes, they should do it all the time. [#93 M-30-P.E.]

Self-assessment has a comparative component; if others can do something, it is clearly feasible. But teachers vary in what they can do, and the efforts of other teachers are often invisible:

There are so many intangibles. It is very difficult to evaluate a teacher. ...One teacher may be marvelous at getting across subject matter—the children may have suffered every minute they were in there but they learned something. Another teacher may not teach quite as much but what she teaches, she teaches well and certain ideas that she gets across to them have very lasting value, though they might forget little things that she taught them. Self-evaluation is the most difficult of all. [#28 F-26-3d]

I think it is very difficult. You don't have any means of comparison. . . . You have no idea of what is going on across the hall or next door. . . . You know what people tell you. You take that with a grain of salt. [#38 F-35-3d]

The perplexities teachers face in goal-setting reflect the structure and culture of the public school. The instructional objectives stated in the curriculum do not resolve the concern of the Christian believer who would relate history and God; they do not help the teacher who worries lest he misjudge the level of demand appropriate for a particular group of students. Terms like "student potential" prove to be of little use in concrete situations. Self-evaluation is complicated by the realization that teachers have divergent competencies; these differences, however, do not receive formal acknowledgment in the cellular structure of schools. The mutual isolation of peers makes it difficult for the individual teacher to verify collegial claims. Thus not only is it difficult to ascertain whether one has realized given objectives, but for some the objectives are themselves unclear.

The Issue of Timing

When does the teacher know whether his efforts have had a lasting and desirable effect on students? Questions of this type seem to underlie the worries of some teachers:

I wonder at times if I'm doing the best possible job. After all, only the life the students lead afterward is the ultimate proof of it. . . . Students have a lot of influences playing on them, some good, some bad, and I hope I'm one of the good influences. [#82 M-34-Biology]

English particularly is so much a business of increasing the ability to think for themselves, to write their thoughts, get them down on paper, that sometimes you don't know until they're seniors whether what you have taught them as sophomores has penetrated at all. . . . Sometimes it doesn't work until they're in college. [#22 F-55-English]

There seem to be two concerns here. One is that the highest hopes of some teachers—moral influence—cannot be assessed until the person's life has begun to unfold. The second is that one's efforts may have only temporary effect on students. Those trained in behavioral science are used to accepting short-run measurements as evidence of effectiveness; it would be easy to assume that these teachers do not want to confront the possibility of low impact on students. But one wonders: styles of thought which pervade science may not work for those who take personal responsibility for the development of children. Science moves ahead through deliberate and sophisticated simplifications of reality, but there is little to suggest that this is the approach of classroom teachers.

The Scope of Teacher Effectiveness

Some teachers are particularly concerned with the goal of reaching all their students, as we observed in chapter 5. General impact is implied by the ideal of equitable treatment which is supposed to mark public education. Uncertainty on this count emerged in the responses of some teachers who talked about whether they were meeting such standards; as in the first responses discussed in this section, these responses are not strictly logical answers to the question which was asked:

> I know my greatest fault is that I neglect the brightest children. I work with the slow group first. Then I feel guilty about the brighter ones, that I haven't given the time that I should but there are just so many minutes in the day. [#59 F-58-1st]

> Particularly with some of the lower groups... that don't act interested—they will try their darnedest to get you working in any other area with them. But then somehow something happens that it kind of shows you that they have been listening a little bit. They become discouraging to me but there is always a little bit of something that makes me realize it's been worthwhile. [#49 F-26-Homemaking]

The two quotations cited, the first from an elementary teacher and the second from a high school teacher, point up a pattern observed in the data. Elementary teachers show concern about the disposition of time with a fixed group of students throughout an entire day; the high school teacher's day is broken into parts with separate classes. The elementary teacher can exercise more discretion, therefore, in allocating time (e.g., to slow or bright students). If the high school teacher's classes are tracked he may, of course, put more energy into his work with some and less into others. But the high school teacher faces fewer choices.

One respondent went on at great length about the problems of assessment and the deep feelings of discouragement he and others experience. The following excerpt is highly condensed—his original answer ran some fourteen hundred words:

> Yes, at times you wonder are you doing anything, see, and does it pay to do this, see?...More times than not you have no idea and it's very

easy to get discouraged. I think teachers work very hard...out of the one hundred kids you meet, seventy respond but the thirty that don't they kill you...the reason why teachers will blame the preceding grade is not for the sake of blaming them and excusing any deficiency but because they know they are working their fool heads off and they don't seem to be getting anywhere.... Why can't I get this kid? I can knock down ninety-nine others but it seems as if this kid can undo all that he's trying to do for the others and it seems to stand out in his mind....

This is why teachers so often cry in their beer to each other about this and...start releasing all their fury or tensions as I am doing now and they begin to realize that I'm not really so bad after all and this is rather common and it's not really the fault of the elementary school. It's that darn fool kid and really I'm doing a better job than it looks on the surface...and realize you just can't teach every kid...you're going to get a certain percentage who don't know anything. So you kind of console each other. [#17 M-37-English]

One of the more interesting features of this response is the linking of informal relationships among teachers with anxiety about goal achievement. It suggests that a significant function of peer grouping is to help individual teachers cope with feelings of self-doubt and worthlessness. One of the reassuring themes, it appears, is the impossibility of teaching every student; such informal groups, in short, support views which run contrary to the formal, ideal statements of public educators.

The problem of the scope of a teacher's effectiveness, to make a brief aside, deserves considerably closer inquiry than it has received. There are articles, of course, which document the tendency of some teachers to favor the offspring of higher-status families (Brophy and Good 1970; Rist 1970; Yee 1968). There has also been a growing tendency to specialize teachers for work in the "inner city." Yet we have paid little attention to the general problem of the *range* of teacher effectiveness with children of different personalities and social backgrounds. Many schools continue to have considerable diversity within single classrooms; school systems assume, in using batching procedures, that any teacher can (or should) reach all types of students. How plausible is this assumption? Could it be that such generalist assignments—by inducing teacher anxiety—foster discriminatory treatment of students?

The Question of Authorship

In occupations where it is possible to win fame (and sometimes fortune), elaborate mechanisms may be developed to make attributions of authorship and priority of discovery as reliable as possible. This is in large part true in the fields of art and science.[6] Although fame rarely (if ever) comes to a classroom teacher, there are still problems of authorship—the teacher himself wants to establish that he has influenced students. Alternative explanations are always possible when credit for success is at issue; credit might belong to the students themselves or to other teachers:

> I had a very good group this year. I feel that they've done well, but how much have I actually done with them? Some of them could really do a lot on their own of what I have, you know, gone through with them formally. [#46 F-61-2d]

> Other teachers have worked with them, too. You work from appearances, in tests and that sort of thing. But of course what you think is important and good, another teacher might not. [#83 M-38-English]

As we remarked earlier, the punctilious find it hard to award themselves the rewards of accomplishment.

The Absence of Authoritative Reassurance

That teachers spend most of their working hours outside the view of other adults has consequences for monitoring their results. Some wish there were witnesses who could help in their self-assessment:

> Yes it is. I don't have anyone criticize me. Like my principal, sometimes I wish she'd give me a compliment or a word or two on how I am accomplishing something. When I test I try to evaluate. . . . Only by evaluating myself do I feel that I am doing all right. Nobody says anything to you. [#37 F-29-4th]

> Lots of times you wonder. The principal never comes to see you or you never see some of the other teachers and you wonder, well, what do they think of you—are you doing a good job? How do you feel yourself? You've got to evaluate yourself, I think. [#69 M-30-P.E.]

The isolation of the cellular structure and its attendant privacy reduce the joy of respondents such as these—they crave reassurance which, for them, could only come from superordinates or teaching peers.

In the first section of this chapter, we reviewed some a priori grounds for expecting that teachers might find it difficult to assess their work performance. We derived certain expectations by concentrating on intangibles in the craft; the expectations would hold only if the occupation lacked a technical culture which "solved" such recurring problems. We have seen that more than half of the teachers in two samples said they encountered difficulty in assessing their work perfor-

149

mance, and in Five Towns the actual difficulties reported were close to those predicted on a priori grounds. Issues of timing and authorship were made explicit by respondents; the instability of outcomes was connected to problems in timing assessment. Goal-setting and ascertaining change in students are complicated by the presence of multiple criteria and the absence of concrete, consensual models. Other problems arose which were not anticipated using the intangibility perspective. One, the problem of the scope of teacher effects, was discussed in the last chapter and the other, the lack of official reassurance, has roots in the cellular structure of schools. The emotional tone of many respondents underlines the degree to which problems of work assessment threaten the work achievement and psychic rewards of classroom teachers.

It is likely that teaching has a greater degree of uncertainty in work assessment than many, if not most, other fields of work; few combine so many intrinsic assessment problems with so little cultural definition. The subculture cannot be seen as highly developed when it fails to provide evaluative criteria for many who are engaged in the occupation's tasks. Critical, recurrent problems remain unresolved in the daily work of teachers—uncertainty stalks as they try to determine whether they are influencing students. It seems, moreover, that teachers are largely alone in such matters—the mutual isolation of their work arrangements reduces chances for turning to colleagues and superordinates for informed assistance. School officials can exacerbate difficulties by emphasizing ideal goals (e.g., reaching all the students) which many teachers simply do not find feasible.

The bimodality of the responses on the assessment issue needs further investigation—we need to understand better why teachers differ on this. The fact of bimodality itself, however, has consequences for the occupation—it indicates a lack of consensus on core problems. Deeply concerned teachers will find that some colleagues do not sympathize with their uncertainty; some who see uncertainty as endemic will feel that "the sure ones" are either arrogant or too easily satisfied. Those who doubt may find themselves labeled incompetent ("they cannot see results because there are none"), and nondoubters may be accused of avoiding painful truths. It seems probable, therefore, that the issue of performance assessment blocks communication among teachers and may in fact produce fissures in their group solidarity.

Fragilities of Relationship

Establishing and maintaining relationships with students is, as we saw in chapter 5, the other side of the teaching craft; in the eyes of our respondents it is integral and stands alongside instructional results as the mark of good teaching. We have also seen that teachers do not view such relationships as automatic, assured outcomes of teaching. They reserve special praise for colleagues who demonstrate the capacity to sustain evocative ties with their students. In this section, we seek insight into why teachers consider relationships with students problematic. What prevents them from taking them for granted?

In earlier comments, I identified three special issues in relational aspects of teaching: (1) the lack of voluntarism, (2) the incomplete socialization of students as workers, and (3) the grouped context within which instruction takes place. These conditions suggest that the leadership role of the teacher is particularly delicate. Is there evidence to support this viewpoint? We shall explore this question using two kinds of data from Five Towns. The first kind consists of teachers' responses to a question on the reputation they wish to have with students; the second revolves around shameful experiences in the classroom.

The Delicate Balance of Teacher Leadership

There are aspects to the teacher's leadership role which do not always lie easily with each other. First, there is universal agreement that the teacher must establish and keep sovereignty over classroom affairs; pedagogical experts, school administrators, and the public agree on this (Gallup 1969). School practices reinforce it, and beginning teachers soon learn that if their capacity to maintain "classroom control" is in doubt they may be fired. Waller's argument is probably as true today as it was in his time—teachers who fail to keep control over students soon find that teaching is intolerable work (Waller 1961). This is not to say that all schools expect the same level of control or that all teachers within a given school hold children to the same rules. Variations exist.[7] But the central point is not affected by these variations: the teacher must be in charge and must be so perceived.

The teacher, moreover, is expected to elicit work from students. Students in all subjects and activities must engage in directed activities which are believed to produce "learning." Their behavior, in short, should be purposeful, normatively controlled, and steady; concern with discipline and control, in fact, largely revolves around the need to get work done by immature, changeful, and divergent persons who are confined in a small space. Eliciting work in these circumstances requires attention to scheduling activities, coordinating student efforts, keeping supplies coming, dealing with emergencies, and so forth; a considerable amount of managerial work is called for in classroom teaching. Teachers make strong efforts, therefore, to establish working rules for class

Chapter Six

activity; as Smith and Geoffrey (1968) put it, they "groove" the students into regular patterns of joint action. The "crowd" described by Jackson (1968) cannot be permitted to become a mob.

The teacher therefore must "motivate" students, within the constraints described, to work hard and, if possible, to enjoy their efforts. He cannot count on voluntary enthusiasm; the teacher must generate much of the positive feeling that animates purposeful effort. All this, moreover, must be accomplished within a group setting and with persons who (in many cases) have not yet acquired the capacity for sustained effort. Interactionists since George Herbert Mead (1934) have argued that social action is complicated by the instability and unpredictability of people as social objects; Parsons and Shils (1952) built their theory of action on the need for regularization in human intercourse. The difficulties are particularly great when joint action must be carried out by partially socialized and physically immature young people: they are less able than adults to govern their own behavior in terms of rules and expectations.

These comments suggest the complexity of the teacher's classroom situation—control must be maintained, work must be ordered, and the students' interest must be aroused and sustained. These objectives must be met within a group over which the teacher presides; although there are dyadic contacts, a simple bit of arithmetic discloses that teachers can hardly spend more than a few minutes with each child in the course of a working day.[8] Most of their teaching behavior, therefore, must be addressed to groups of children. Thus the teacher, willy-nilly, must successfully perform the emotional (or "expressive") tasks involved in sustained leadership. The tasks set for students must be accomplished, but this also entails coping with the emotional needs individual children bring to the classroom. The teacher must handle these various aspects of leadership in a visible situation where inconsistencies are quickly observed by students.

Bales (1956) has argued that there is considerable strain between two kinds of leadership—getting tasks accomplished by a group and attending to expressive needs. He maintains that the personal orientations and dispositions needed to keep a group moving toward work goals differ from those involved in satisfying participants' expressive needs. Yet teachers cannot sidestep either leadership function, nor can they delegate them to students; doing so would sacrifice leadership resources needed in maintaining control. If Bales is right and strain exists in the performance of these two leadership functions, then teachers should experience tension between them. We can test this expectation by examining some relevant Five Towns data.

Five Towns teachers were asked to describe the kind of reputation they wanted to have with students; since their responses were detailed, it was possible to classify them according to the kinds of relationships projected for the classroom (Question 56, App. B-1). The specific themes discerned in the analysis can be categorized as expressive or task-oriented. Two themes are classified as task-oriented: "the students learn" (45) and "the teacher is not easy" (21). The numbers in parentheses refer to the number of mentions. Expressive themes include "fairness" (43), "warmth and understanding" (17), "teacher is thought nice or is liked" (16), "teacher is respected" (14), and "students enjoy the class" (11). It is suggestive that more mentions dealt with expressive considerations (101 versus 66); perhaps American schools, with a cellular organization which is not usually offset by external examinations, foster this orientation.[9] But both sides of the leadership coin are mentioned; respondents are evidently concerned with both task and expressive leadership functions.

How do respondents relate the two facets of leadership? Can we find out whether they see them as mutually supportive or as competitive? To deal with this question, we need evidence that (1) some teachers mention both facets in their responses and that (2) their answers signal a belief that they are antipathetic. The first test is simple: one counts how many times a respondent's answer falls either on one or on both sides of the leadership dichotomy. More than half the respondents (56 percent) mentioned both sets of leadership functions; more respondents who mentioned only one chose socioemotional considerations.[10]

The second criterion for establishing perceived antipathy is more elusive. I noticed, however, that the two kinds of leadership roles were frequently linked by the conjunctions "yet" or "but"—a linguistic structure which normally signifies opposition rather than consonance between two ideas. Here are some examples:

I think they'd understand that I'm a teacher who doesn't stand for any fooling around *but yet* you can have fun in the class. Someone that you can learn well from and some teacher they would enjoy spending a whole year with. [#55 F-25-6th]

Most teachers want to be liked. But I would like the reputation of being a nice guy, as the kids say, he's a good egg or he's a good guy. At the same time, an effective teacher. I would like them also to say he's a good guy, *but* you work considerably in his classroom and you learn. [#26 M-34-Reading]

Well, I would like to hear them say difficult, a hard teacher, you can get instruction, I mean, I want them to feel that they have learned something and not...an easy teacher...they still can feel free to talk to me, for additional visits and help if they don't understand the work *but* I'd like them to consider me as a teacher that knows her subject matter. [#71 F-26-Business]

Protocols were available for thirty-eight teachers who cited both task and socioemotional themes: coding conservatively, slightly more than half the respondents opposed one or more instrumental qualities to socioemotional ones. The use of quantitative logic is puzzling when one is dealing with such "volunteered" data—respondents were not systematically asked whether they saw the roles as antipathetic or supportive. (Those who did not oppose the two types of leadership, however, did *not* assert that they were mutually supportive.) Given these ambiguities, the prudent conclusion is that some Five Towns teachers perceive tension between task and expressive aspects of their role.

The more specific oppositions are worth mentioning, for it appears that the patterns of perceived antipathy may break into subtypes worth pursuing in future research. One was the implied conflict between asserting authority and the warmer aspects of teaching:

I would like them to say that I helped them. I'm strict, but I helped them. [#46 F-61-2d]

And another teacher told me that one of the children said to her, "Mrs. W. makes us mind, but we like her." So to me, if you can get that, that's everything. [#50 F-67-4th]

I like to be their friend and yet to know when hilarity and fun stops. I think they know where the line goes.... You have controlled discipline all the time. [#30 F-41-P.E.]

Researchers who have observed classrooms have estimated that about 40 percent of a teacher's actions are directed toward maintaining order (M. Hughes 1959). This adds up to a large number of acts, and the probability is that some will be mistaken—the teacher might, for example, reprove the wrong child. Some teachers worry that a reputation for strictness might carry the undesirable companion of alleged unfairness:

He is a good disciplinarian but he is fair. I like to be fair with no favoritism. That's what I would like but I don't always succeed. It's pretty hard to stay uninvolved with them. [#33 M-39-6th]

I don't mind at all when children think I'm strict just as long as they don't think I'm mean or anything.....It's much easier to start out that way and to let up...you can't change in the middle of the stream and you cannot bear down after because they lose respect for you. They become very fresh and they can really make life miserable. [#2 F-25-6th]

He's not easy to get around or something like that, he shows no favoritism...a good teacher. I don't want to try and play favorites at all and I want to have a well-disciplined class. [#51 M-26-Science, Math]

Teachers who feel that task and expressive leadership functions are at odds probably believe that they cannot optimize both work leadership and responsiveness to the emotional needs of students. If they assume conflict, it follows that demands on students and consideration for them can each be carried too far; excessive demands for effort will produce alienation, but excessive consideration will lead students to "take advantage" of the situation. We can think of teachers, therefore, as selecting a point in their classroom behavior (it may, of course, vary from time to time) where the two competing requirements meet in a balance they find acceptable. In the term used by March and Simon (1958), such teachers "satisfice" by accepting X goal achievement and Y relational conditions. To the extent that teachers think their productivity is restricted by the need for such trade-offs, the psychic rewards of teaching seem intrinsically scarce. We saw in chapter 5 that teachers want both results and appropriate relationships with students; to believe that one must be sacrificed for the other is to feel that the supply of each is limited.

There is little evidence that teachers have been educated to observe such contradictions within their roles or to analyze the issues involved; they do not explicate the subtle problems we have discussed. Those who train and supervise teachers might allege (with some justification) that the available knowledge base is weak; behavioral science has much to learn about group and leadership processes. But whatever the reasons for the lack of attention in teacher preparation, the gap in conceptualization underlines the low utility of the conventional wisdom of teaching and the incompleteness of technical knowledge in the occupation. Again we encounter uncertainty: individuals must solve recurrent problems largely unaided by systematic, relevant knowledge.

The Erratic Self: Despoiling Relationships

The role of the classroom teacher puts the major obligation for effective action on his shoulders; it is the teacher's responsibility to coordinate, stimulate, and shepherd the immature workers in his charge. Student groups have a deficit of work capacity (by adult standards) which the teacher alone can make up; the efficacy of school systems rests on the capacity of the aggregate of teachers to provide leadership in their separate classrooms. Task and expressive leadership in classrooms must emanate from the teacher, who, it is presumed, corrects for the capriciousness of students with the steadiness, resolve, and sangfroid of one who governs. The austere virtues, moreover, must be complemented by warmer qualities like empathy and patience. It becomes clear, then, that the self of the teacher, his very personality, is deeply engaged in classroom work; the self must be used and disciplined as a tool necessary for achieving results and earning work gratifications.

If the foregoing analysis is accurate, we will expect teachers to hold themselves accountable for fulfilling their obligations; that is, behavior should match the requirements of the role. Conversely, teacher sentiments should be violated when they fail to meet the obligations they have taken on. The reasoning can be tested with data from Five Towns which deal with teacher perceptions of serious error—their definitions of the mistakes which are important enough to merit feelings of shame (question 33, App. B-1). By telling us what concrete events lead to feelings of shame, teachers are informing us on the content of their work consciences and about the norms which undergird their daily work (Lortie 1967). As we shall see, these data reaffirm the centrality of relational issues; teachers feel shame when they act in ways which undermine their relationships with students. The big mistakes, then, are interactional.

Teachers do not always manage to handle themselves in the way they consider right. In citing sources of shame, 55 percent of the Five Towns teachers talked about times when they lost their temper with students.[11] It was clear that the public display of impulsive anger was the most emotionally disturbing of the shameful events in which they had a hand. Loss of temper was linked with lashing out at students, usually verbally but sometimes physically. These excerpts illustrate the range of behavior connected with teacher anger:

> The one big thing I regret whenever I do it is when I lose my temper and stamp my foot and scream. Because it's very undignified, it doesn't get you anywhere. [#67 F-24-3d]

> Losing my temper. I try never to say "shut up" in my room but I have done that and my children know, I mean I say to them, don't use "shut up." I don't want you to use "shut up" and then I come out and say it to someone. It doesn't look too good, you know. I've lost my temper twice in the time I've been teaching here and both times I felt

terrible about it...it makes you feel terrible that you have stooped that low. [#55 F-25-6th]

Well, years ago I hit children. Of course I wouldn't, you can't do that now but I have done that which I felt badly about....Recently...I have taken work I didn't like, I've just crumpled it up and threw it in the wastebasket. And afterward I have thought what a terrible thing to do because maybe that was the child's best effort. [#8 F-58-1st]

One day coming home from a track meet the kids performed poorly, and they weren't at all dismayed....This puts me in a bad mood when the kids perform poorly and don't give a damn....I decided to let them have it and tell them off. One kid, I think, probably didn't hear me, didn't stop talking, and I belted him across the back of the head. I was terribly embarrassed....I was sort of worried about relationships with the team....It was out of character....I think it was more that they were disappointed in me than anything else. Frankly, I also thought he might talk about it at home. [#17 M-37-English]

Waller talks about the controlled anger teachers learn to use to quell a disturbance or control a student, but the outbursts reported by Five Towns teachers were not intended (1961, p. 206). They described impulsive behavior which erupted despite their knowledge of its potential harmfulness and despite their intention not to give vent to such feelings:

You make a vow that you will never do that again, but then will come another day when my patience is just worn too thin and you explode again. [#70 F-65-1st]

I know yelling at her wouldn't do any good and every now and then I'd just get to the end of my rope and I'd yell at her. You'd just wished you'd bitten your tongue. [#67 F-24-3d]

You should stay out when you're really sick...this is when you are mean to students. [#14 M-33-6th]

It can build up over weeks and then you undo in a very short time something which has been building up, a hasty word or not being understanding in a particular situation. [#60 F-59-6th]

My emotions got away with me. [#18 M-36-1st]

The responses revealed that teachers feel shame on two major bases: behavior which violates their responsibilitiy to students and behavior which damages their relationship with students. (We shall focus on the latter here.) Teachers believe that angry impulses and wrongful punishment injure the ties with students which they seek both as ends in themselves and as key resources in forwarding student accomplishment. The self-inflicted nature of the damage rankles; they fret as they see their own loss of control shatter the rapport they strove so hard to achieve:

[The relationship with the class] sort of goes whsssht....Nine out of ten times you've probably lost them for the rest of the session, depending on how quickly you recover your own equilibrium. [#38 F-35-3d]

There are certain occasions, like if I have raised my voice....I think you can feel the tension with the children. [#52 F-47-3d]

The relationship with a single student can also be damaged by anger. A male elementary teacher, telling how one student teased him about his part-time job in a liquor store, continued:

We had an art lesson...[he] drew a picture of a whiskey bottle and the label read, "Oh, Mr. ———." I was angered by it...I called Jimmy up. I explained to him that I had a family to take care of....Maybe I was too harsh with him...he started crying....I think...I was angered that I probably spoke to him more harshly than I should have. As a result, I don't think we had the best relations....It wasn't good for him or me. [#18 M-36-1st]

In chapter 3 we found that teachers place interpersonal qualities like patience, consideration, and warmth at the heart of their "subjective warrant" for teaching—they mentioned such characteristics oftener than intellectual qualities. We can appreciate, therefore, why the angry outburst is so threatening to a teacher. It attacks his personal sense of competence. There are, of course, risks connected with external responses to teacher anger—parents may become angry themselves and try to retaliate. But the comments of Five Towns teachers stress their own feelings of embarrassment, self-accusation, acute discomfort, remorse, and other self-punishing emotions. The mistake which most rapidly unravels the teacher's self-assurance as a competent teacher is the release of unbridled anger.

Our examination of teacher mistakes, though brief, provides additional insight into their relationships with students and how fragile they seem to them. We also see how relational fragilities can prove costly to the teacher; feelings can be evoked which mar pleasure and pride in one's work. Teachers have little choice about control—it falls to them to organize the activities of youngsters. Yet the exercise of control requires continual attempts to direct children in particular ways, and they can and do balk. The teacher's exasperation must somehow be contained and his anger defused; otherwise he will regret his spontaneity. There are endemic tensions within the task-oriented, controlling aspects of the teacher's role, and individual teachers must find ways to cope with those tensions in noninjurious ways. The costs are not only instructional; teachers suffer as a consequence of their own angry impulses. Experiences in which anger boils over may leave the teacher uncertain about the future. Will it happen again? If Waller was right in thinking that teachers develop a somewhat constrained personality, it may not be surprising that this occurs. The negative outcomes of spontaneity can be severe.

The outside observer is again impressed by the lack of specific attention to these matters in teacher training, the literature on teaching, and the talk of school administrators. Social workers, clinical psychologists, and psychotherapists are routinely educated to consider their own personalities and to take them into account in their work with people. Their stance is supposed to be analytic and open; one concedes and works with one's own limitations—it is hoped—in a context of self-acceptance. The tone of teacher interviews and their rhetoric reveals no such orientation; I would characterize it as moralistic rather than analytic and self-accusing rather than self-accepting. It does not appear that their work culture has come to grips with the inevitabilities of interpersonal clash and considerations of how one copes with them. Teachers seem lonely; they fight battles alone with their consciences and, it seems, frequently lose.

The Structural Exacerbation of Uncertainty

Endemic uncertainties complicate the teaching craft and hamper the earning of psychic rewards. Intangibility and complexity impose a toll; built-in difficulties include assessing performance, balancing demands and relationships, and managing the self under provocation. In each instance the technical culture falls short of resolving the issue; it is most unlikely that so many teachers would experience difficulty if effective solutions were at hand. Although an individual teacher may escape some of the problems we have discussed, it is highly improbable that anyone can avoid them all. Some kind of uncertainty usually accompanies classroom teaching.

People in other occupations also encounter work uncertainty; one thinks, for example, of those in mental health vocations like clinical psychology, psychiatry, and psychiatric social work. Yet I believe the situation in teaching is more serious; it is exacerbated by teaching's somewhat unique structural characteristics. Two in particular appear germane: the pattern of eased entry and the unstepped nature of the career line.

In another place (Lortie 1968) I have compared how classroom teachers and professors are inducted into work; the analysis was organized around the functions of shared ordeal in work socialization. (Some of the ideas were referred to in chapter 3.) Basing the comparison on research done by Hall and others, I pointed out that graduate students in arts and science typically share ordeals which forge their identities as members of the occupation. Doctoral examinations are a case in point. Hall (1967) found that graduate students who worked together to prepare for such experiences underwent greater identity change than those who worked alone; in that sense, collective strategies for dealing with a common problem were rewarded. Such ordeals differentiate members of the field from nonmembers; they also strengthen the self-esteem of those who persist and, in the aggregate, the self-esteem of members of the occupation. The neophyte's readiness to experience demanding trials demonstrates his commitment; older members of the field are reassured that newcomers "care" about their work. Examination procedures require that senior colleagues attest to the fitness of those who are accepted; in moments of self-doubt, those who have passed through the system can reassure themselves that they were tested and found acceptable. The same processes take place where protracted apprenticeships govern training and entry; the "graduate" knows that his capacities have been examined and certified.

The contrast with teaching is striking. Teachers are inclined to talk about their training as easy ("mickey mouse"); I have yet to hear a teacher complain that education courses were too difficult or demanded too much effort. Teachers do not perceive their preparation as conveying something special—as setting them apart from others. Eased entry is the psychological as well as logical opposite of shared ordeal. We saw in chapter 3 that teachers do not consider training the key to their legitimation as teachers. That rests in experience. But as we also noted, the experience of teachers tends to be private rather than shared. The "sink-or-swim" pattern is individual, not collective; there is little to suggest that it induces a sense of solidarity with colleagues. Nor does it seem stringent enough to warrant the neophyte's commitment; my impression is that one demonstrates commitment to teaching by staying with it for some years, a criterion no beginner can meet. It seems likely that the functions performed by shared ordeal in academia—assisting occupational identity formation, encouraging collegial patterns of behavior, fostering generational trust, and enhancing self-esteem—are slighted in classroom teaching. We do know, for example, that teachers tend to underestimate the rank of their occupation; that finding suggests that teachers have, if anything, a deficit rather than surplus of self-esteem (Charters 1963, p. 748). The induction processes of classroom teaching, then, do not appear to augment the "reassurance capital" of classroom teachers.

Perhaps the most relevant experiences, however, are those of experienced teachers; probably all beginners have doubts about their capacity. The career line of teaching gives the occupation an unusual quality; once tenured, a person can work for years without public recognition for his greater mastery of core tasks. We observed in chapter 4 that the situation is different in the established professions and traditional crafts; there we find regular turning points which highlight shifts in status as the person moves along. The important figures in a lawyer's life know what it means to be appointed partner; and the social set of the academic is sensitive to gradations of rank and promotion. Mental health workers usually march up career lines demarcated by title and income; journalists move through graded assignments and editorial posts. Crafts employ a lexicon of status terms such as apprentice, journeyman (divided into classes), and master craftsman; and business and government organizations identify career turning points with formal hierarchy and informal privilege.

The study of social stratification has taught us that status channels the flow of deference to individuals. Deference can reassure people of their worth and competence; moving through a series of statuses therefore provides a gradient of increasing psychological support. Repeated indications of others' respect can quell self-doubt. Deference, in short, can help people who work with uncertainty and ambiguity. Yet we have seen that teaching careers typically offer little support of this kind; most starkly, a teacher with forty years of experience may be replaced by a rank beginner. Older teachers, in fact, may find that students tend to give more deference and affection to younger colleagues; seniority cannot be used to order the reponses of students. The career system of teachers, unlike that in most kinds of work, does little to offset the subjective discomfort caused by intangibility and relational complexity.

Eased entry and unstepped careers exacerbate rather than alleviate the feelings of uncertainty provoked by teaching tasks. Uncertainty, under these conditions, can be transformed into diffuse anxiety and painful self-doubt, which reduce the psychic rewards of classroom teaching. It seems likely that teachers treasure the joys of accomplishment the more for their scarcity. It is also likely that they will care deeply about working conditions which they believe increase the flow of work rewards.

7

The Logic of
Teacher Sentiments

People in a similar line of work are likely to share at least some common thoughts and feelings about that work. Such convergence can arise from the diffusion of a subculture; on the other hand, it may derive from common responses to common contingencies. Whatever the source of the shared sentiments, however, it is essential to know their nature if we are to grasp the ethos of an occupation.

Sentiment is a broad term. We can facilitate analysis, I believe, if we subdivide that idea into three components—preoccupations, beliefs, and preferences. Colleagues are likely to show similar preoccupations—they heed particular aspects of the environment and are indifferent to others. Thus does the world look different to geologists and painters. Beliefs can also vary along occupational lines; members of an occupation develop theories (implicit as well as explicit) to account for events which are important to them. Thus policemen and social workers are likely to use different theories to explain similar behavior. Members of different occupations have different preferences in working arrangements and such: whereas the "big-ticket" salesman is sharply individualistic, ironworkers count heavily on the intimate coorperation of their four-man teams.

What work sentiments do teachers share? That is the first question we shall address in this chapter; we will analyze survey data and open-ended interviews to identify some of their shared preoccupations, beliefs, and preferences. The data will cover a variety of issues, including the circumstances teachers associate with high points in their work, the nature of their discontents, and the changes they would like to see in their work context. We will search for general sentiments which permeate different aspects of their work; where we succeed, we should gain insight into teacher perspectives and, quite possibly, teacher behavior.

There is a second major objective for this chapter—a more ambitious one. That goal is to understand as much as we can about the underlying logic of teacher sentiments. The assumption is that teacher sentiments represent an adaptation to their work situation; if we understand the problems of teachers, their sentiments should prove more understandable. We will look for such understanding by connecting our findings on sentiments to what we have already learned about the occupation. More is required, however. We cannot afford to overlook limits imposed on teachers by their particular status. Teacher tasks and teacher status are related, and an examination of teacher sentiments must reflect that relationship.

First, I will recapitulate some of the major points made so far, connecting them with the teacher's stake in school organization; I will draw certain corollaries and test them with survey data. Second, I will analyze teacher tasks and the imperatives which flow from them to see what tensions arise between the tasks teachers perform and the status they occupy.

Priorities of Teacher Allegiance

The argument of the last three chapters carries implications for teachers' views on their work setting. In chapter 4, we observed that psychic rewards have special significance for teachers and that such rewards are linked to achievement with students. Chapter 5 argued that teacher purposes revolve around classroom events; in chapter 6, the problematics we identified arise in the immediate work setting of the teacher. But what about the school and the school system? How do teachers view the organizational context in which they work?

If teachers cathect classrooms, it means that other settings and relationships have less importance for them. Two corollaries follow. First, teachers should care less about tasks and activities rooted in organizational matters than about those rooted in classroom matters. Second, when a conflict arises between organizational and classroom demands, teachers should favor those originating in the classroom. We can test these corollaries with data from Dade County.

When asked how they would choose to spend additional work time,

Dade County teachers overwhelmingly selected activities related to classroom rather than schoolwide matters (question T4, App. B-2). Ninety-one percent of the respondents chose teaching-related activities such as more preparation (40 percent), more teaching (28 percent), counseling students (19 percent), and parent conferences (4 percent).[1] Nine percent gave first choice to committee work on school operations, instruction, and public relations. Their press is toward effort where psychic rewards occur—in work directly connected with their students. (The choices have an interesting side implication; they throw doubt on teachers' allegations about wanting greater control over curricular affairs at the school system level.) It is also interesting that 91 percent of the first choices are individualistic; they are all tasks which teachers normally perform alone. As an indication of preference for classroom versus schoolwide activities, the responses are unambiguous; the vast majority of respondents—5,448 out of 5,991—chose to spend additional time on classroom tasks rather than working with the school at large.

Two kinds of data speak to the question of which claims, organizational or classroom, teachers prefer to meet. The first consists of responses Dade County teachers gave to a question on school organization.[2] They were asked to choose between more freedom from organizational authority and greater efficiency through rules; an attempt was made to balance the evident appeal of freedom by mentioning an explicit benefit of rules. The results were clear-cut: 66 percent chose greater freedom, 29 percent prevailing arrangements, and 4 percent more rules and efficiency. If anything, these teachers want to loosen organizational claims in favor of teacher decision-making in the classroom.

The second set of data consists of answers to a question we discussed in chapter 3; we may recall that 59 percent of Dade County teachers said that the good teacher monitors his own efforts in the classroom. By the most generous count, 7 percent of the respondents emphasized superordinate judgments as the most appropriate source of work monitoring. Since the line of vertical authority symbolizes organizational goals and claims, its relegation to such infrequency indicates secondary allegiance to the organization at large.[3]

These data seem to support the corollaries which have been drawn; in the available data, teachers prefer classroom tasks over organizational tasks and classroom claims over organizational initiations. Their impulses are organizationally centrifugal; their primary allegiance is to the classroom. What makes these tendencies interesting (they are understandable given the reward structure) is that teachers are not seen as entrepreneurs seeking psychic rewards; they are defined as employees of school systems and are hired to implement board policies and administrative rulings. As we shall see, the tension between teacher impulses and status realities has consequences for the nature of teacher sentiments.

Task Imperatives and Status Constraints

Since teachers assign priority to classroom tasks, we would expect their sentiments to reflect that concern. The question arises: What circumstances are likely to advance or retard realization of their classroom aims? For if teachers have a stake in task performance, they are likely to be deeply concerned with conditions which affect that performance.

To get a fresh perspective on teaching tasks, let us compare teaching with other occupations which include similar tasks. What is the relationship between rights and obligations and what people must do in their work? More abstractly, how are status realities and task imperatives related? Task imperatives refer here to the necessities involved in performing duties; for example, in order to make arrests, a police officer must be able to use force in overcoming resistance. In teaching, the imperative of maintaining classroom discipline requires that teachers be able to punish other people's children—an unusual right. In this instance, the status of the teacher and his task imperatives are congruent. But as we shall see, alignment is not always present; tension can obtain between task imperatives and status realities.

Teachers strive to *"reach"* students. They *manage* groups of young people at work. Teachers are also expected to *perceive and act on* the needs of individual learners. The foregoing tasks can be found in other occupations. The first requires communication with, and penetration of, a group of people in a face-to-face situation. This requirement occurs in several occupations—we will choose the theater for comparison. The occupation analogous to the second set of tasks, the management of work groups, is more obvious; industrial or business managers perform similar tasks. The need to observe individuals and to prescribe suitable procedures and monitor their progress is similar to the tasks of the psychotherapist.

Although teaching is a long-range, continuing activity, in contrast to the short-range, immediate impact sought in the theater, both teachers and actors face similar task imperatives. They must overcome the influence of distractions and mobilize the attention of initially uninvolved audiences. Without full attention, neither learning nor dramatic experience is likely to take place. In theater work there is a complex division of labor aimed at reaching the audience; directors, stage managers, actors—to say nothing of the playwright—work together. The teacher typically works alone and is forced to play all those roles simultaneously. The theatrical setting, moreover, is usually manipulated to concentrate audience attention; lighting, scenery, properties, and costumes all contribute to monopolizing the audience's attention. The teacher, on the other hand, works under comparatively humdrum conditions, with fewer resources for riveting attention. (We should also recall that students, unlike theater audiences, have not come voluntarily.) Teachers, in short, face some of the same imperatives as theater people without possessing equal resources.

The teacher has an additional handicap in maintaining attention; unlike the director of a play, the teacher has little "artistic control" over the enterprise. Teachers cannot select or reject scripts; they frequently must follow curricula which bore students or are beyond their capacities. Nor is the classroom a stage over which the teacher can legitimately assert full authority; as part of the school, its activities are subject to review by higher officials. Teachers have difficulty in sealing off disruption. Administrators may intervene and peers may interrupt; students may break the spell a teacher has sought to develop. The teacher must work with supplies furnished by others and may in fact have trouble getting enough. In addition to having fewer resources, the teacher has less control over the situation than those directing theatrical productions. The teacher's status, in short, is less suited to imperatives of communication and penetration.

Although one hears references to "classroom management," teachers are rarely described as managers. Perhaps the position of teachers as subordinates, coupled with the lower prestige accorded to work with minors, accounts for the tendency to overlook similarities between teachers and managers. Both set goals for groups of subordinates and try to lead them toward accomplishment. Both must decide how to allocate time and other scarce resources to get work done. Both must balance task and socioemotional considerations. Both distribute rewards and punishments to those in their charge.

It is a truism of organization that administrators need a degree of autonomy and authority to carry out their responsibilities (Parsons 1958). The statuses of teachers and managers are nowhere more different than here; teachers work *under* administrators—the latter term is used to distinguish managers from teachers. Without the title to identify their managerial functions, teachers do not benefit from the principle of administrative discretion. Nor are they expected to show the personal qualities (e.g., independence in decision-making, aggressiveness) which mark the manager. Teachers rarely have budgetary discretion and the other prerogatives which are part of the manager's working equipment. In status terms, teachers are disadvantaged compared with managers; imperatives which flow from their managerial tasks are likely to be misaligned with their formal status.

Although teachers have difficulty meeting individual needs in the grouped structure of public schools, they are expected to make individual assessments and decisions about students. Such work with people involves considerable judgement; to prescribe particular remedies for learning difficulties, for example, is not a cut-and-dried matter—it involves intuition as well as explicit reasoning. One's judgments, moreover, need time to reveal their merit or inadequacy; others must be willing to extend trust until the results are in. Similar conditions apply to the practice of psychotherapy; diagnoses and treatment interact over time as the therapist tests various possibilities. But although the tasks and imperatives may be similar for teachers and therapists, there is normally a large difference in their prestige. Therapists may be licensed psychologists or physicians; where that is so, their claims to trust are buttressed by impressive qualifications based on protracted study.

Although it would require separate research to find out how willing members of the public are to trust teachers' judgments about individual students, that trust rarely matches that extended to qualified therapists. Teachers are certified to teach in schools without demonstrating expert knowledge of individual psychology. There is evidence, moreover, that parents question teachers' judgments and do not feel constrained to "wait it out"; one hears of administrators overruling teachers' judgments.[4] Again we find that the imperatives of teaching and the status of teachers are misaligned.

In each comparison, we found that persons performing tasks similar to teachers' enjoyed greater status rights. Teachers have fewer resources, and less control over them, than theater directors. Teachers have less discretionary power and fewer resources than managers. Teachers have less formal recognition to support their judgments than do psychotherapists. Teachers therefore can be said to be comparatively poorer in the status resources which facilitate accomplishment of the tasks listed here. Recalling how deeply teachers feel about their psychic rewards, we would expect them to develop ideas about these points of stress and tension. They are inhibited in impulses toward autonomy, more resources, and control over the work situation—that, at least, is a reasonable inference from our analysis so far. On the other hand, teachers have been socialized to a subordinate position within school systems. We know, too, that they are dogged by painful uncertainties.

How do teachers cope with these tensions? Do their sentiments focus on status limitations? Or do they accept such difficulties as unavoidable features of their work?

Preoccupations, Beliefs, and Preferences

The researcher's delight can be the writer's bane. Certain key sentiments appeared and reappeared in several questions I asked Five Towns teachers; that repetition convinced me of their importance. Yet discussion of repetition could prove tedious. I will therefore mention the range of responses to each question but emphasize new themes as they come up.

High Points for Teachers: The Good Day

One of the most useful questions in the Five Towns interviews asked respondents to describe "a good day" in their teaching; the question was developed after pilot research indicated that teachers used the phrase in discussing their work (Question 31, App. B-1). The question meets the criteria we used in chapter 5 to assess the quality of interview data: it is personal, concrete, indirect and cathected. The vast majority of respondents gave graphic and detailed answers. Since the material was valuable, it was analyzed in three distinct ways—each tells us something about how teachers see those occasions when things go very well.

Invariant Themes. Lindesmith argued that social scientists should give special attention to invariant findings—that is, occasions where one cannot find exceptions to patterns in one's data (Lindesmith 1947). All respondents made certain points (explicitly and implicitly) in answering this question. Of the three invariant themes identified, two are familiar to us and can be discussed briefly.

The first commonality was that all respondents readily accepted the assumption of variability built into the question and based their answers on that assumption. These teachers evidently see their work as "up and down" in nature and view the flow of accomplishment and rewards as erratic. This observation fits in with earlier discussions of teacher rewards and uncertainty.

The second invariant theme was that every teacher, regardless of grade or specialty, based his answer on the same locale. In each instance he focused on events within his immediate work area, whether classroom, gymnasium, woodworking shop, or laboratory. Other settings (e.g., assemblies, lunchrooms, or corridors) were alluded to in negative terms; good things were not linked to them. We have already discussed teachers' cathexis of classrooms and their secondary involvement in other facets of their work; responses to this question underscore that point.

The third similarity in the answers revolves around the actors identified in the events which mark a good day. The pattern is striking; positive events and outcomes are linked to two sets of actors—the teacher and the students. (Students occasionally produce negative references connected with discipline cases.) But *all* other persons, without exception, were connected with undesirable occurrences. Negative allusions were made to parents, the principal, the school nurse, colleagues—in fact, to anyone and everyone who "intrudes" on classroom events. The cathected scene is stripped of all transactions save those between teacher and students.

This third theme introduces sentiments we have not yet discussed. From the evidence of this question, teachers attach great meaning to the boundaries which separate their classrooms from the rest of the school and, of course, the community. Teachers deprecate transactions which cut across those boundaries. Walls are perceived as beneficial; they protect and enhance the course of instruction. All but teacher and students are outsiders. That definition conveys an implicit belief that, on site, other adults have potential for hindrance but not for help.

It's a day when you really have the children to yourself. You accomplish a lot. At the end of the day you feel you've taught them something. [#34 F-45-4th]

A good day for me...is a smooth day. A day when you can close the doors and do nothing but teach. When you don't have to collect picture money or find out how many want pizza for lunch or how many want baked macaroni or how many want to subscribe to a magazine. If you could have a day without those extra duties—that would be a good day. [#39 F-31-1st]

I think, to me, a day is good without interruption—the several days during the week that I spend mostly in the classroom. There is no gym, no TV, no programs that take the children out of the room, but those days are getting less all the time....I like to be right in the classroom and have the children there. Some days can be rather hectic here. You just don't get that much done. You look up and where is Johnny? He's taking a lesson. Sometimes the children are out of the room and you don't even realize it. It is hard to keep track of some of the things and extras. I think they are extras in some cases and interfere with the teacher's day. [#14 M-33-6th]

169

Well, when things you planned go well. For example, you have a subject to teach that's not always an interesting subject but one of the dull factors that has to do with mechanics and suddenly you get results. You see that the youngsters see what you have and get it easily and quickly and apply it and it comes back to you as you want it to come back. I think that is a satisfying day—a day when you feel you've accomplished your job as a teacher. You taught something.

[Could you contrast this with a bad day?]

Well, just the reverse—when everything you do just does not go all right. Sometimes I wonder if the days have to have a great many interruptions and we have those unfortunately. It's a day you're being pushed for reports, you're being pushed for this and you don't feel as though you have the time and sometimes the energy to put across the subject that you need to put across in your classrooms and so your approach is perhaps not as calm as it would have been on a good day and, as a result, you don't get results and you feel it's been a completely frustrating day. I think it usually comes when you're being pressed for reports on time or you have a great many interruptions. Things of that kind. It used to be an extremely difficult day when we used to give the polio shots, for instance, in the gym and this room, this corridor out here, was Grand Central Station. You had youngsters crying, you had mamas, you know, in and out, and mama would see you in the room so she would burst right into the class and say, "Oh, hello Miss ———, it's you." A day like that could be a very bad day and yet it was something to be able to do that in itself. A bad day to me is something that you can't do anything about. [#22 F-55-English]

All because there are so many interruptions. You start to teach something and one of the teachers might come in, or the principal comes in or a supervisor comes in and before you know it, you've lost their attention entirely and might as well just not bother to even teach. As far as that goes with that particular subject because you're not about to get their attention back and that's my idea of a bad day. [#55 F-25-6th]

The quotations remind us of the comparisons between teachers and theater people; distraction is the enemy. Teaching can be marred when others interrupt its flow; the teacher may be pulled away to activities which, in his view, have nothing to do with teaching. In the teacher's idyll, there is a continuous, productive exchange between teacher and students; others have little to offer in advancing that exchange. Schoolwide tasks are defined in negative terms—they take energy and attention away from the primary setting, the classroom. It appears that teachers want to establish and maintain a time-bound but definite monopoly over students' attention and involvement. A key belief shown in these responses is that attention and response flourish when the classroom is a bounded, protected space. Teachers clearly prefer boundedness. In interpreting such sentiments, it is important to remember W. I. Thomas's dictum: it is not objective "truth" but what people believe to be true that affects their outlook. Teachers apparently think that their lives would be happier and their work more effective if they had more occasions when their relationship with the students matched their wants. They strive for a kind of privatization. Yet note that they are reporting on the rarity of such occasions; they are describing *high points* in their work. Teacher status does not ensure conditions they consider favorable to their work; the imperatives they value are infrequently satisfied. The impulse to build boundaries collides with status reality.

The Events of a Good Day. What happens within the classroom on a good day? What do teachers and students experience when all goes well? To answer such questions, responses were analyzed on a sentence-by-sentence basis; all comments made about the teacher and students were listed and coded. Different categories were developed for the two parties. We begin with teachers' perceptions about their own actions and experiences on a good day.

Of the comments made about the teacher's role on a good day (124 in all), some (29) referred to what the teacher brought to the day, some (69) dealt with the teacher's actions throughout the day, and the rest (36) described the teacher's feelings about such a day. The main idea conveyed in the first category—what the teacher brought to the day—was that the teacher *begins* feeling well. The day starts with a motivated teacher who is in a "good humor," "feels good," "is rested and well." The responses were comparatively homogeneous; the teacher begins in the right frame of mind for teaching.

More distinctions were made when respondents discussed the teacher's actions during the day. The largest number of comments (26) stressed effectiveness in permeating student awareness: they referred to "stimulating students," "being enthusiastic," "getting across," "reaching." Other statements concentrated on the handling of time constraints; some (almost all elementary teachers) stressed that on a good day they finished their work plans. Other respondents used general language indicating higher teacher performance (13); they said "the teacher performs well," "the teacher gets and sees results," and "the teacher reaches his goals." Some commented (8) that preparations proved effective, and others (5) said that the teacher worked hard on a good day. From what we have seen in earlier chapters, it should come as no surprise that the feelings teachers associate with such a good day—the third category of responses—are positive. Some (15) talked about the sense of accomplishment they felt—they feel vindicated as teachers. Others (11) contrasted it with other days, stating that they did not feel aggravated or tired at the end of the day.

To sum up the teacher's role on a good day, then, we can say this. The teacher starts off ready for work, feeling good and having high energy. The day is marked by getting through to the students, finishing one's plans, and effective teaching; plans prove viable and one works hard. At the end of the day, the teacher feels worthy. He has earned his way.

How do respondents define the students' contributions to a good day? The emphasis here is somewhat different; students contribute by responding and cooperating (62), behaving themselves (29), and demonstrating positive feelings (11). They are excellent followers of the teacher's leadership. They participate actively, show interest, and give their full attention. They work hard. They behave themselves by conforming to the teacher's rules. They show positive affect by "wanting to learn," "being in a good mood," and "enjoying the classes."

The outcomes for students are instructional; forty-five of the statements dealt with student learning and accomplishment. The teachers said things like "the students learn," "they get it," and "they grasp the lesson." The benefits reaped by students and teachers are different but complementary; student learning is matched to the teacher's sense of accomplishment.

Most of the themes disclosed in these observations have been discussed in earlier chapters. We note that the teacher is reaching the students; instructional goals are met. We also note that relational complexities are mastered and assessment worries allayed; the students' enthusiasm affirms the teacher's leadership skill and reduces anxiety about effectiveness. One theme is somewhat novel; teachers believe that the teacher is the essential catalyst for student achievement. Teacher leadership stands at the center of this benign and desirable activity; it is portrayed as the sine qua non of student learning. The role of the teacher approaches the heroic.

The themes of distraction and attention also emerged in comments which were not coded in the scheme we have just reviewed. Teachers described unlikely times for good days; they mentioned Mondays and Fridays, days before and after major holidays, and days immediately before major school events—particularly in high schools—such as dances or important games. In such instances the teacher finds it difficult to claim and hold student attention; the underlying belief is that when outside influences are at their highest point the teacher's is at its lowest.

A zero-sum conceptualization appears to be at work; the belief that student attention belongs to other activities *or* to the teacher is probably connected with the wish to separate classroom activities from the rest of the world.

The events of a good day reaffirm earlier analyses. They occur behind boundaries in the cathected classroom setting; they yield treasured rewards and reassure teachers. We see the fusion of achievement and satisfaction and the belief that teachers are the essential catalysts of student learning. There are times when difficulties in teaching are overcome and when sought-after goals and relationships are attained. One wonders, then, Can teachers ensure the occurrence of such days? We turn next to the issue which underlies teacher answers to that question. What do they believe causes a good day?

Uncertainty Reiterated: Subtleties of Mood. The advantages of a question which uses indirection to provoke spontaneity are offset, unfortunately, by disadvantages; one sometimes wishes more specific probes had been used. In trying to ascertain the "theories" held by respondents, it is difficult to be sure when causation is implied. Did those teachers who stressed boundedness intend to say that boundedness "caused" the good day? Or were they merely mentioning a necessary but not sufficient cause? In deciding to check on this, I identified all instances in which respondents made clear-cut statements on the cause of a good day. To my surprise, most of those statements (33 of 44) dealt not with boundedness but with psychological states of teachers and students.[5] Obviously one must treat such counts with caution; but it is useful to note that a proportion of Five Towns teachers feel that a good day requires more than boundedness.

The preoccupation with psychological states, and the attributions of cause and effect, revolved around what we can call factors of "mood." Some respondents (13) explained the good day in terms of the mood of both teacher and students; it arose only when both were in the appropriate frame of mind. Sometimes mood itself depended on external events like health or environmental conditions (e.g., the time of year, the weather). But other respondents located mood origins in the interaction between teacher and students; their talk reminds one of the processes discussed by students of collective behavior (Blumer 1957). Thus a good day evolves as students and teacher positively reinforce one another—there is an emphasis on rapport. (Some made comments such as "there's sort of a two-way radio between the children and me" or "the children and teacher seem to be in tune all day.") This suggests that further research might inquire into two discrete kinds of theories among teachers to account for points of high productivity and satisfaction. In one individuals react primarily to external influences, and in the other the emphasis is on a cycle of mutual sensitivity and positive reinforcement.

Some respondents, however, select either the teacher's or students' moods as controlling. A teacher who feels bad may infect sutdents with the same attitude. For example:

> If you didn't get enough sleep the night before...the children won't be as interested...more discipline problems. [#6 M-24-5th]

> Like when my husband was sick...that reacted on the children. [#46 F-61-2d]

A few teachers said that a good day depended on the mood of students. "Students may tune you out," for example, or "many are going to come in and are not going to learn anything no matter what you do." Another teacher talked about "bad actors" and remarked, "Sometimes a good day is when those students stay home." Student moods are frequently depicted as volatile; one teacher said snow falling outside on a December morning means "that is the end of it, they have been distracted." Student moods are seen as will-o'-the-wisps; they are unpredictable, quixotic, and ultimately mysterious.

The fact that some teachers explain good days (and the attendant results and satisfactions) in terms of subtle, changeful moods is provocative. The explanatory theories they are relying upon do not, in such instances, emphasize rational choice. Strategy counts for less than chance when mood is king. Such a view underlines the transitory, uncertain course of teaching; it also magnifies psychological processes which are usually thought to be beyond intentional control. One suspects that most people think of mood as something that happens to them, not as something they select. To link teaching effectiveness and rewards to mood is to make them contingent rather than manipulable—it connotes caprice rather than craft. Those who hold to such a view telegraph uncertainty rather than sure control; good days—and their benefits—are not something one orders up at will.

Summary: High Points. The teachers in our samples are preoccupied with classroom matters; they attach secondary importance to organizational affairs. Five Towns teachers talk largely about efforts to get and hold student attention and their attempts to permeate student awareness. The testimony in this chapter reaffirms the central importance of psychic rewards, instructional goals, and evocative relationships. Respondents evidently resent incursions on their teaching time; whatever distracts teachers or students, assuming that the interaction is essential to learning, is counterproductive. Respondents obviously have difficulty in warding off such incursions; their status does not provide them with the power to do so. Yet it is not clear that they believe boundedness is enough to ensure high results; some respondents emphasize the importance of subtle, difficult-to-control flows of mood. They seem to believe that short-term productivity and key rewards have an element of caprice.

What these teachers want matches their preoccupations and their beliefs—they want to teach. Since they also believe that the teacher is the essential catalyst in the learning process, they feel their impulses are legitimate. Whatever impedes their efforts impedes student progress. They want to concentrate their efforts on the core tasks of teaching, not on distractive organizational duties. One senses their yearning for uninterrupted, productive engagements with students.

The Anatomy of Discontent

Teacher complaint is almost ritualized in quality—its major components have been heard many times. In order to keep the same base for analysis, I shall present the responses to questions about dissatisfactions asked in the Five Towns interviews (questions 46, 48, App. B-1). There is an additional advantage to using those data, since they were open-ended and it was possible to analyze details which are usually omitted in questionnaire studies. Table 4 presents the results to two questions using conventional survey coding; in the text, we will discuss an additional analysis of the same data.

Respondents talked about two major sources of difficulty in their work. The first deals with their tasks and their use of time; the second refers to relationships with students, co-workers, and parents. We will discuss tasks and time use first and then briefly discuss interpersonal difficulties; the latter will receive considerably more attention in the next chapter. We are again faced with the scientific benefit but aesthetic problem of repetition. As we shall see, the difficulties teachers discuss are the other side, in large part, of what we have learned about their wants. I shall try to be concise, therefore, in reviewing the data.

Tasks and Time Use. Since teachers assign priority to classroom work with students, we can better understand their specific complaints if we make a simple distinction between two kinds of teacher time. The first can be called "potentially productive time." It refers to occasions when the teacher is engaged in either direct instruction of students or activities closely related to it (e.g., preparation, counseling). The second kind of time is "inert time"; this refers to occasions when the potential for learning is absent or very low because the teacher's activities are not instructional. The classification builds on *teacher* perceptions; teachers link students' learning to teachers' activities and, of course, to their psychic rewards. To them, potentially productive time can be salutary for students and personally rewarding; inert time is neither.

TABLE 4. COMPLAINTS OF FIVE TOWNS TEACHERS

Area of Complaint	Question 46 Mentions	%	Question 48 Mentions	%	Total Mentions
Tasks and Time Use					
Clerical duties	29	34	16	19	45
Interruptions, time pressures	16	19	29	35	45
Duties outside class	13	15	7	8	20
Large classes, schools	7	8	—	—	7
Grading papers, etc.	7	8	—	—	7
Fringe subjects	3	4	—	—	3
Interpersonal Relationships					
Troublesome students	19	22	25	30	44
Administrative superordinates	20	24	9	11	29
Parents	14	17	6	7	20
Fellow teachers	7	8	13	16	20
Other					
Income and prestige of occupation	5	6	—	—	5
Facilities and supplies	—	—	5	6	5
Miscellaneous	10	—	11	—	21

The content of table 4 makes sense when we bear that distinction in mind. The three most frequently mentioned problems and irritants (clerical duties, interruptions and time pressures, and extra duties) all involve inert time. Clerical duties usually originate in organizational needs for reports, forms, and so on; extra duties refer to supervising areas outside one's own domain, such as playgrounds, corridors, study halls, and lunchrooms. Interruptions occur when the flow of teaching is broken by the principal's making an announcement over the public address system, a parent's making an unscheduled call, or a fellow teacher's "visiting too long." Time pressures refer to sudden requests (usually from administrators) or short deadlines which require that planned activities be put aside. In each instance time is lost.

The time dimension to the other complaints listed in table 4 may be less immediately apparent. Large classes increase the proportion of inert time by requiring more clerical work, greater attention to managerial issues, and more disciplinary activity. Large schools increase the administration's managerial load; the result is probably an increase in administrative requests of staff members. Grading papers is notoriously time-consuming; some teachers, moreover, do not consider it instructionally productive. They resist evaluating students comparatively, possibly on philosophical grounds and possibly because it increases the social distance between them and their students. References to fringe subjects were made by elementary teachers who would prefer to spend the time required for art and music on "basic" subjects like arithmetic and reading; interestingly, they often support their objections by disclaiming any talent in the arts.

Teachers' objections to inert time are understandable, but one or two points are worth making. First, we can think of time as the single most important, general resource teachers possess in their quest for productivity and psychic reward; ineffective allocations of time are costly. Second, from one perspective teaching processes are ultimately interminable; one can never strictly say that one has "finished" teaching students. At what point has one taught every student everything he might possibly learn about the curriculum? More broadly, when can one feel that one has taught everything any particular student should learn? The theme of concern about incompleteness ran throughout the interviews; unfortunately, it occurred in various places, making systematic collation next to impossible. Presumably teachers develop defenses against overexpectation for themselves; yet these defenses do not always seem to work. If one is inwardly pressed by a feeling of not having finished one's work, inert time must be particularly galling.

Interpersonal Relationships. Table 4 identifies four categories of people who stimulate teacher complaints. Students can disrupt the teacher's plans and day, and one child who acts out can create considerable difficulty for a teacher.[6] Overall, however, adults are mentioned more often than students; how do administrators, parents, and fellow teachers pose problems for the classroom teacher?

There is a common theme in the complaints respondents registered about administrators, parents, and fellow teachers; time and again they said that they failed to give them sufficient "support" in their work. The specifics of support apparently differ with each category. With administrators, complaints centered on sudden, interruptive demands and the principals' failure to protect teachers against parental intrusions and harassments. Respondents criticized parents for either interfering in the teacher's classroom work or for not backing him up at home.

177

Colleagues were berated for avoiding their fair share of what Hughes (1958) calls "dirty work"; fellow teachers who fail to participate equally in unpopular tasks of hall duty, lunchroom supervision, and so forth increase the others' load. "Support" seems to mean that those who work in conjunction with the teacher should contribute to rather than detract from favorable work conditions; they should forward the teacher's strivings for boundaries, time control, and effective relationships with students.

The responses listed in table 4 were analyzed in another fashion. In all instances where teachers complained about interpersonal relationships, the responses were coded in terms of this question: What grounds does the respondent supply for his complaint? The results bring us back, strikingly, to concerns with time usage; sixty-two of the ninety-eight reasons given for complaint dealt with time erosion or the disruption of work flow. Some quotations reveal how those who intruded on the teacher's potentially productive time evoked annoyance:

> I think last-minute interruptions more than anything else. To go along with the classroom interruption business we have a P. A. system. It is overused. Instead of sending a notice around at the beginning and end of the day, and telling us what he has in mind for a particular thing . . . if you were in the middle of an arithmetic lesson, you'd just be hammering a point across and the loudspeaker would come on and the principal would talk for two or three minutes. By then, they are gone. Some kiddo will come in wanting to borrow our paper. The milk collection boy or the attendance book coming through the room . . . these things irritate me very much. I hate like the devil to be in the middle of a lesson and have this happen. You are in the middle of a lesson and a youngster will walk up to the wastebasket to deposit a piece of paper. . . . This burns me to no end. They learn it early in my class that this I don't go for. I think interruptions more than anything else bother me. [#18 M-36-4th]

> I do think that sometimes too much of our actual school day has to be taken up with collecting things or making our reports and so forth. It isn't that I object to doing them, but I do object to the time it takes away from my class. The only practical thing is, I guess, for the teacher to do it, but it does take away from—the children should be here—the town's paying to have them educated—not to have you collect milk money and I mean there are so many little things like that. I suppose maybe that's what is dissatisfying to teachers. [#70 F-65-1st]

> I don't know that they bother but I think we have so much secretarial

work, so many other things to do besides teach. Sometimes it seems to me that teaching comes last instead of first. And so I think that would be the part of our teaching for which all the secretarial work would be the parts for which we have the least training really, and yet more and more and more we have to do that . . . fill out insurance papers and take care of all the P. T. A. notices, collect money for this and for that, and all these other odd jobs that we have to do that are so time-consuming. By the time that we do all that there's not too much time left to teach. [#66 F-54-English]

Interruptions. Interruptions during class time. Additional duties that are actually not assigned that you just pick up along the way. In other words, you may have something planned, you may have a free period, and you may plan on doing some work, and you get a call saying, well, cover a class, or cover study hall. Changing of programming at times by them in other words, you're on a schedule, you're on a routine perhaps if you want to call it that, and you have things planned because you have to plan ahead, and all of a sudden, the P. A. system says, well, there'll be no first period today, or today's first will be tomorrow's third or sixth or something like that. This aggravates me. Or that some event will take precedence over the classroom time. For instance, a football rally or something like that. [#10 M-38-Soc. Stud.]

The reader will see that there is a note of hurt, of dignity offended, in this talk about disruption and managing time. Intrusions on teaching carry a symbolic meaning—they depreciate the importance of those tasks the teacher considers central. The principal who interrupts the class with an announcement about a football rally can be thought to feel that teaching is less important than boosting athletic contests. Accounts must balance, but when administrators stress receipts for milk sales, they are not signaling grave concern for instruction. There is an undercurrent in these responses, then, of more than annoyance at work disrupted and time lost. Those who intrude on the teacher's scarce time are doing more than inhibiting work processes; they are manifesting a lack of respect for what teachers consider their core functions. The frustration of the teacher is doubled. Potentially productive time, already limited, is reduced, and the teacher's craft is depreciated. Such lack of "support" is the opposite of the reassurance teachers apparently need to offset the uncertainties of their work.

The second major set of grounds for complaint about other persons centered on issues of status—on instances where others offended the teacher's dignity. (It is obvious that the distinction between the two sets of grounds is subtle; perhaps we cannot get an accurate count where meanings become entwined as they do in this instance.) The following quotations illustrate such instances (27) and the third, smaller category (9) illustrates cases where colleagues irritated respondents by failing to do their share of the dirty work:

I don't like the caste system in school today. It seems, you know the old joke, the teacher's afraid of the supervisor, the supervisor's afraid of the principal, and the principal's afraid of the superintendent, the superintendent's afraid of the school committee, the school committee's afraid of the parents, the parents are afraid of the kids, and the kids aren't afraid of anything. The teachers are at the bottom of the ladder. Everybody counts but the teacher. [#47 F-32-1st]

The hiring of so-called specialists who don't work directly with the teacher, that rather talk with the principal who knows little or nothing about work problems and then once the decision has been made, the teacher is the last to be consulted. [#7 F-34-5th]

I think the thing that aggravates them most is that no one else takes their job, considers their job as seriously as do teachers. I think teachers consider their job most seriously and expend themselves no end in it and I think it bothers them because people are not aware how they feel, how important this particular job is and I think it annoys them no end. [#17 M-37-English]

The trend in recent years has been to pacify the parent and do what the parents want. In any situation involved with disputes with parents, in my opinion, all too often the supervisory people back down and give in. My own instance several years ago I was keeping a boy back and my own principal had gone over the records and decided it was the best thing for him. The parents complained and the principal just automatically let him go. Things along that nature. [#14 M-33-6th]

Well, there's no question that it's having another teacher question your authority. That is—in my way of thinking, that's the worst of all, you know, for example, say a kiddo is late leaving the gymnasium and you write him a note and send him to another class and the teacher won't accept the note. Well, that really burns you. [#69 M-30-P. E.]

I probably do more corridor duty than the average teacher but I am quite conscious of the need of it. I think that I don't overlook the discipline in the corridors and I know it, it annoys me when other people don't do their work. I think that is one thing that does bother me, the fact that other teachers aren't cooperating and doing their job. [#64 M-60-Bookkeeping]

Waller discussed the special sensitivity of teachers to issues of prestige and dignity; my data suggest that his observations are not outdated (1961, p. 388). But the reasons which underlie that sensitivity may rest in the imperatives of teaching and their misalignment with teacher status. It is one thing for teachers to prefer boundedness, to want autonomy and more potentially productive time; it is another thing to get them. Teachers cannot take such matters for granted—their complaints reveal that others complicate their work by witholding the support they consider their due. Thus teachers cannot act as if they were fully independent workers. Since they cannot "command" the assistance of others, they must hope that these will be voluntarily forthcoming. They are thus *dependent* on the readiness of administrators, fellow teachers, and parents to grant them the work conditions they desire.

There is a dilemma built into the situation of the classroom teacher—a tension between his sentiments and his status realities. He cannot prevent others from eroding his potentially productive time, and so he has limited control over the flow of psychic rewards. (This is in addition to the inherent uncertainties he faces.) Were his position more powerful, he might move away from other people, counting primarily on his personal capacities in teaching students. But his status proscribes this withdrawal, at least as the sole strategy; he must temper his self-isolation by seeking the support of others whom he needs in order, ironically, to make autonomy work. A kind of ambivalence is inherent in his role; we shall have occasion later to note the significance of this ambivalence for his interpersonal relationships with adults.

The Changes Teachers Want

Information on what changes teachers would like to see in their work arrangements can test the arguments I have advanced in this book. If the orientations described in chapters 2, 3, and 4 are significant, teachers should reveal them in their proposals for change—their suggestions should be conservative rather than radical, individualistic rather than collectivist, and present- rather than future-oriented. They should be closer to tinkering than revolution, in short, and consist of minor adjustments rather than demanding reforms. If they reflect the sentiments I have described in this chapter and immediately preceding chapters, suggested changes should reflect tensions between task imperatives (as seen by teachers) and status constraints.

My data on changes desired by teachers are taken from the Five Towns interviews and consist of responses to two questions. The first asked respondents what changes would help them to be more effective in meeting their teaching goals; the second asked what changes would augment their satisfaction with teaching (questions 35, 45, App. B-1). It will surprise no one by now that the responses were largely similar; the fusion of work achievement and satisfaction was again manifest. The responses to both questions are displayed in table 5.

TABLE 5. PROPOSALS FOR CHANGE: FIVE TOWNS TEACHERS
(Number of Times Mentioned)

Area	Effectiveness (Question 35)	Satisfaction (Question 45)
Time Use		
Smaller classes	18	15
Less clerical, extra duty	17	18
Fewer interruptions	13	—
More time for basic subjects	9	8
Fewer sections	8	4
Longer school schedules	7	—
Miscellaneous time factors	8	5
Subtotal	80	50
Better Facilities	25	10
Curricular Improvements	14	4
Better Students	11	5
Improved Administration	7	6
Better Parents	7	6
More Money, Promotion	—	21
Better Profession	—	7
More Autonomy	3	4
Changes in Self	7	3
All Other	4	4
Subtotal	74	70
Total	154	120

More than half the proposals which respondents linked with work effectiveness dealt with time use. Most have already been discussed in the preceding section. The novel ones are "fewer sections" and "longer school schedules"; in the first instance, some junior high school teachers wanted to have more time with fewer students by rearranging the schedule. Those advocating longer school schedules did so with comments about "not telling my colleagues," joking that they feared retribution if their views were known. It is a point worth making here that the concern respondents showed about potentially productive time took place *within* their allocations of life space discussed in chapter 4. Few were ready to advocate longer school days or years; the vast majority wanted to reapportion inert and potentially productive time within their existing commitments. But again we witness the overriding preoccupation with time and the preference for teaching versus other tasks.

Comments about facilities centered primarily on books (respondents wanted more, better, and more up-to-date books), more audiovisual equipment, and, in some instances, more or better-designed space. (Physical facilities seem to matter more to teachers in physical education, science, and home economics, where equipment plays a major part in instruction.) Teachers criticize complicated curricula, preferring those which increase student options, include recent developments, and feature good articulation. Wistful comments were made about students; some teachers wished aloud for ways of ridding themselves of those who are troublesome, and other teachers, particularly in the high schools, wished they would be assigned brighter students. Improved administration referred primarily to remarks about "better-educated" administrators and superordinates who would lay less emphasis on organizational rules. Parents would be "better" if they interfered less and helped more—at home. A very small number called for greater autonomy for teachers. A handful responded by referring to self-improvement; these were elementary teachers who lamented their teachers college training or yearned for opportunities to observe colleagues at work, saying they thought such observation would help them improve their own performance. It is clear, however, that the vast majority, when asked what changes would improve their performance, thought in terms of structural change or change in the behavior of others.

Responses to the question on increasing satisfaction were similar (table 5). There are suggestive differences, however. Respondents linked money and promotion to satisfaction, but not to effectiveness; that distinction raises a question about the allegations of union and teacher association leaders that more monetary rewards will yield greater productivity. These teachers, at least, do not link them. A few respondents said their satisfaction would increase if colleagues were better ("better profession") but did not link this preference to effectiveness. Perhaps they see the occupation's reputation in terms of reward rather than performance; such respondents, who complained about other teachers, possibly find inadequate colleagues frustrating but do not consider them serious obstacles to their personal work goals.

How do these responses fit with the orientations we mentioned above and with previous observations on teacher sentiments? They appear consistent with conservatism, individualism, and presentism in several respects. The structural proposals, for example, are hardly radical; they are familiar themes heard for many years and do not question the basic assumptions of the schooling system. They call for modifications in practice which are consistent with established ways of acting and thinking; they are "a little more" or "a little less" kinds of suggestions. The hopes that others will behave differently may be somewhat utopian, but they cannot be called radical; the norms they apply to others (e.g., better behavior by students, more democratic administration, helpful parents) are consistent with accepted social definitions. Nor do we find departure from individualistic or presentist orientations. There is no call for notable changes in collegial relationships or protracted programs of action directed toward a different tomorrow.

Some information is added, however, to our understanding of teacher sentiments; the proposals for change emphasize the importance teachers attribute to more and better resources besides time. Greater concentration of time on potentially productive activities is of course reiterated, but we also see that teachers desire better facilities and more flexible, workable curricula. They also express views on students, but they seem unsure about how such preferences might be fulfilled. There is an underlying possibility which is rarely permitted to surface in the talk of these teachers; perhaps they want greater personal control over resources as well as more ample supplies. Such a wish, of course, edges toward open conflict with the school hierarchy; it raises the issue of managerial discretion. In Five Towns few apparently wanted to make that issue explicit; they did not seem to propose striking new departures in the allocative mechanisms of school systems.

Teachers have been criticized for advocating programs which are "more of the same"; those who think present educational circumstances are critical view such proposals as seriously inadequate (Fantini 1972). One can argue whether the criticism is justified or moot; one can understand how teachers might feel they have not been given the chance to show what they can do. But the "more of the same" description seems largely accurate; the foregoing proposals, for example, do not represent a major shift from the pedagogical strategies of the past. The beliefs and preferences expressed suggest individualistic teachers who want more elbow room to practice their craft. But the state of the craft does not come under review. Respondents voiced little concern about teachers' limitations in ensuring predictable results; doubts expressed in other parts of the interview did not come into play here. The underlying critique is directed toward the organization of teacher effort and the behavior of adult coparticipants. There is no discernible preoccupation with deficiencies in the technical culture of the teaching occupation.

Summary: The Roots of Ambivalence

The sentiments of teachers mirror their daily tasks and the realities of classroom life. The world of those teachers who have shared their feelings with us is more complex than it looks at first glance. The key rewards are hard to come by, and the daily demands are not easily met. The complexities draw teachers more deeply into their involvement with classroom events; they foster preoccupation with influencing students and with conditions which seem to increase that influence. Our informants seem harassed by a lack of time; protracted instructional contact with students seems scarce. Nor do they feel sufficiently well-supplied with physical materials. They worry about how others treat them. Others intrude and disrupt their teaching rather than help them reach the students. They wonder if their central purposes are understood and appreciated.

Teachers in Five Towns see boundaries around the classroom as useful; principally, they ward off the constant threat to task completion and the ever-present sense of time eroded. They believe that the teacher is the essential catalyst of student effort and learning and fret when their energies are used up in tasks they consider trivial. Yet they do not seem certain that a bounded classroom is quite enough to ensure high results; some believe that high points require a lucky conjunction of moods. When our teachers think about improving things, their thoughts turn to concentrating time and effort to more teaching. If only others would let them, they seem to say, they could do much more. They picture themselves as constrained, undersupplied, and underappreciated; their aims and their context do not jibe.

What teachers want seems to revolve around their preoccupations and their beliefs. The teachers we interviewed want to pinpoint their effort; the time and energies they have for teaching ought not, they feel, be splayed over a range of organizational tasks. They want to focus on instruction; they wish others would understand that and respect their wish by helping them fulfill it. They clearly feel that obstacles are placed in their way—and they cannot order them removed. Some reveal a certain prickliness, a sense of dignity offended: instead of reassurance and support, they sense denigration. They want to do their jobs as they see them and get the rewards that (sometimes) result.

These feelings are easier to understand, I think, if we recall the imperatives we linked to getting and sustaining attention, managing work groups, and coping with subtle individual differences. Teachers seem to want conditions which favor more control over student involvement, more discretion to make decisions, and greater trust from principals and parents. Yet one senses a reluctance to press the case to its logical extreme; it is as if these teachers half accept and half reject the limitations imposed by their status. Their status clearly does not grant them control over the conditions they believe are important and necessary; they are not permitted to arrange instruction in a driving, aggressive way. They would like abler or more compliant students, but have no concrete suggestions on how to get them. They cannot order superordinates, parents, and peers to support their efforts. Yet they hold back from asking for full autonomy and official independence. There are, of course, informal norms which permit some degree of teacher autonomy in the classroom, but such norms remain informal, fragile (particularly when trouble arises), and limited. These respondents do not suggest that teacher independence be formalized or that they be granted official discretion and control over resources. They do not challenge the basic order. They accept the fact that students, space, supplies, and schedules are "owned and controlled" by others and do not assert that they should control the means of production. They want more favorable dispositions within the prevailing system; but they apparently accept the terms imposed by the organization. For at the base of teacher status is the indisputable constraint that without access to a position in the schools the teacher cannot practice his craft.

There is a certain ambivalence, then, in the teacher's sentiments. He yearns for more independence, greater resources, and, just possibly, more control over key resources. But he accepts the hegemony of the school system on which he is economically and functionally dependent. He cannot ensure that the imperatives of teaching, as he defines them, will be honored, but he chafes when they are not. He is poised between the impulse to control his work life and the necessity to accept its vagaries; perhaps he holds back partly because he is at heart uncertain that he can produce predictable results. In any event, the feelings I have discerned among Five Towns teachers are internally contradictory and reflect dilemmas in the role. In the pages which follow we will see how relationships with others represent attempts to balance the tensions between independence and dependence, autonomy and participation, control and subordination.

8
Sentiments and Interpersonal Preferences

Psychic rewards and teacher sentiments rotate around classroom events and relationships with students; the cathexis of classroom life underlies much of what teachers feel about their work. Tensions arise in the opposition of teacher sentiments to their position in the organization. Impulses flowing from core tasks collide with status limitations, since the urge to go it alone must be tempered by reliance upon others. Relationships with other adults do not stand at the heart of the teacher's psychological world; being shaped by deeper commitments to students, they are secondary and derivative in nature. If my reasoning is accurate, we should be able to trace connections between teachers' preoccupation with classroom phenomena and the expectations they hold for other adults. Interpersonal preferences should fit with the teacher's drive to increase classroom-centered rewards.

We will examine teacher relationships with parents, peers, and the principal in this light. Using data from Five Towns, we will explore the issues provoked by each relationship and review teacher preferences for their resolution. The analysis is intensive and largely qualitative; I will emphasize modal tendencies but will mention internal differences which could be amplified in subsequent research. My central concern will be to establish linkages between the core sentiments of teachers and their feelings about the adults with whom they work.

Analysis of teacher preferences in relationships with other adults will constitute the bulk of the chapter, but there are three other shorter sections. The second section summarizes recurrent themes in teacher preferences: What are the general properties of their expectations for others? In the next section, we will connect teacher sentiments to the course of collective bargaining. Can we find relationships between the two? Finally, we will discuss the sentiments and the orientations we found in earlier chapters, looking into their mutual relationships.

Teacher Preferences and Derivative Expectations

The Teacher and the Parent

The ideology of public education upholds the importance of close working relationships between teachers and the parents of their students. There is also a record of scholarship, primarily in sociology, which reports on the complexity of relationships between teachers and parents—some researchers have looked beneath the conventional definitions of such interaction to find bases for conflict. Waller pointed out that parents and teachers differ in their perception of the child. To the parents, he is a special, prized person; to the teacher, he is one member of the category "student" (1961, p. 69). Sykes (1953) analyzed parent-teacher associations as formalisms directed toward reducing potential conflict between teachers and parents.

In a sensitive analysis, Naegle (1956)noted that students reveal much of the inner life of families to teachers both in conversation and in action. The teacher comes to know "guilty secrets" which can lead to strain in his relationship with parents. Working-class mothers often have bitter memories of school and show their children unsympathetic attitudes toward teachers (Rainwater, Coleman, and Handel 1959). The socialization functions of the teacher require that he prepare the student for an achievement-oriented society by grading him in comparison with others (Parsons 1959; Dreeben 1968). Teacher judgments may shock and repel parents, particularly if they have idealized their child's capacities. Teachers, moreover, can be perceived by parents as socialization competitors; if the values they emphasize do not coincide with the parents' values, parents may feel undercut in their efforts to raise the child. Some parents may become hostile on emotional grounds—they may envy the teacher who excites the child's affection and respect.

Teachers can have their reasons to distrust and even fear parents. In the American public school way of doing things, parents have considerable rights in tending to the school affairs of their children; localism is often vindicated as "keeping school close to the community and/or parents." Parents may complain directly to teachers or to administrative superiors;

repeated or serious complaints can affect the teacher's standing within the school system. We have observed that teachers have the license to discipline other people's children, but there are conditions on that license. The teacher who gives vent to anger may fear parental sanctions; some parents bring lawsuits against teachers. Teachers have a certain vulnerability, then, to parents, particularly when parents have higher than average resources of collective or status-based power.[1]

We noted in the previous chapter that parents can hinder the work of the teacher. How is this so? I believe it rests on the fact that teachers must create and maintain a viable instructional group ("a class") under difficult circumstances. They try to construct a universalistic social order in which rules are consistently and fairly administered. If they fail to do so, students—and sometimes parents—become alarmed. A parent who asks for special treatment for his child (or even seems to do so by frequent visits) places the teacher in a conflict situation; the teacher may be forced to choose between parental initiations and his own rules. The situation is more complex if several parents make contradictory requests; a barrage of parental interventions may make the teacher fear that his social order is beginning to unravel. The underlying tension is increased by the fact that the students "belong" to the parents, not to the teacher. Teachers are trying to build and sustain a social order with people over whom they have only limited and specific, place-bound authority.

Teachers are doubly dependent on parents. Since parental involvement is legitimate, teachers count on them to show voluntary restraint; if the boundaries of the classroom are to be respected, parents must choose to avoid "excessive" intrusion. But there is another aspect of the teacher's dependency on parents; parents have considerable influence over their children and can affect their readiness to participate—in ways the teacher values—in their schoolwork. Parental actions, in short, can range across strong help, indifference, and open hostility; the parents' choice can have an important effect on the student's behavior in class.

In light of these considerations, what do teachers want from parents? Specifically, what do Five Towns teachers see as ideal relationships between themselves and parents? What connections can we find between the content of teacher expectations and their stake in classroom events?

Information was gathered on the nature and extent of contact between Five Towns teachers and parents and on the preferences of teachers in this respect (questions 60, 61, App. B-1). Few would describe the amount of contact as extensive. One finds regular parent and school staff gatherings (PTA and the like) occurring four or five times a year; teachers depicted such occasions either as "a waste of time" or as interpersonally awkward. (Parents ask questions about their children's progress and teachers find it difficult to respond frankly because of the lack of privacy which usually prevails.) Teachers reported seeing parents primarily when the teacher invited the parent in to discuss a student problem. The modal rate of contact was two or fewer interactions a month, but a quarter of the teachers reported three to six contacts monthly. Elementary teachers, as one would expect, had more contacts than secondary teachers.

Most Five Towns respondents said they wanted more contact with parents, but they qualified that statement; they wanted to see parents when their children were having trouble in school. Very few expressed interest in more interaction with the parents of successful students; for these respondents, contact with parents was justified only when difficulties arose.

Some internal differences are too striking to ignore, and since they occur in other studies as well they should be mentioned here (McDowell 1954). In the lower-status elementary schools, 88 percent of the teachers wanted more contact with parents, compared with 23 percent of teachers working in higher-status schools. The answers illuminate the reasons for the difference; the problems teachers encounter with parents are different in the two contexts. In lower-status schools, parents often fail to respond to teacher invitations to come in and discuss the student; in the higher-status schools, parents are likely to show up without invitation. Few teachers expressed enthusiasm for such spontaneous visits.

In what way are teacher preferences about contact with parents derived from their work sentiments? It seems to work this way: when the student is performing adequately (as defined by the teacher), there is no impulse toward parental contact—boundedness is preferred. But when the student is performing below the teacher's expectations, the teacher seeks the parents' help. The implicit relationship places the teacher in the superordinate role—the teacher wants to define occasions which justify parental involvement and does not legitimate parental concerns (i.e., parental definitions of adequate or inadequate performance). The respondents' comments about parents who came in without invitation had critical overtones; they are depicted as academic hypochondriacs worrying and fussing without cause. These preferences reflect teachers' assumptions that they are best qualified to define when parents have a part to play at school; if teachers initiate contact parents should come, but other visits are "interruptions." The teacher is the gatekeeper.

Respondents' descriptions of the "good parent" are consistent with the data on interaction preferences (question 62, App. B-1). Two central themes appear to underlie the specific responses; parents should not intervene and parents should support the teacher's efforts. The most frequent response (51 percent) was "the parent is interested in the child's schoolwork," and the comments suggest that teachers judge the parent's interest in terms of demonstrated support for school. Other responses included "cooperates without interfering," "is realistic about the child's potential," "sees to it that the child's work is done," "backs up the teacher with the child," "follows the teacher's suggestions," "respects education," and "responds to invitations to appear." The good parent, in short, takes his lead from the teacher—there is no contest for leadership. Other respondents defined the good parent strictly in terms of home responsibilities: the good parent provides moral, physical, and emotional care for his children. Home is the proper place to exercise parental authority; the parent, under the teacher's guidance, should take ameliorative action there. My respondents project a clear sense of territorial proprieties. There is "teacher territory" and "parental territory," and leadership on school affairs rests with the teacher. Teachers, in sum, want the parent to be a "distant assistant."

The implied advantages for the teacher in these views are consistent with what we have seen of work sentiments and the tension between autonomy and dependency. The wish to control the workplace is combined with the wish for support from influential others—independence and dependence are contained in a formula based on boundedness and teacher initiation. The teacher's concerns are placed at the center of the ideal relationship; parents should comply with arrangements which meet teacher needs. Complications we discussed earlier are reduced by separating the territories of teachers and parents. The cooks do not work in the same kitchen. There is no indication that respondents worried about the relationship they projected as asymmetrical; perhaps they feel that since they do not intervene in home affairs, parents ought not to intervene in "theirs"—the classroom. These teachers, then, seek to ensure both independence *and* support, and the mechanisms they invoke are physical separation and teacher control over parents' access to the school.

Teachers do not, however, possess any Aladdin's lamp to grant their wishes, nor does their formal status permit them to enforce the relationships they prefer. They are not like doctors who can issue "orders" to patients and their families. They are not like university professors who claim that their instructional decisions are beyond administrative review. The ideology of the institution legitimates parental concern, and the employee status of the teacher makes him subject to control by superordinates. Upper-middle-class parents can insist on visiting the school without notice and can criticize the teacher to the principal; working-class parents can refuse to honor teachers' requests. Teachers do not possess the status resources to make parents comply or to withstand their attacks; their vulnerability is genuine.

I will anticipate discussion of the teacher-principal relationship to point out the interconnection between internal and external relationships for teachers. The teacher's preference for particular kinds of relationships with parents involves the principal. Because of his higher status, he can assist the teacher in various ways, or he can make his life more difficult. The principal can use his position to protect teachers against intervention or not; he can help teachers see reluctant parents or not. The authority and standing of the principal is a potential resource for the teacher, and so teachers have a stake in its use.

One can see that teachers face a dilemma in the triad of teacher-parent-principal relationships. To obtain leverage or autonomy vis-à-vis parents, the teacher may rely on the principal to initiate contact or to serve as a buffer, thus indebting himself for favors received. Where parental relationships are troublesome, the teacher may find himself in a "double bind" situation in winning autonomy; to fend off parents' intrusion or gain their assistance, he may have to accept a greater degree of control from the principal; the principal, after all, may collect his debts by expecting more compliance. I wish to underline the interlocked nature of teacher relationships; what takes place with parents influences transactions with the principal. Teachers not only have to contend with the tension between task imperatives and status constraints, they may well have to choose between alternative resolutions of that tension—none of which eliminates the need to sacrifice personal preferences to organizational demands.

The Teacher and Other Teachers

From what has been said in this book, the reader might conclude that relationships among teachers are marked by mutual indifference. The cellular form of school organization, and the attendant time and space ecology, puts interactions between teachers at the margin of their daily work. Individualism characterizes their socialization; teachers do not share a powerful technical culture. The major psychic rewards of teachers are earned in isolation from peers, and they can hamper one another by intruding on classroom boundaries. It seems that teachers can work effectively without the active assistance of colleagues, since teacher-teacher interaction does not seem to play a critical part in the work life of our respondents.

But other observations should alert us against a too casual view of the significance of peer relationships. Surveys of teacher opinion, for example, reveal that teachers consider faculty relationships to affect their professional achievement (NEA 1967, p. 48). Researchers have shown that collegial norms influence newcomers (Hoy 1969). We found earlier that teachers see each other as the primary source of useful ideas; we also noted that some elementary teachers assess their progress by comparing it with that of other teachers.

Obviously, relationships among teachers are complex; we should avoid the simplification of describing them in either-or terms. It is true that in comparison with those in many other lines of work (e.g., construction workers, actors, members of an engineering team), teachers do not work together closely. Yet although teachers center on their classroom affairs, they do have an interest in those who work alongside them—they are at least sources of help and, sometimes, mirrors for assessing one's performance. We also recall that teachers resent colleagues who fail to hold up their end of the less pleasant schoolwide tasks. One might expect some tension, therefore, between the impulse toward distance and the need for proximity—between the wish for boundedness and the search for assistance. We turn now to the norms teachers hold on mutual relationship; using data from Five Towns, we will examine the patterns of interaction they currently sustain and their definitions of appropriate colleagueship.

There is considerable variation in the amount of spontaneous, informal cooperation Five Towns teachers engage in. Almost half (45 percent) reported that they had "no contact" with other teachers in the course of their work; 32 percent reported "some contact," and 25 percent "much contact" (question 65, App. B-1). We can give clearer meaning to such terms by describing the behaviors involved.

Teachers who reported "much contact" mentioned jointly planning classes, jointly reviewing students' work, and, on some occasions, switching classes for particular purposes. Some elementary teachers had participated in a special program which required close cooperation, but "much contact" respondents were usually persons who worked in a pair arrangement with another teacher. Such pairing is based on informal mutual choice and apparently rests on bonds of friendship. But it is worth noting that even in these instances of high cooperation, none of the respondents chose to teach the same students at the same time. Cooperation could be extensive outside the classroom, but teachers preferred to keep the boundaries intact when they actually worked with students.

In instances where cooperation was less intensive ("some contact"), respondents mentioned intermittent consultation on matters such as grading, sharing class preparations, and comparing notes on student progress. Some elementary teachers exchanged classes in such "fringe" subjects as art and music. None, however, reported that they exchanged students in basic subjects like mathematics, reading, and writing.

The variations in voluntary cooperation are important to understanding norms among teachers on collegial relationships; the reported differences, plus the comments of respondents, make it clear that norms are permissive rather than mandatory. The subculture found in Five Towns defines the degree of cooperation as a matter of individual choice. There was no suggestion that teachers try to influence each other toward more or less mutual effort; those working alone did not express negative views on cooperation or vice versa. Such choices are apparently made without normative pressure. Normative permissiveness has a self-evident function; it encourages individuals with different needs to satisfy themselves along lines they find most rewarding. The summative effect is to augment the gratification of the aggregate of group members; the permissive norms of these teachers foster individual responses to the question of proximity to or distance from colleagues.

Another set of data, however, discloses that there are limits on the degree of self-isolation teachers permit one another. I refer to answers to a question on "the good colleague" (question 68, App. B-1). Five Towns teachers expect peers to be ready to share and to act in friendly, open ways. More than half (54 percent) said the good colleague is willing to share. He shares ideas and work supplies and helps beginning teachers. The good colleague also does his share of schoolwide chores like hall patrol, lunch duty, and study halls. A large proportion (43 percent) of the respondents depicted the good colleague as friendly, sociable, and open; a good colleague is a reassuring, warm associate who does not manifest snobbery or arrogance. Senior high school teachers laid particular emphasis on the technical performance of peers, a difference which might justify further inquiry.[2]

How does the good colleague act toward his peers? We have seen that Five Towns teachers are vague on the amount of mutual cooperation expected—that is left to the individuals. But there is no license for haughty standoffishness—one should respond when called upon. Thus responding to collegial requests for help and meeting schoolwide obligations are expected. The individual teacher is not permitted to "put on airs," but should share in the egalitarian spirit which marks these expectations. Egalitarianism rules out imposing one's views on others; one should respond to requests for help but not expect special privileges for doing so. The etiquette rule seems to be "live and let live, and help when asked."

Collegial norms can be said to arbitrate tension between the quest for individual autonomy and the desire for collegial assistance; work uncertainties may make the latter particularly valued. The norms respect the individual's right to choose between association and privacy; they also protect individual teachers against unsolicited interventions by others. Mutual assistance is permitted and, at one level, encouraged. Those who want close relationships with peers can undertake them, but all are supposed to render assistance when asked. The expectation of equality, in fact, enhances mutual assistance; it reduces the prestige costs of those who ask for it. The norms have an element of ingenuity when seen in the light of teacher ambivalence—they provide for both affiliative and disaffiliative tendencies.

From the perspective of the group as a whole, the norms we have described encourage both individualism *and* sharing of technical knowledge. Freedom to select one's level of association permits a teacher to maximize psychic rewards; depending upon personality differences, one can be a "loner" or work closely with others. Norms which stress sharing and equality foster mutual communication without requiring conformity; individual teachers can pool their knowledge resources; this is not, of course, systematic, formal codification of knowledge but rather exchange of useful "tricks of the trade." The exchanges implied remind me of research I did on young Chicago lawyers and the "share-office" arrangement found among some solo practitioners (Lortie 1958). Some beginning lawyers agreed to share the expenses of practice (e.g., rent, clerical help, library) but not profits. Each man kept whatever he earned beyond his contribution to common expenses. Five Towns norms are similar in that teacher colleagues are expected to share the costs (e.g., extra duties) and help one another upon request, but no arrangement exists for sharing "profits"; each teacher works alone with his students and earns whatever psychic benefits he can. The analogy suggests that we can think of teachers as "entrepreneurs of psychic profits"; from that vantage point, their norms are calculated to reduce organizational influences and to ensure that they have no more "bosses" (that is, influential colleagues) than already exist. Egalitarianism, in short, may serve to protect autonomy.

Other functions may be served by these norms. The expectation that teachers should be sociable, for example, may result from the controlled nature of classroom work; teachers report that they must be careful about acting spontaneously in class.[3] It seems likely that after hours of self-control, teachers want to relax and, in Simmel's definition of pure sociability, enjoy interaction as an end in itself (1950). Perhaps that is why we hear reports that teacher lounge conversation is rarely business-like; I suspect much of it is cathartic.

Other functions which may be served by teacher norms on collegial interchange are reassurance and envy control. When we recall how painful dry periods are (chapter 6), one can appreciate the preference for warm and supportive co-workers; an arrogant colleague would increase one's despair. Perhaps teachers turn to each other to compensate for the absence of a formal system of reassurance. The issue of envy control is more difficult to document, for teachers are reluctant to talk about their feelings when others receive extraordinary amounts of student affection and esteem. One suspects envy may creep in; it seems likely that arrogant, prideful behavior would exacerbate such feelings. Egalitarian, friendly colleagues, on the other hand, are less likely to pour salt on psychological wounds. Envy corrodes group solidarity; to the extent that norms of colleague behavior reduce its effects they contribute toward firmer bonds among teachers.

The Teacher and the Principal

The formal powers of the principal are restricted. Although he is the highest official in the school, his control over funds and his capacity to formulate policies specific to his school are normally limited. Budgetary decision-making is usually centralized in the superintendent's office, and local schools rarely possess mechanisms to generate and legitimate local policy.[4] The school board and superintendent promulgate rules for all schools; curriculum planning, for example, is generally conducted in the central office and coordinated by central office personnel. There is pressure to standardize curricular practices in schools within a school district and, in fact, in schools across the nation. Personnel decisions are within the jurisdiction of the superintendent, who hires, places, and transfers teachers; students are allocated to schools, in most places, on grounds of geographical residence. The decision-making range of the principal, in short, is constricted; he must manage a complex enterprise without extensive powers.

We should not take these limitations to mean, however, that the principal is unimportant in the work lives of teachers. Principals may have considerably more informal power than their role description specifies; some principals become visible, popular persons who are better known to their local constituencies than the superintendent. The physical deployment of schools, moreover, affects the relationship between the superintendent and the principals; the interaction within a particular school is greater than interaction across its boundaries, and the principal is the key official within that dense network. "Large decisions" may be made in the central office, but the principal makes many "small decisions" which affect the social life of the school and those who work in it. Experienced schoolmen claim they can assess a principal after a few minutes in his school; whatever the validity of that claim, research by Halpin and others reveals that there are meaningful differences between the "climates" of different schools (Halpin and Croft 1963).

The principal's decisions can vitally affect the teacher's working conditions. He assigns teachers to classes and students to particular teachers; the actual work may be done by assistants, but the principal remains the court of final appeal. The principal is the ultimate authority on student discipline, and parents turn to him for redress when they think their children have been improperly treated. The allocation of materials, space, and equipment is handled through the principal's office, and time schedules are worked out under his supervision. His decisions can, in short, affect the teacher's work duties for months at a time.

As the official head of the school, the principal is answerable for all events that take place there; the superintendent calls him when trouble arises. There are grounds for arguing that the principal faces the classic administrative dilemma—his responsibilities outrun his authority. School rhetoric presses him to be assertive; he is said to be "the instructional leader of the school." The conditions of his office are such that he is under constant pressure to "keep things under control" (McDowell 1954; Trask 1964).

Teachers have a stake in how the principal goes about his work; his position as the real and symbolic head of the school is likely to evoke the sentiments teachers organize around their work. It is the principal who allocates the resources (including time) which matter so much to them. When teachers try to wrest greater control over working conditions, they are liable to collide with the principal's prerogatives. Teachers may need the principal to intercede in relationships with parents and to cope with fractious students. The principal as a symbol is also important; as the "instructional leader" of the school, he is an enhanced senior colleague. Thus he can symbolize professional purpose and competence: he potentially can reassure teachers about the quality of their teaching.

The teacher-principal relationship is obviously complicated. Full understanding of its subtleties would require protracted and extensive research; we can hardly exhaust the ramifications here. My goal in examining what

197

teachers expect of principals is to connect any themes we can discern with teacher sentiments. I will mention some internal differences, particularly those between elementary and secondary teachers. Elementary principals come closer to being "front-line supervisors" than do high school principals; in high schools, authority relationships between teachers and the principal are usually mediated by department heads (Maguire 1970). We will draw our data from Five Towns.

Asked what they would look for in the principal when considering employment in a particular school, a few respondents dismissed the issue; 10 percent thought the principal too unimportant to warrant attention (question 72, App. B-1). The vast majority was not so cavalier. Half (52 percent) emphasized the way the principal uses his authority. They said that he should be "fair." They also stressed their dislike for principals who are "picky" or "rule-conscious." The wish for fair superiors is not limited to teachers, but they probably show special sensitivity on this issue since they are concerned with the equal distribution of resources and unpopular chores. They clearly reject principals who exercise close supervision or constrain teachers by numerous and detailed rules.

Over a third of the respondents (38 percent) mentioned "support." Does the principal back up the teacher in problems with parents and with difficult students? Another third (31 percent) said the principal should be warm, helpful, and accessible—the kind of person one can turn to for reassurance and assistance. Smaller numbers alluded to the principal's competence as an educator, *his* sex (some women preferred male over female principals), and his stance on discipline—strictness was favored. In short, respondents want an approachable principal who eschews rule-making and close supervision and is equitable in his dealings with faculty members. He should be knowledgeable and firm with both parents and students. The qualities teachers mention meet their needs for autonomy *and* support; the principal should moderate his use of authority over teachers but assert it in relationships with parents, students, and dilatory colleagues. These teachers do not question the rightfulness of the principal's authority, but they seek to appropriate it to their ends.[5]

Answers to a question on the principal's responsibilities toward teachers indicated areas of consensus and dissensus among classroom teachers (question 70, App. B-1). They disagreed, for example, on the extent to which the principal should undertake technical surveillance over the teacher's work. Some respondents (particularly in elementary schools) stressed the supervisory aspects of the principal's role—including class-room events. He should make sure that teachers fulfill their responsibilities (29 percent), and some (12 percent) said that he should check for errors in teacher work. Others, however, turned the question around somewhat by stating that the principal should not only be fair (12 percent) but should allow teachers enough freedom to get their work done (9 percent). The idea that the principal should check for teacher errors was found primarily among elementary teachers; 34 percent of them, compared with 4 percent of the high school teachers, made that point. Some respondents held the principal responsible for close scrutiny of the teacher's work, whereas others stressed his obligation to extend autonomy.

Respondents emphasized that the principal should use his authority to facilitate their work. He should support the teachers (38 percent). He should keep them well supplied with equipment and consumables (13 percent). He should ensure an atmosphere favorable to teaching by "providing good administration," a phrase which implies remoteness from classroom events and was used primarily by secondary teachers (52 percent secondary versus 16 percent elementary). A very small number (4 percent) of Five Towns teachers consider the principal obliged to provide them with educational expertise.

There are important points of consensus among these teachers. They do not question the legitimacy of his office: all accept the presence of a superordinate figure and his right to exercise general supervision over school affairs. He should use his powers to augment those of teachers, and his use of authority should lighten their burden. The respondents disagree, however, on the scope they grant to the principal in supervising them; some define his rights as specific while others, using more general rhetoric, consider the principal a somewhat remote, benign overseer.

A similar pattern of consensus and dissensus emerged when respondents discussed their obligations to the principal (question 71, App. B-1). A large proportion (63 percent) said that they owe the principal the fulfillment of their role obligations, the assurance of work fully and conscientiously done. It is as if the teachers are making the principal the personification of their work conscience—they project their sense of duty onto him. But they do not seem to expect the principal to specify the content of their work; it is more that the principal has the right to expect teachers to do what *they* consider their best work. This theme was particularly relevant among secondary teachers, who elected it 80 percent of the time compared with 49 percent among elementary teachers.

Other respondents (again predominantly elementary teachers—thirty-three mentions versus nine) said that the teacher should comply with the principal's requests and rules. The exact meaning of these statements, unfortunately, is moot. Some respondents circumscribed the domain in which the principal should expect teacher compliance: out-of-class affairs were allocated to the principal, in-class matters reserved for the teacher. Others placed no such limits on the principal's right to initiate for them; their silence may mean that they grant the principal hegemony over classroom as well as schoolwide matters. One can speculate that teachers cope with the tensions between autonomy and support in different ways, possibly in terms of their personality characteristics. Some deal with vertical authority by compartmentalizing it—the principal can expect compliance on schoolwide but not on classroom matters. Others, it seems, move toward a general conception of compliance, preferring the principal's support over personal autonomy.

Two additional themes occurred in the responses to this question. Some teachers said they should make sure that the principal is not embarrassed by reports on classroom events; the teacher should inform the principal on anything which might give him trouble. Others talked about the teacher's obligation to "show respect" for the principal and to "be loyal" to him. (The rhetoric suggests an exchange like that between vassals and lords during medieval times. The superordinate is expected to use his power to protect and help those of lesser rank; they, in turn, are bound in fealty to return the appropriate deference and respect.)

To summarize what teachers expect of principals and the relationship they consider appropriate, we find that acceptance of the principal's authority is coupled with definite ideas on how that authority should be deployed. They agree that it should be mobilized to serve teacher interests; parents should be buffered, troublesome students dealt with, and chore-avoiding colleagues brought to heel. Most respondents seem to favor a light rein for themselves; some, however, prefer the principal who checks them closely and carefully. Our respondents stand ready, it seems, to award deference and loyalty to principals who make their authority available to teachers; that authority can help them achieve working conditions which favor classroom achievement and its rewards.

The Normative Appropriation of Resources

We observed in chapter 4 that the reward system in classroom teaching puts a premium on psychic rewards; achievement and the gratification which attends it are consistent with the traditions of the occupation and, unlike other kinds of benefits, are neither fixed nor automatic. In chapters 5 and 6 we saw that teachers' psychic earnings are not abundant; they take solace in less-then-ideal outcomes, and their daily routine requires them to cope with intangible goals and fragile relationships. Their quest for psychic rewards is taxing—benefits flow erratically. Teachers experience periods of genuine distress, and the occupation provides little regular reassurance to allay such feelings.

In chapter 7 we inquired into the circumstances teachers think are beneficial to their work. We found that they want a degree of boundedness around their classrooms; they cathect them, not the organization at large. They want more potentially productive time with students. They depict other adults as intrusive and hindering, and they yearn for more resources as they try to influence their students. Others, they feel, should support them in their work with students—should uphold rather than denigrate their standing. Yet teacher wants are ill-matched to their status resources; as subordinates, they must accept being allocated *for*. As occupants of roles with limited power, they cannot command the cooperation of others or control the disposition of resources.

What teachers want of other adults is related to reward-seeking and the attempt to remove obstacles they think are in the way. There are recurrent themes in their talk about parents, colleagues, and the principal; in each case, they try to strike an acceptable balance between autonomy and support. Some of the specific mechanisms reappear in different contexts.

Take, for example, their preferences concerning parents and teaching colleagues. They want assistance of different kinds from each. Teachers want parents to use their influence with their children to further classroom efforts; they want peers to share useful knowledge, be sociable, and help with unpleasant chores. But in both instances respondents want that assistance at minimal cost to their freedom. They fend off parental intrusion by territorial rules and by maintaining the right to initiate contact; parents are to do their helping at home and come to school only when invited. Control by colleagues is blocked by norms of live and let live and help upon invitation only. The balance these teachers seek is autonomy with minimal control from others. The individual teacher will determine the occasions and conditions under which help is received.

Things are more complicated with the principal. He is an authoritative figure who represents hierarchical authority in the school, governs the faculty, and is the final court of appeal for students. The power at his disposal is valuable to teachers; he allocates prized resources, monitors faculty effort, and has a marked effect on student compliance with school and teacher authority. Chances are that he is respected by members of the community; so he can protect teachers against parental intervention or strengthen their hand when parents show too little interest in their children's problems. We can say that the principal has more of what teachers want than parents or colleagues do; his rank grants him privileges which bear directly on teachers' working conditions. The principal is also (potentially) a senior colleague, primus inter pares, a knowledgeable educator who may offer technical help and timely reassurance.

Teachers do not challenge the concept of an authoritative principal, but they try to appropriate his authority to their purposes. However, they cannot use the same mechanisms to stave off intervention from him that they use with parents and peers. In fact, there seem to be differences in the relationship depending on school level. High school teachers seem to see the principal as somewhat remote; departmentalization probably means that they confront few direct interventions by the principal. Elementary teachers are more exposed. Some erect the shield of territorial jurisdiction, granting the principal hegemony over corridors and assemblies and all other areas save their classrooms. Others seem less inclined to erect defenses; perhaps they lean toward dependency rather than autonomy, valuing the principal's interest as certification of their efforts and warrant against the pain of uncertainty. All respondents seem to want the principal to use his authority to help their classroom efforts; they differ essentially in the bargain they are willing to strike with him.

Despite the variations we have just noted, there is a central tendency in the expectations teachers hold for other adults. They want the most autonomy they can get while simultaneously receiving the help they need. The help they desire is linked to the gap between teacher wants and the constraints built into their status. Analogies spring to mind. One thinks of the entrepreneur who resents "government interference" while pressing government to hold down the costs of production. One is reminded of the established craftsman who insists on his right to arrange space and tools and fashion his product as he wishes. Or we can visualize the professional asserting his full independence and expecting others to accept the consequences. But the analogies break down at a crucial point; teachers, unlike freewheeling businessmen, established craftsmen, and professionals, cannot escape a painful reality. They own no means of production and have no formal rights to support their preferences; they are employees in a formal organization and hirelings paid out of community tax funds.

What teachers expect of other adults contradicts the realities of their position. Yet we note that the expectations we have reviewed *deny that fact*. Teachers expect parents to accept the subordinate position of "distant assistants," and they press colleagues to stay out of their affairs except when invited. Teachers expect to use authority conferred on them by school boards in their own ways. Teachers seem to substitute normative expectations for powers they evidently wish they possessed;

they act as if they had considerably more freedom and power than they do. They overlook the realities of their status and try to get others to do the same. All of this is highly informal. Teachers could not openly aver that their expectations merely express recognized principles of school organization —and they do not. Nowhere are parents recorded as subordinate to teachers. Live and let live violates dominant conceptions of organizational responsibility; officially, teachers are presumed to have the interests of all students at heart. The principal is presumed to use his authority to further the attainment of organizational objectives, not simply to serve as the protector of teacher interests. Teacher preferences run counter to formal definitions; it is interesting that such opposition is *not* found in the collective pronouncements of teachers. For, as we noted earlier, teachers have avoided challenging the major tenets underlying public school organization.

Finally, one notes the individualistic tenor of these interpersonal preferences. Teachers talk about collegial relationships in much the same way as other relationships; they are ancillary to the main theater—the classroom. There is no flavor here of "solidarity forever" or comradeship. One senses little commitment to the occupation and its fate. The major impression is that each teacher is trying to strike the best personal balance he can get—to earn whatever psychic rewards he can.

A Note on Collective Bargaining

Collective bargaining between teachers and school boards is a recent development. From what we know about similar movements in other parts of our society, bargaining content and bargaining mechanisms are likely to change as the entire process moves through different stages (Hiller 1928). Some first-rate studies have already been done on the initial phases of collective bargaining; the dynamism of this kind of conflict means that we will need continued and intensive study of these aspects of the occupation (Cole 1969; Perry and Wildman 1970; Rosenthal 1969). I will make some observations here from the perspective of teacher sentiments, observations intended more as leads for research than as conclusions. In chapter 9, I will explore some of the consequences bargaining might have for teachers.

Considerable energy has been expended in the beginning stages of "teacher militancy." It is no small effort to organize employees, mobilize them for militant action, and conduct effective bargaining where no mechanisms have previously existed. The situation in teaching has been complicated by the presence of two kinds of organizations—teacher unions and the newly aggressive associations. Competition between the two kinds of organization has itself consumed additional energies; efforts are being made to find ways to unite teachers into nonrivalrous groupings. The need to construct new arrangements for bargaining carries its own imperatives—as does competition between organizations. The actions of leaders within the occupation, therefore, can be fully understood only in the context of these organizational imperatives; it is naive to read all collective actions by teachers as pure expression of their job-related wants (Blumer 1947). We must exercise caution, therefore, in interpreting the relationship between collective activities and the preferences of rank-and-file teachers.

Teachers' demands in the initial phases of bargaining have emphasized material benefits, particularly money income. This emphasis is not surprising; there are understandable reasons for it. Teachers thought they were underpaid and the public agreed; so they initiated demands with the balance of public opinion on their side (Gallup 1969). They began militant action in times of increasing inflation (a condition which is particularly difficult for salaried people) and rising need for teachers; teachers had both the incentive and the opportunity to get higher salaries. Such benefits also suited the situation of their leadership; money, being a general value of interest to all, served to mobilize teacher support without creating internal divisions. It neutralized differences of interest within the occupation.

The form of the monetary demands proved continuous with previous practice; teachers concentrated on raising beginning salaries, and benefits were accrued "up the line" from that base. Although some contracts have reduced the time needed to reach maximum earnings, little has been done to increase the ratio of incomes of experienced and inexperienced teachers. One suspects this reflects the political exigencies of a high turnover occupation in which people with limited experience have considerable voice. The form of money demands has not challenged the career system we discussed in chapter 4; money rewards are still "front-loaded." Economists are better equipped than I to analyze the influence of collective bargaining on the distribution of the sexes within teaching; it seems likely that emphasizing beginning salaries will increase the attractiveness of teaching for women more than for men. In any event, it does not appear that collective bargaining has so far made a major change in the structure of the reward system.

How do the nonmonetary demands of teachers relate to the sentiments we have been discussing in this chapter and the previous one? A recent survey of contract provisions indicates that nonmonetary bargaining has centered on classroom concerns and resources we have identified as important to Five Towns teachers (Perry and Wildman 1970). Teacher organizations have made some demands for inclusion in school system decision-making, but they have not pressed such demands very hard. Nor is there evidence that their claims and victories have made any fundamental difference in the way school systems make major policy decisions. Perry and Wildman (1970, p. 188) conclude:

> While myriad "policy" and "professional" subjects have received attention in school bargaining, collective negotiations has [*sic*] not yet resulted in any wholesale restructuring of the traditional control patterns affecting basic school district policy or its implementation.

The authors tell of one incident which is interesting in light of our earlier discussion of the low interest teachers show in organization-wide affairs (p. 174). After winning the right for teachers to participate in selecting the curriculum and textbooks, one teacher organization found that it could not ensure that they would regularly attend curriculum meetings. It consequently had to wrestle with the issue of whether such absentee teachers should be "docked" for not attending the required number of meetings! Teachers have not used collective bargaining to challenge the way public school systems are organized; they have worked *within* the prevailing structure.

The preoccupations we found in Five Towns apparently have influenced teachers on the points they have brought to the bargaining table. They have fought to get control over the use of their time; many contracts have detailed specifications on the extent to which management can make time demands on teachers. Contracts are likely to concentrate on "extra" time outside the regular working day, limiting the unpaid effort which can be asked of teachers. Teachers have bargained to reduce the proportion of inert to potentially productive time in the working day; they have pressed for free lunchtime periods, less clerical work, and control of their "free" time. They have managed to get reductions in the number of class preparations expected of a teacher; they have also favored employing teacher aides to relieve them of tasks they consider nonprofessional.

Contracts have also included restraints on principals' exercise of authority (Perry and Wildman 1970, p. 119). Teacher representatives have won contract provisions in which principals are required to allocate resources and make appointments on the "objective" basis of seniority; the net effect is to reduce the scope of managerial discretion. Some contracts specify that the principal must support the teacher in dealings with recalcitrant students. More and more contracts now provide for grievances in which superordinates can be cited for infractions of the contract. We do not yet know how seriously such arrangements cut into the principal's power; there are some indications that early predictions of administrative erosion were exaggerated (Berg 1973).

Reviews of contract content do not mention efforts to keep parents from intervening; this would probably be extremely difficult to do overtly. Yet this may be affected by the reduction of principal powers. Principals with limited discretionary powers would find it hard to act upon parents' complaints, and so parents would find that their displeasure had fewer consequences for teachers. The point merits close observation.

Some aspects of collective bargaining represent teachers' efforts to reduce the tension between status constraints and task imperatives. Their major strategy seems to stress containing vertical authority and shaping it by contract provisions. That approach is continuous with the historical emphasis on reducing the impact of administrative authority rather than augmenting the positive powers of classroom teachers. In that respect, collective bargaining does not represent a sharp break with the past.

It is difficult to estimate how successful teachers will be in using bargaining to codify their preferences about school practice. Theoretically, the future course of collective bargaining might test the efficacy of teacher beliefs on productivity in the classroom. Reducing intervention by principals and parents and disruption by students should, according to their logic, raise performance. Spending a higher proportion of time on potentially productive tasks should also increase their effectiveness. Yet one can imagine alternative outcomes: successful bargaining may raise the level of teacher expectations. If that happens, they may escalate their definition of satisfactory working conditions. It should be interesting to watch these developments; perhaps "autonomy" and "support" will prove to be relative rather than absolute conceptions.

What about "support"? Can it be increased through collective bargaining? Teachers apparently expect others to offer constructive assistance, which involves more than simply not hindering. Thus a principal may be expected to overlook the rule book in a particular instance and show sensitivity to a teacher's special problem. But if teachers rely primarily upon legalistic procedures to control principals' behavior, will they not invite legalistic retaliation and less flexibility? Given the present disposition of formal authority in school systems, are teachers likely to win any such struggle short of a major overhaul of the authority system? One also wonders about parents: How will they react if a principal says he can do nothing when they complain about teachers? Will discontent among parents produce hostilities which children will carry into the classroom?

Other questions arise on the limits of collective bargaining. Shanker has stated that the provisions in specific contracts reflect administrators' "abuses" of authority; teachers seek to offset specific administrative behavior by writing proscriptions into the contract.[6] Yet if such restrictions are made general rules they can have unintended consequences. A rule designed to prevent administrators from calling unnecessary meetings may turn into a maximal statement on teachers' readiness to participate in staff meetings (March and Simon 1958). Some teachers, fearing collegial displeasure, may hold back from initiating activities which require joint planning. A rule designed to curb administrators may become a general constraint on teacher activity; and observers may become cynical about teachers' "commitment" to their work.

Teachers may find there is a trap in efforts to correct status deficiencies through collective bargaining. Attempts to improve status in one respect (i.e., consonance with task imperatives) may weaken it in others; the reputation of teachers and their social standing may be reduced. For by using restrictive rules to enhance tasks they cathect, they may appear uncaring and uncommitted; various publics may conclude that the work rules are intended to reduce total effort rather than to enhance teaching effectiveness (e.g., many people are upset when teachers refuse to stay after hours without extra pay). Earlier, I argued that status is affected by public attributions of motive and function; occupations which are defined as "service" gain from that designation (chapter 1). If teachers' actions are construed as little more than attempts to get greater benefits for less effort, they will lose the advantages of reputation which have made teaching something more than simply a job.

It may be that there are intrinsic limits on the utility of collective bargaining for reducing contradictions between teacher status and teacher tasks; future research should concentrate on this possibility. Teachers may find those limits unacceptable and find it necessary to devise new stategies to cope with their work problems.

The Sentiments and the Ethos

In chapters 2, 3, and 4 we examined the processes which keep the occupation going—recruitment, socialization, and the system of rewards. We found that such processes foster particular outlooks among teachers, specifically the orientations of conservatism, individualism, and presentism. More recently we have concentrated on the tasks of classroom teachers, using phenomenological and microsociological approaches. The question now arises: What is the relationship between task-related sentiments and the structurally derived orientations? Are they congruent or contravening? Are they likely to influence the ethos in similar or in divergent directions?

I will attack these questions by reviewing the connections between each orientation and the relevant sentiments. After considering each orientation separately, we will be able to estimate the contribution of the sentiments to the ethos of classroom teachers. We will identify congruent relationships and points where internal strains arise.

Conservatism and the Sentiments

Educational goals are often stated in global, even utopian terms. In chapter 5 we observed that teachers "reduce" such goals into specific objectives they use in their daily work. This reduction apparently involves two conservative tendencies: relying on personal convictions and obtaining high satisfaction from outcomes that are less than universalistic. When teachers cannot use stated goals to guide their actions, organizational objectives give way to personal values; the personal values of teachers, as we saw in chapter 3, are heavily influenced by past experience. The elitism implicit in taking satisfaction when a limited number of students learn is probably unintended. But it links present practice to historical rather than recent standards—egalitarian concerns in teaching lose out.

Teaching tasks are marked by difficulties of assessment and relationship (chapter 6). Assessment problems have the same effects (in general) as unusable goals—they encourage the employment of personal standards and the use of mechanisms (e.g., tests, compliance) associated with traditional forms of instruction. The teacher's dependence on student response mixes tendencies toward continuity and toward change. It is often said that children are conservatives, resisting change; earlier we pointed out that they can become socialized to particular school practices. Yet older children are influenced by "youth culture" and by the mass media; teachers comment that they must stay abreast of popular culture if they are to communicate with the students. (This belief reminds us of Simmel's insight into the relationship between the leader and his followers; followers influence the leader as well as vice versa [Simmel 1950]). There is therefore some pressure on teachers to "move with the times." It would take specific research to establish whether these two tendencies (the conservative and the changeful) offset one another or result in a balance favoring one. I believe that as other cultural influences play on students, schools gradually accommodate to changed tastes and dispositions. The increased power of the mass media since Waller's time means that schools today are probably less aptly described as "museums of virtue" (p. 34).

Teaching problematics can produce uncertainty among teachers, and uncertainty, because of the lack of a reassurance structure, can be escalated into feelings of anxiety. A little anxiety may stimulate effectiveness, but more than that will impede intellectual performance. Anxious teachers are likely to give up the search for superior solutions and to cling to what they know from the past. In begetting anxiety, uncertainty may reduce innovation and serve conservative ends. This is a possibility which deserves further inquiry; if it should be validated, it establishes a connection between organizational objectives, evaluative procedures, and the balance of continuity and change.

There is clear congruence between teachers' preferences and conservatism of outlook. What teachers consider desirable change can be summed up as "more of the same"; they believe the best program of improvement removes obstacles and provides for more teaching with better support. They want arrangements to "unleash" their capacities. Their approach is implicitly conservative; in assuming that current instructional tactics are adequate if properly supported, the blame for deficiencies is laid upon the environment. Remedies lie in changing the environment, not in finding more efficacious ways to instruct.

Teacher sentiments toward other adults move toward an equilibrium organized around autonomy and support; my respondents do not seek *basic* changes in their interactions with others. When their expectations are met, teachers "bootleg" more freedom than their official status prescribes. Other adults are assigned to supporting, nonintrusive roles. Teachers are using collective bargaining to codify relationships according to their preferences. So far the outcome is moot; bargaining may initiate a Hegelian dialectic of thesis and antithesis or simply crystallize relationships. Only time will tell.

Relationships among teachers may deepen and broaden. Considerable effort is being expended today to foster closer working relationships among teachers; for example, many new schools are built with open space arrangements which facilitate teacher teaming. Solidarities induced in bargaining may generalize into classroom-related activities. But as I have already pointed out several times, there are substantial impediments to close working relationships among teachers. (We will discuss this further in chapter 9.) Yet teachers may decide that the great effort to intensify collegial work ties is worth the price.

It is much easier to find congruence than antipathy in a relationship between conservatism and the task-related sentiments; the drift is toward continuity rather than change. The ways teachers see their tasks reinforce a conservative frame of mind—a preference for doing things as they have been done in the past.

Individualism and the Sentiments

A reward system which emphasizes psychic rewards based on somewhat indeterminate criteria for achievement reinforces individualistic orientations. The teacher who is burdened with ambiguous criteria must select his own indicators of effectiveness; this gives him the chance to align his goals with his own capacities and interests. Having worked out a satisfactory balance, a teacher is likely to resist conditions that would force change—he has a stake in autonomy. The ideology of individualism serves teachers' purposes; it undergirds psychic rewards; the circle is closed.

Craft problematics encourage individualism. Individual personality comes into play in selecting proximate criteria for assessment. The teacher's self is also deeply implicated in classroom leadership; the lack of standard technique, coupled with "sink-or-swim" socialization, means that teachers learn to cope on their own. The individual plays a large part in forming himself as a teacher; the fact that such shaping takes place without extensive analysis does not make it any less important. Individuals find personal ways to cope with provocation and anger, guilt and shame; institutionalized arrangements do not provide the teacher with common definitions and solutions. (It is possible, of course, that informal relationships play a part in such processes; it will take research to clarify this point.)

I argued above that uncertainty and anxiety may push teachers back into their pasts. Uncertainty may work against the orientation of individualism and evoke the need for conformity. Anxious people may lean on others for reassurance or may rely on orthodox doctrines to buttress their self-confidence. I suspect that this happens among teachers, leavening their individualism and infusing it with a querulous quality. The term "individualism" may connote self-assured crustiness or even arrogance; but those qualities were rare in the Five Towns interviews. Teacher individualism is more guarded and cautious—it lies behind a formal rhetoric given to praising cooperation and denying conflict. Teacher individualism is not cocky and self-assured; it is hesitant and uneasy.

Our respondents want boundaries around their core teaching tasks—
they assume that students learn best when the teacher works without
interruption. Individualistic assumptions are evident in teachers' preoccupation with resources; they have a kind of "unleash me" stance. The
preoccupation with potentially productive time assumes that the individual teacher is the critical ingredient in student learning. We did not
encounter talk about system resources—about the importance of combining the contributions of individuals into a more effective whole. The
point of view is aggregative rather than systematic; school is perceived as a
collection of individual teachers inflencing students. Improvements
suggested by respondents centered on strengthening the hand of the
individual teacher, not on arranging a more stimulating total environment
for children.

Individualism is also visible in the relational preferences of the
respondents. They stress the desirability of limited, specified, and
circumscribed cooperation; they do not endorse denser and more intense
relationships among adults. The quality of interactions they see as good is
more hesitant than impulsive and more prudent than open. The
individual teacher is shielded.

The task-related sentiments reassert the theme of individualism. We
find this in the reward system, the problematics of teaching, and
teachers' preoccupations and preferences. But there is a countertendency; anxiety may induce conformity in teachers. That countertendency
probably accounts for the muted quality of teacher individualism.

Presentism and the Sentiments

I linked presentism to the "front-loaded" career of teachers in chapter 4,
finding that few teachers plan to teach for a long, continuous period.
Presentism can be seen in the lack of enthusiasm teachers show in working
together to build a stronger technical culture; it gets help from teacher
individualism. Presentism is also related to the special nature of teaching
tasks, as teachers find it hard to achieve a sense of full mastery, even with
experience. They do not signal assurance about their future performance.

Teachers perceive their psychic rewards as scarce, erratic, and unpredictable. They are vulnerable to the ebb and flow of student response;
even highly experienced teachers talk about "bad years." Uncertainties
in teaching inhibit the feeling that future rewards are ensured, and such
doubts support the position that it is unwise to sacrifice present
opportunities for future possibilities.

Means-ends relationships in teaching are not well understood, particularly for long-range instructional goals. It may well be that the emphasis
in pedagogy on breaking teaching up into short units (e.g., lesson plans,

study units) stems from this lack of knowledge about long-range instruction. Teachers are more likely to experience reward if they can punctuate their work, concentrating on short-range outcomes as a source of gratification.

Today we usually think of knowledge-building in terms of scientific methodologies. A scientific approach, however, normally begins with the assumption that there is an underlying order in the phenomena under study. It is not clear that all or most teachers make that assumption about their world. Some see teaching outcomes as capricious and describe short-term results in almost mysterious terms. If that viewpoint is widespread, it is not surprising that teachers do not invest in searching for general principles to inform their work. If they suspect that classroom events are beyond comprehension, inquiry is futile.

The preference for boundedness exemplifies how individualism combines with presentism to retard the search for occupational knowledge. Teachers who work in isolation cannot create an empirically grounded, semantically potent common language; unless they develop terms to indicate specific events, discussion will lack the clarity it needs to enlighten practice. We see a similar theme in the relational preferences of teachers—they have a constricted conception of colleagueship which discourages extensive interaction.

In sum, sentiments attached to teacher tasks intensify the presentist orientations built into a "front-loaded" career system. The logics of reward favor immediate gratification rather than long-range perspectives. Individualism supports presentism by inhibiting work with others in a search for common solutions. Teachers do not undertake the collegial effort which has played so crucial a role in other occupations.

Summary

The ways teachers define their tasks and the feelings they attach to them are largely congruent with the orientations induced by recruitment, socialization, and career rewards. Approaching the ethos from two different perspectives, we find the same themes. Conservatism, individualism, and presentism are significant components in the ethos of American classroom teachers.

There are points of internal tension and we will examine more of these in the final chapter. We have noticed that collegial relationships are moving toward greater intensity in collective bargaining. We have seen that individualism is contained by uncertainty; teachers may welcome changes which would reduce their uneasiness about classroom work. Not all teachers use the language of caprice to describe their work. Under the influence of behavioral science and close empirical analysis (e.g., analysis of microfilmed instruction), recently trained teachers may show greater interest in systematic inquiry. Future researchers will have the opportunity to watch whether the ethos we have described is beginning to shift under the pressure of change.

I have concluded my analysis of empirical data and my description of the occupational ethos. The following chapter takes a different approach: it consists of speculations about change. It also includes examples of interventions which might play a part in shaping the future of the public schools.

9

Speculations on Change

It is fitting that I conclude this study with speculations on the future of teaching; we began with time and now we end with it. Intervening chapters have featured what anthropologists call the "synchronic" perspective; we have overlooked changes which might be taking place in the components of the social system. That "point in time" approach is useful in exposing interconnections within a social system, but it risks overestimating its stability. A direct attack on questions of change should help to offset that tendency.

Change is inescapable in education today. Constant discussion of change has methodological implications; it can create the impression that fundamental alterations have already taken place, particularly when journalists announce the arrival of an educational "revolution." The parameters of any such revolution, to say the least, are clouded. What is changing and in what direction is it moving? It is paradoxical that although in recent years millions have been spent on educational development, the quality and quantity of reporting on school actualities remain seriously inadequate. It is certain that large-scale intervention in schools will produce unintended consequences; if policies are not to be undermined by such outcomes, we will need close monitoring of trends coupled with sufficient flexibility to make corrections when policies go awry. Thoughtful speculation about the future might help those who plan systems of data-gathering to locate points where information will be particularly salient.

We will raise three kinds of questions about change in teaching. First, What kinds of change are likely to occur? Second, What are the implications of projected changes for teaching and how do they relate to what we know about the ethos of the occupation? These two questions will be addressed in the first section of this chapter. I will construct alternative scenarios and assess likely impact on the occupation.

People interested in education are likely to have a concern for its betterment; few of us can be dispassionate about the way each generation is introduced to our society and our cultural heritage. The third question, therefore, deals with the malleability of the forces in operation and the likelihood that they might be shaped by inquiry-based intervention. I will cite specific ways we might cope with apparent tensions and strains between the historical ethos of teaching and the (apparent) demands of the future. The primary purpose here is not to promote specific remedies—it is to illustrate the possibilities which lie in combining action and research. If the occupation we know today is largely the result of past decisions, it seems likely that future decisions can have significant influence.

Three Scenarios

One cannot discuss trends without guesswork; to label any phenomenon a "trend" is to assume that it will continue. I am loath to make long-range predictions, since the longer the vista, the larger the possible number of branchings and the smaller the chances of making the right choices from the manifold possibilities. It seems best to look ahead only a few years at a time and to make statements which lend themselves to empirical testing. Imaginative scenarios can probably help us get germane, reliable, and periodic information on school realities—they point up events which bear watching.

These scenarios focus on different aspects of the occupation and are based on somewhat divergent perspectives. The first focuses on cultural change—on alterations in thought about practice. The second has a more structural cast in that it centers on likely changes in the status of teachers. The third scenario unfolds against the backdrop of political and governmental affairs; it deals with the possibility that schools will become centralized bureaucracies. I know of no sure criteria for assigning probabilities of outcome to the several scenarios. I shall therefore note the implications of each scenario and their relationship to the ethos of teaching, identifying points of stress and tension. In subsequent pages we will concentrate on recurrent issues.

Scenario 1: The Erosion of Tradition

Culture can be variously defined; the concept is one of the major definitional problems of modern anthropology and sociology. Despite the disagreements, however, there is a consensus that culture includes the way members of a group think about social action; culture encompasses alternatives for resolving problems in collective life. The storehouse of ideas may exceed the variety of observable behavior within the group, for some possibilities may not find expression. The distinction between what is now theoretically possible and what actually happens in schools is important, for it is a likely source of change.

The number of alternative approaches in education has increased sharply over the last two decades or so. During the first two centuries of American education, no special machinery existed for generating new pedagogical ideas and practices. An occasional book could carry noteworthy influence, but there were no institutionalized arrangements for developing, testing, and diffusing pedagogical strategies. The specialized system created to train teachers originated in the nineteenth century and blossomed into high influence in the twentieth; but it was not until 1950 that a national program to upgrade the quality of public education began. An increasingly complex apparatus has been built since then to create and disseminate new approaches to public schooling. Today thousands of people are engaged in research, development, and dissemination, and the machinery for producing educational knowledge is still abuilding. The superstructure of people involved in education but working outside schools is increasingly influential. The result of all this activity is a marked increase in the options available to those making educational decisions at all levels. The cultural homogeneity of the past is coming under increasing pressure as alternative possibilities are developed.

Another consequence of this knowledge-building system in universities, federally supported organizations, and private companies is a new set of interests—interests in the process of change itself. It entails new university units struggling for recognition, government agencies busily forming constituencies, and business investments to be protected and enhanced. It affects thousands of careers; in addition to those charged with producing new approaches, others are engaged in "field services," "dissemination," and "sales." Such people stand to benefit when school personnel change their behavior; such change, in fact, defines their success. Other fields of expertise are also affected—the growing speciality of educational evaluation is a case in point. We are witnessing the institutionalization of the press toward change.

Any comprehensive list of options available today which did not exist twenty years ago would be too long for replication here—it would touch on all aspects of school operation. One finds sharp alternatives in architecture, whereas not long ago all school buildings were remarkably alike. Today one finds numerous curricula for a given subject and a given grade; there are growing numbers of ways to order the school day which replace previously sacrosanct schedules. Some schools have replaced the familiar grades with new systems; others display a variety of patterns for deploying school personnel. Novel schemes project widely different conceptions of the student's role in learning; they include heavy reliance on drill, the use of computers, and emphasis on considerable student independence. Many of the novel ways of teaching students are systematically disseminated by change agencies; government and private donors have been known, moreover, to offer incentives to school systems, rewarding those which are prepared to adopt particular innovations. Government uses its leverage to foster new linkages between universities, research centers, and school districts, and the outcome is a series of new networks of mutual influence. The ideas being developed in research and development are backed by considerable weight.

The sheer knowledge of existing alternatives has an effect on the decision-making climate in schools and school systems (Lortie, 1970). Nowadays the decision to do the usual thing is clearly a decision—it is not merely showing one's commitment to "good practice." For today, "good practice" itself requires specific assessment as older verities give way to a new outlook which stesses rigorous goal specification and empirical validation of claims. The dilution of traditional ways of thinking supports those who uphold "rationality" in school decision-making. Yet it is risky to jump to the conclusion that the aforementioned revolution has taken place. It seems that some of the announcements of the death of the old order are premature; like Tom Sawyer, the deceased has a way of showing up at the funeral.

What does exist is the *possibility* for greatly increased pluralism and visible discontinuity in American public schooling. Options are multiplying fast enough to permit considerable differentiation between and within school districts; were all existing alternatives put into practice, the resulting permutations could result in schools appreciably different from one another and from their standardized predecessors. As far as teachers are concerned, instructional approaches are already sufficiently diverse that attempts to create various mixes of elements could produce a variety of teacher roles. (Specifically, think of the various outcomes possible if one put together conventional modes of instruction, differentiated staffing, and computer-assisted instruction.) Yet we do not see anything like this variation in actual school practice; those making serious reports on schools, starting out with hopes of finding fresh, new approaches to teaching, have almost invariably been disappointed (Mayer 1961; Goodlad 1970; Silberman 1970). If there has been a revolution, I suspect it has occurred in people's expectations for schools, not in practice; the gap between the possible and the actual has become an issue. That issue is likely to grow in importance in the years ahead; it could serve as a point for concentrated inquiry.

What should one look for in studying the hiatus between the possible and the real? One potential avenue of research is studying how school systems respond to pressures for change. We should learn more about the mechanisms school boards and administrators use in deflecting pressures they do not welcome. There are indications, for example, that large school systems sometimes use new approaches in showplace schools while resisting their widespread adoption; this tactic can "cool out" enthusiasts until their ardor has waned. Another device is to change the rhetoric of school practice while leaving the substance intact; some school systems proclaim commitment to "team teaching" when in fact they are merely taking public notice of voluntary patterns of cooperation which have existed among teachers for some time. The absorption of the Teacher Corps is an excellent example of how school systems can turn intended "reforms" to conventional purposes (Watson 1967). I do not cite such instances to argue that all large school systems reject change. Some do not. But we must be careful to avoid assuming that the presence of alternatives, even though thousands of people are motivated to diffuse them, automatically produces change. Acceptance of new approaches is obviously contingent, and research could center on the nature of the crucial contingencies.

We will understand the diffusion of new options only if we find models of diffusion which are appropriate to the shool situation. Models which identify the critical processes in business and agriculture, for example, may mislead us in studying public education. Business executives, for example, can normally ensure that the expensive equipment they purchase is put to proper use—their authority is equal to that task.

Yet one hears that the opposite occurs in schools, where purchasing officials make decisions which are not implemented by school personnel; equipment may go unused or be improperly employed. (Is the allegaion apocryphal that school basements are filled with unused television equipment?) Business buyers are sometimes forced to buy equipment and productive processes regardless of personal preference; differences in productivity, coupled with competitve realities, may give them no choice. Agricultural innovations have reportedly been diffused most effectively by demonstration; effective processes become obvious to the farmer's neighbors. Teaching differs from both these fields, of course, in that productivity is neither as coercive as it is in business nor as tangible as in farming. Our models must take such differences into account.

It would probably be a mistake to visualize the agencies of change as leviathans clearing away all before them; organizations involved in promoting change are also vulnerable. Businesses can lose money, university units be disbanded, and government agencies undergo budget cuts. Where resistance cannot be overcome, we can expect that research and development efforts will falter as support is withdrawn. One might hypothesize, therefore, that the movement toward change will prove to be not linear but erratic; the forces of change and resistance will probably interact contrapuntally. The outcome may be a kind of seesawing between change and stability as the opposing forces gain temporary advantage.

What issues are teachers likely to confront as the result of proliferating options? What tensions will arise between their orientations and sentiments and the demands which will result from the erosion of traditional ways?

The most obvious consequence is that teachers will have to adapt to a context where conservatism, particularly reflexive conservatism, becomes increasingly suspect. This is not to say that teachers will have to accept all the options presented to them; it seems unlikely, however, that a dogged commitment to the past will work if options continue to multiply and norms of rationality take hold. Groups of teachers who openly resist change will run the risk of being labeled "reactionary" and "obstructive"; such conflict may take place in the arena of collective bargaining. Individual teachers may find that the expectations around them gradually shift to new techniques and more frequent innovation. There will be a generalized pressure toward adaptability.

One can think of specific challenges which will tax the decision-making capacity of individual teachers and of the occupation as a whole. Let us say, for example, that highly structured instructional programs are

219

developed and are said to be highly effective. Teachers might find such programs distasteful; they would cramp individuality and autonomy and quite possibly be based on principles of pedagogy which are alien to teachers. (Such programs are usually developed by people whose orientations are different from those of classroom teachers; for example, they are likely to favor general impact and widespread adoption, both of which contravene teacher sentiments.) How will teachers cope with such innovations? What mechanisms will be available to warn teachers of the disadvantages? What intellectual resources will they have to counter such programs?

One can visualize a future in which teachers must select from a wide range of possible alternatives in instruction. (Let us assume that they have found it impossible or undesirable to reject all proposed changes.) Individual teachers may find themselves unable to get the information they need to make a choice consistent with their preferences and convictions. Groups of teachers may be involved in transactions with school management and be unable to advance substantiated defense for one approach rather than another. They may be somewhat suspicious of information provided by business, university, or government proponents: Where are they to turn for reliable information which is geared to their interests and perspectives? Intelligent selectivity, in short, will require substantial support from organizations committed to teacher concerns. Although some teacher organizations currently conduct research, the resources of most local and state groups are limited; teachers have not been sufficiently collegial in outlook to demand and pay for advanced evaluative and instructional assistance from their organizations.

There will be other problems for teachers. Research and development will probably spawn new techniques which could become specialties; we may already have an example in computer-assisted instruction. How will teachers go about deciding on, and influencing, the division of labor within schools? Will they be able, as has medicine, to absorb new technologies? Or will they find themselves "encroached" upon by people with widely different orientations and commitments? If that happens, will they find themselves losing the power they have worked so carefully to acquire?

The examples cited point up the general problems which may face teachers as tradition erodes and alternatives increase. Their conservatism will be under serious challenge, and political risks will follow from intransigent opposition to all change. They will find themselves sharing new problems for which solutions do not exist, and they will need to cooperate to find acceptable answers. The issues will frequently be highly technical, and the forces pressing for change will be equipped with impressive resources of intellectual prestige and power. Selectivity will therefore be problematic; they will need their "own" experts. Informal forms of mutual assistance may prove inadequate to the demands imposed by complex innovations developed by superstructure personnel. The changes I have projected point up the need for greater adaptability, more effective colleague relationships, and more sharing in issues of knowledge and expertise. The ethos stresses contradictory themes; we have noted its emphasis on conservatism, individualism, and presentism. It seems probable that the erosion of tradition will induce powerful strains between the historical ethos of teachers and the demands of the new situation.

Scenario 2: Bargaining and Backlash

We need not assume that collective bargaining will be the same in the future as it has been in the past; as we have noted, there are discernible stages in the unfolding of employee-employer conflict. We may be nearing the end of an initial period in school system bargaining during which teachers have confronted ill-prepared, vulnerable school boards; school boards will probably be less likely to give ground in the future. Bargaining implies exchange—a process of give and take. Well-established unions in the private sector have found it necessary to make counterconcessions. (Industrial unions, for example, have generally accepted management's right to introduce technological changes and to lay off employees.) I can see little reason for believing that teacher organizations will not have to concede points in their confrontations with school boards; should current patterns of teacher oversupply continue, teacher organizations may find bargaining increasingly difficult.

A scenario for collective bargaining should take account of certain peculiarities on the educational scene. First, there is the historically rooted status of teachers and the probable effects teacher aggressiveness will have on that status. It appears that teachers have received a degree of "ritual pity" in the past; it was conventional to lament their low pay and refer to them as "dedicated"—workers who gave more than they received. The moral position of teachers made it difficult for others to demand more of them; teachers subsequently were exempted from high performance expectations and rigorous public scrutiny. But such relationships undergo change when teachers assert their collective power and win significant gains. The use of calculative strategies invites the use of calculative counterstrategies.

A survey conducted by the Gallup Organization in 1969 (Gallup 1969) revealed that compared with ten years before a smaller proportion of the public considered teachers "underpaid." It seems highly probable that teacher militancy in the intervening years belied their image as victims of a penurious public. Some have claimed that teacher victories in collective bargaining signal a "new dignity" for members of the occupation—they are more than likely right. Little emphasis has been placed, however, on the usual consequences of increases in rights; they frequently imply greater responsibility. For teachers, I believe that increased responsibility takes the form of reduced exemption from public review; the clamor for teacher "accountability" has risen since teachers have become militant in their relationships with school boards.

There is another way teacher aggressiveness affects public opinion. The subordination of teachers to boards and administrators has previously exonerated them from responsibility for decisions made by school authorities; unpopular school policies were not associated with teachers, who had no share in their formation. Today, the visible assertion of teacher power changes the impression received by the public; when teachers win the right to participate in school policy-making (whether or not that option is exercised), another exemption evaporates. Furthermore, their readiness to sign contracts which do not contain changes desired by other publics aligns teachers with the administration; their agreement may be taken as willing compliance with features of school operation which some publics resent. There is a loss of political innocence; teachers become potentially culpable for school system practices which they could previously disclaim.

Teachers share particular problems with others who try to adapt collective bargaining approaches to the public sector. One of the most obvious examples is the matter of public inconvenience; the sanctions used by public servants almost invariably affect the lives of citizens who are not party to the negotiations. Anger is often evoked; in the case of schools, this can be particularly difficult for leaders of teacher organizations, since local citizens hold the ultimate power of the purse. The public is known to be unsympathetic to teacher strikes (Gallup 1969). Thus teachers face a dilemma when deciding whether to strike; short-term gains may be offset by long-range losses brought about by taxpayer alienation. Public resistance to financing schools has, in fact, been rising over the last few years; one wonders what part of that reluctance to pay more taxes for schools stems from dismay over teacher aggressiveness.

Criticism of public schools has increased sharply over the last decade or so; it seems that the number of groups who give more-or-less automatic support to public schools is shrinking. Schools have always had their critics—the perennial ones have been conservative taxpayers alleging waste of funds and academics critical of the intellectual standards of the schools. Yet today we have important segments of the black and white communities embroiled in struggles over control of schools and busing of students. We have conservatives and liberals urging that public resources be allocated to private ventures in education ("voucher plans"). The public has been exposed to a steady series of critical books, films, and articles in the popular media; radicals are urging the complete rethinking of education and schooling (Illich 1971). Even those staunch historical allies of public schools—members of the upper-middle class—seem less than certain nowadays; some are leading experiments with "free schools" and other alternatives to the common school.[1] This criticism and disaffection may prove to be a passing phenomenon; it may reflect a mood of general dissatisfaction with institutions which has marked the country of late. On the other hand, it may mean that public opinion is being prepared for fundamental changes in educational practice. Protracted criticism of public schools may loosen the public's affiliation with the common school concept developed and institutionalized during the middle years of the nineteenth century. In the short run, it reduces the standing of teachers as participants in a questioned enterprise and increases their vulnerability to public opinion.

Yet public disaffection need not go to extremes to imply changed expectations of teachers; fewer exemptions for teachers, anger aroused by strikes, and a climate of criticism are probably enough. I suspect that the process has already begun; one hears increasing criticism of teachers' tenure, automatic pay increases, and slow acceptance of change. There is the growing movement—as yet rather undefined—toward "accountability." It is difficult to ascertain at this point whether increased demands will focus on higher productivity or on contingent rewards for teachers. They might include both. The concept of attaining stipulated outcomes (using tests of student achievement) is already employed in "performance contracting" where school boards pay business firms only if they manage to produce a specified level of student learning (Campbell and Lorion 1972). One hears more complaints today about the schools' inability to discharge incompetent teachers; despite chronic resistance by teachers, the concept of "merit pay" refuses to die. Teachers may be vulnerable on issues they fought and seemingly resolved years ago; the public may not be convinced of the necessity for assured tenure and automatic pay increases.

School boards, backed by state departments of education, may launch various kinds of counterassertions to teacher power. They may hold teachers collectively accountable for the performance of the group; this could take the specific form of demands that teacher organizations participate in the discharge of teachers who fall below acceptable standards. They may demand increased use of differentiated payment for teachers; differentiated staffing patterns (e.g., teams with ranked members) open up possiblities for using position classification as a basis for variable salary payment. Boards may press for the adoption of particular technical innovations despite teacher opposition; this will most likely occur when a program is reputed to increase student rates of learning while reducing costs or holding them constant. Whatever boards decide to do, however, teacher negotiators will probably find it harder to "get something for nothing" in the years ahead.

As in the tradition erosion scenario, status changes will require considerable adaptability from teachers. They will need a quality of detachment as they cope with consequences of their power struggles; tenets of an older orthodoxy will prove less relevant. There will be fewer gratifications associated with the dedicatory image and fewer exemptions from criticism. Self-concepts based on earlier realities (if dialectics of bargaining intensify) will prove inconsistent with the expectations others hold for teachers.

Since teachers have mobilized power through collective means, responses from bargaining opponents will probably focus on collective obligations; teachers' individualism will come under pressure as school boards make demands on the entire group. Agreements signed by teachers' representatives will carry the obligation to ensure that members adhere to the stated terms; the need for internal discipline will increase as teachers are forced to prove their reliability as bargaining partners. Counterdemands would add to the points on which the group, acting through its leaders, will be expected to control individual teachers. Voluntaristic ties among teachers will be supplemented (and perhaps replaced) by increasingly coercive rules. Yet leaders may balk at enforcing such rules, refusing to engage in what they will call "management obligations." A dilemma will be provoked; teachers will have to choose between more collegial discipline or the greater exercise of authority by administrative superordinates. In either case the autonomy of the individual teacher will be reduced—the issue will be what kind of external power is preferable. In light of teacher sentiments, these are deeply difficult issues; it will take extraordinarily effective interchange among teaching colleagues to find and implement consensus on them. There is irony here: whether teachers choose more collegial control or more authority for administrators, they will need strong mechanisms of collegial action in order to make a viable decision.

Finally, the issues raised by changing reciprocities and teacher status will involve complex technical matters; take, for example, differential payment for differential results with students. Specialists in psychometrics and evaluation find the issues so presented extremely difficult to resolve; teachers will have to make joint decisions about what stands they will take on intricate questions of that sort. The advantages and disadvantages of alternative staffing patterns are most difficult to assess—the evaluative problems cut across several disciplines. Teachers will need trustworthy technical advice in reaching such decisions; mobilizing such technical assistance will require them to become increasingly sophisticated consumers of technical expertise. They will in all probability find it harder to rely upon their historical mentors on such matters; professors of education and school administrators will not necessarily identify their interests with classroom teachers. It seems likely, therefore, that teachers will find it necessary to develop cadres of technical specialists if they are to continue with protracted power contests.

Scenario 3: Trends toward Centralization

A casual observer might conclude that decentralization of authority is taking place in the public schools; he could get that impression from the news media. The efforts of urban blacks (particularly in New York) to attain "community control" over schools have been widely publicized; "free schools" make colorful stories. Innovations like "informal education" and "open classrooms," and other instances of liberalized authority, attract considerable attention. Yet the underlying trends may be of quite another order. One can argue that schools are likely to undergo greater centralization in the disposition of authority.

Two major developments point toward the centralized governance of public schools. The first lies in the enhanced potential of state governments in administering local school systems. The second originates in the increasing mean size of school districts; the number of school districts declined from 94,926 in 1948 to 18,000 in 1970 while school enrollment doubled.[2]

One hesitates to predict the course of relationships between the federal government and the states in the years ahead; at present their respective roles in public education are controversial, and probably fluid. Yet there are signs that state governments may appropriate powers currently held by local districts. These indications include: (1) the tendency for collective bargaining to be conducted by teacher units larger than the local school district, (2) doctrines of the "New Federalism" which stress the value of state rather than federal control over domestic expenditures, and (3) the growing concern over equalizing educational opportunities by equalizing expenditures within state boundaries.

Teacher organizations normally cut across the boundaries of individual school districts; local teacher groups frequently call upon state and national bodies for assistance. There is a movement today to merge unions and associations. Powerful teacher organizations have been able to bring great force to bear on school boards; Thomas reports, for example, that local boards in Michigan were forced to turn to the state for financial help to meet teacher demands.[3] Large employee organizations invite the creation of large counterassociations of employers; in the case of schools, this could move collective bargaining to the state level as a matter of course (Perry and Wildman 1970, p. 228). Thus state officials may become directly engaged in bargaining; since personnel expenditures are the major item in school budgets, they would be making critical decisions about the conduct of local schooling.

The Nixon administration sought to decentralize control over some types of domestic expenditures by backing tax sharing with the states. Although the ultimate fate of this approach is unclear, it has generated considerable support and it is evident that the direct financial contribution of the federal government has leveled off in the past few years. Although the Supreme Court did not uphold the principle that equality of educational expenditures should be mandated for the states, some states are increasing contributions to offset local inequalities. Should this social movement continue to grow in importance, it would require that state governments increase their participation in school affairs, if only to ensure that their increased contributions are spent in the legally appropriate way.

It is generally thought that the locus of financial support is vital in matters of control; Bailyn argues, for example, that the decision to finance schools through property taxation placed control in the hands of local property owners (1966). Is it not likely, therefore, that changes in the source of school financing would reallocate authority in favor of greater state hegemony?

One should not overlook, of course, the inertia which results from entrenched tradition; state governments have historically refrained from exercising their full constitutional powers over local school districts (Campbell, Cunningham, and McPhee 1965). Such conventions will not be dismissed out of hand, since state officials will fear attack from upholders of local control. Yet it is probable that occasions will occur when local officials create difficulties in the use of state funds; such events, and even scandals, are not unknown in education. Under such circumstances, it is probable that state officials would act to protect themselves; few political figures care to be embarrassed by the actions of others. Since fiscal responsibility without administrative control spells vulnerability, one would not be surprised if state officials responded by promulgating and enforcing "guidelines" for local school officials. Custom would come under strong pressures of political exigency.

Will individual school districts continue to decline in number while growing in size? The process of aggregation among local school districts should be carefully observed in the years ahead; it could play a crucial role in centralization. There are the immediate effects on schools and school personnel; larger school systems are more likely to develop bureaucratized structures. But there is the further question of ease of control by state government. If the number of districts continues to dwindle, it should become easier for states to grasp effective control over operations; it is simpler to control a smaller number of units. (There is a span of control issue among government units, I believe, which is similar to that among individuals in an organization.) The two kinds of centralization might ultimately link up, producing a considerably more unified system of school government than currently prevails.

How would such centralization affect classroom teachers? One important issue can be identified: teachers would find themselves confronted with a crisis in the definition of their employment status, for a state-dominated system would raise the question of classifying teachers as state employees, as bureaucrats within the governmental structure. Intervention by local citizens would matter less and the hierarchy of state officialdom would matter more. Movement to a bureaucratic, governmental context would raise serious issues for teachers who value their autonomy. Informal understandings which currently soften vertical authority could erode under steady pressure toward bureaucratization; governments have long experience in attaining close control over civil servants (Kaufman 1960). One might object, Isn't it true that professors in state colleges and universities enjoy considerable autonomy in their work? Quite so. Yet one cannot be sure that the formulas developed for academics will be applied to classroom teachers. The status differences between teachers and professors are longstanding and apparently stable. The role of the professor developed largely in private institutions and was transferred to public institutions; the continued existence of private universities continues to reinforce a nongovernmental model. It would be incautious to assume that teachers would automatically receive the autonomy granted university professors.

One can imagine a future tribunal where teachers are pressed to justify their wish to be exempted from close bureaucratic supervision. (The "tribunal" would probably consist of state legislatures, executive hearings, and courts.) How could teachers buttress their claims? They would be on safer ground if they could point to significant changes taking place within the occupation; if they did not, hearing officials might simply conclude that the transfer of supervision from local school officials to state officials was a matter of detail. An emphasis on change could justify increased autonomy for teachers. Teacher spokesmen would be more convincing if they could argue that teaching is a highly organized occupation in which peer judgments have considerable weight; the principle of collegial authority could be invoked to offset the threat of increased vertical authority. Claims for exemption from rules and rule enforcers would be strengthened if teachers could argue that it takes highly technical preparation to make the difficult judgments involved in classroom work. Autonomy, in short, could be advanced on the basis of teacher qualifications and the nature of teaching tasks. But we must recall that the tribunals in question would probably require proof of these allegations. Teachers would be expected to document their statements that their work was dynamic rather than static, that collegial judgment played a key part in decision-making, and that teachers acquired arcane, indispensable training to prepare them for the high demands of teaching.

Another way to say this is that teachers will stand a better chance of winning autonomy within a state-dominated system if they can persuade decision-makers that they are a "professionalizing" occupation. But the axes of professionalization I have mentioned (there are others) run against the ethos of the occupation; unless there is a shift in teacher orientations and sentiments, it is not likely that they will be able to document the allegations I have put in the mouths of their future spokesmen. Conservatism will not result in a dynamic, changing occupation. Individualism will not produce intricate arrangements for collegial judgment. Presentism will not eventuate in growing, arcane knowledge possessed by teachers alone. In sum, unless teachers substitute professionally oriented values for those they currently express, they will be hard pressed to claim professional status in a centralized system of public education.

On Accommodating to Change

We cannot know which scenario will be most important in the years ahead. But if any of the projected sequences occurs, we can expect some strain between the occupational ethos and the demands of change. The actual unfolding of any one scenario will require that teachers adapt to altered circumstances, forge firmer collegial bonds, and improve their technical knowledge. The present ethos seems ill suited to the putative needs confronting teachers.

Components of the ethos apparently reinforce each other: conservatism, individualism, and presentism work together to produce features of the occupational subculture. The ethos, moreover, has deep roots in the history and social position of the occupation; time and the absence of major crises have permitted considerable integration in the social system and the ethos. One would not expect the occupational order to wither at the slightest touch; it will prove resistant to change.

Some consider resistance a basis for despair and conclude that the occupation can never change. Pessimism of this sort rests on the assumption that the structure of teaching and its task organization are immutable. Yet we can trace the decisions which have shaped the structure and organization of work; future decisions could have different consequences. The assumption that change is impossible, since it discourages effort, tends to be self-confirming. The challenge lies in finding points where intelligent intervention can make a difference.

This final section will illustrate how we can use the analyses in this study to cope with problems of change. I shall present examples of how we might mediate the tension between the ethos of teachers and the contingencies of change. Since various parts of the ethos are mutually supportive, a comprehensive program would prove extremely complex, and so some simplification is necessary. I shall discuss the recurring demands of change adumbrated in the preceding section, concentrating on their connections to particular themes in the teacher ethos. I hope the approach achieves my major purpose in writing this section—to stimulate further dialogue and inquiry.

Adaptablility and Reflexive Conservatism

Significant change will demand from teachers the capacity to make effective adaptations.[4] The ethos tends toward automatic conservatism; reflexivity is induced by teachers' recruitment, socialization, and task organization. I will not argue that teachers should become enthusiasts for whatever is new; not only is reflexive adherence to the novel as irrational as its opposite, but it appears that teachers will have to exercise considerable selectivity in the years ahead. They will confront options in educational practice, alternative responses to public expectations, and difficult organizational decisions. The target for intervention, as I see it, should be *reflexive* conservatism; teachers ought not to reject change out of hand or be unwilling to give serious thought to alternative ways of attacking pedagogical problems.

Conservative proclivities nest in selection and socialization into teaching, and some aspects of task organization reinforce these tendencies. I shall suggest a few countervailing actions which might offset conservatizing influences built into current occupational arrangements.

People attracted to teaching tend to favor the status quo (chapter 2). We hypothesized that this is especially marked when entrants live out earlier identifications with teachers. Selection procedures could be altered to contravene the tendency for teaching to perpetuate its ways through recruitment. Specifically, students could be carefully screened before admission to training; if the current oversupply continues, training institutions could raise their standards. Advances in psychological testing should make it possible to distinguish between applicants who are wedded to the past and those who can revise ideas and practice in light of new experiences. Longitudinal studies could be conducted to study the relationship between personality and subsequent teaching behavior, and specific programs could test the effects of deliberate selection policies. One could test a variety of possibilities: for example, do counter-identifiers innovate more and show greater readiness to accept change in school organization? Such inquiry and action would take a few years to bear fruit; so it would be wise to bear in mind that making major changes in the occupation will take time. One cannot undo centuries of tradition with a few simple alterations.

Programs of teacher preparation could foster orientations of selectivity and personal flexibility; students who survive screening but prove incapable of change could be routed to other lines of work. Training experiences could be diversified to encourage resilience; assuming that teaching techniques will undergo accelerating rates of change, personal versatility should be an important quality in the future. Courses and fieldwork could be designed to expand the student's ability to cope with ambiguity and complexity and to acquaint students with a wide variety of teaching approaches.

We observed in chapter 3 that education students have usually internalized—in part unconsciously—the practices of their own teachers. If teachers are to adapt their behavior to changed circumstances, they will have to be freed of unconscious influences of this kind; what they bring from the past should be as thoroughly examined as alternatives in the present. There are perplexing psychological questions in this regard;

what teaching methods will be most effective in helping students to gain cognitive control over previous unconscious learning? How can this be done without exorbitant cost or the invasion of privacy? I suspect that ingenuity can provide ways to achieve this; the trick will be to get students to dredge up their previous experience and subject it to thoughtful scrutiny. Autobiographies of students might be used; microfilmed lessons by various teachers might help to stimulate recall. Novels and biographies could also evoke recollections. I believe that strenuous efforts should be made in this direction, for unless teachers-to-be are aware of their preconceptions and internalizations, the varieties of instructional methods they study may be wasted. The goal is not to have future teachers reject their entire past—that too would be wasteful. The aim should be to increase the person's awareness of his beliefs and preferences about teaching and to have him expose them to personal examination. At that point he can become truly selective and work out a synthesis of past and current practices in terms of his own values and understanding.

The preparation of teachers does not seem to result in the analytic turn of mind one finds in other occupations whose members are trained in colleges and universities. One notes, for example, that few teachers (I observed perhaps two or three in Five Towns) connect their knowledge of scientific method with practical teaching matters. One hears little mention of the disciplines of observation, comparison, rules of inference, sampling, testing hypotheses through treatment, and so forth. Scientific modes of reasoning and pedagogical practice seem compartmentalized; I observed this even among science teachers. This intellectual segregation puzzles me; those in other kinds of "people work" (e.g., clinical psychology, psychiatry, social work) seem more inclined to connect clinical issues with scientific modes of thought. This separation is relevant because it militates against the development of an effective technical culture and because its absence means that conservative doctrines receive less factual challenge; each teacher is encouraged to have a personal version of teaching truth. Perhaps the segregation arises from compartmentalized instruction; education students may not be expected to apply substantive knowledge in behavioral science to practical matters. It may reflect distrust of principles of pedagogy. Short of close observation of the process of teacher socialization, one hesitates to prescribe offsetting arrangements. It seems, however, that integration in formal preparation programs leaves much to be desired. Students should be pressed to forge more connections between theory and practice.

Since the apprenticeship in teaching is relatively undeveloped, it seems to offer opportunities for countering reflexive conservatism among teachers. The number and diversity of classroom mentors should be increased; teachers in training could be expected to observe, evaluate, and justify their assessments of a wide variety of teaching styles and approaches. They could be pressed to explicate the rationales which underlie their choices. Is that rationale consistent with what is known about human behavior? How does it connect with their expressed central values in teaching? Research could be an integral feature of such apprenticeships, and alternative patterns could be assessed to find which ones enhance flexibility, adaptability, and classroom effectiveness.

The current organization of teaching tasks fosters conservatism of outlook. Change is impeded by mutual isolation, vague yet demanding goals, dilemmas of outcome assessment, restricted in-service training, rigidities in assignment, and working conditions which produce a "more-of-the-same" syndrome among classroom teachers. My previous suggestions could be implemented by those charged with selecting and training teachers before employment; but alterations in working arrangements will obviously require the intervention of school officials and the accord of those who conduct negotiations for teachers.

One hears much these days about team teaching and differentiated staffing, but I believe the vast majority of classroom teachers continue to work apart from other adults. Opportunities for mutual consultation are limited during the working day, and contacts between teachers are peripheral to their major obligations. Much could be done to encourage mutual involvement in teaching affairs short of requiring that teachers share the actual instruction of students. (Where teachers choose teaming of a highly integrated type, this problem fades.) Arrangements could be made to "conference" individual students and bring various specialist observations to bear; teachers might learn something from physicians in this respect.[5] Time could be set aside to have teachers observe special lessons taught by peers and visitors. Exchange of classes (an informal practice some teachers engage in) could be encouraged on a school- and system-wide basis; time could be set aside for exchange teachers to compare their observations on class and individual phenomena. In short, serious efforts could be made to reduce the intellectual narrowness induced by mutual isolation and to foster closer exchange among faculty members. Reflexive conservatism is less readily sustained when people confront others who do things differently but well; the "critical mass" phenomenon applies to ideas as well as to atoms.

Some conservatism probably derives from the career frustrations of older teachers who feel stigmatized because they are still in the class-room; since change requires effort, teachers whose bitterness causes them to invest outside teaching reduce the adaptability of the occupation as a whole. Serious attention should be given to suggestions for careers *within* teaching—to progressions in status which can occur without shifting to administrative positions. Keppel and Benson have made provocative proposals in this regard; I do not think that their potential for reducing frustration and the attendant resistance to change has been sufficiently realized (Keppel 1961; Benson 1961a). Any full discussion of alternative career patterns in teaching is beyond our scope here, but problems associated with the prevailing career system need not be thought irrevocable. Ways could be found to differentiate teaching careers which would be acceptable to teacher organizations and school administrations.

We have seen that vague but demanding school goals create difficulties for classroom teachers; they contribute to a sense of nonaccomplishment. Utopian statements of intent probably press teachers back to conservative, relatively concrete outcomes; they discourage the risk-taking required for creativity. It seems clear that school officials should work out more effective patterns for goal-setting with teaching staffs; such vital activity should be considered an integral part of the teacher's working day.[6] I doubt that public opinion is much impressed by the extravagant claims made in many statements of school objectives; "oversell" contributes little. In fact, the growing tendency toward consumerism might be heeded by those who write such advertisements.

Uncertainty about classroom outcomes plagues many teachers, as we found in chapter 6. Depressed feelings about nonaccomplishment will not produce readiness for change; constriction is the more probable result. Greater clarity on this issue might release the energies of teachers who are currently troubled; they might question their assumption that the tried is true. More training in evaluation before teaching might help. But a better solution could lie in adding skilled personnel with training in evaluation at the school level. Some universities have found professors responsive to assistance of this kind; upon invitation, the consultant helps in formulating course objectives and devising ways to measure their realization. A voluntaristic approach might work well with public school teachers; it almost goes without saying that specialists of this kind should play no part in official evaluations of teachers. Their function would be to help individual teachers resolve some of their worries about their effectiveness; by helping them to target particular points for improvement, they could help to channel anxiety into productive effort. Coupled with clarification of organizational goals, the presence of such specialized competencies could reduce some of the ambiguity currently attached to teaching tasks.

"In-service training" in American public schools rarely rises above a superficial level; it seems to consist primarily of occasional short "workshops," faculty meetings, and infrequent visits to the classroom by central office supervisors. School systems generally have not assumed responsibility for systematically improving staff performance through serious training programs. I have speculated earlier that this stems from financial stringency and narrow localism; it may also be connected with a reluctance to invest in the future of staffs with high turnover. The lengthening average period of service among teachers, however, may change the attitudes of school boards and senior administrators; state and federal donors, moreover, are more likely to take a broad view of manpower resources in teaching. If school systems are to play a significant part in increasing the adaptability of teachers, in-service education will have to receive considerably more cultivation.

Teachers are like practitioners in other fields—they are reluctant to try new approaches unless they feel sure they can make them work and avoid damaging their reputations; obvious mistakes embarrass established practitioners in any field. To offset this concern, school systems could establish subschools where specialists work with classes of students on a rotation schedule while the regular teacher serves as an assistant (Lortie 1967). The subschool specialists could teach specialized content in a subject or use unfamiliar techniques with conventional content; the situation could be defined to avoid stigma for the regular classroom teacher. The periods of instruction (possibly a few weeks at a time) should be long enough to permit the regular teacher to gain mastery over the content or techniques involved—sufficient "mastery," that is, to permit him to use the approach himself. Over time, large numbers of regular classroom teachers would bcome familiar with a range of new ways of teaching; conservatism based on anxiety about trying the unfamiliar should be reduced. Serious efforts at in-service training could be the object of special grants and research monitoring; before-and-after observation of teacher attitudes and behavior could test the validity of the general approach and inform selection between specific kinds of alternatives within it.

(I wish to remind the reader at this point that I am concentrating on conservatism and the teacher ethos; I am not examining all sources of conservatism in schools. It is conventional knowledge within education, and I believe accurate, that imaginative teachers can be discouraged by cautious or rigid administrations. A thorough discussion of conservatism would have to deal with the constraints affecting school boards and administrators as well as teachers. Such analysis would take us afield in this context, but we should bear in mind that the orientations and sentiments of teachers are not the only obstacles to adaptability in public schools.)

I shall conclude this section with a few observations on the "more-of-the-same" syndrome discussed in chapter 7. Teachers have a built-in resistance to change because they believe that their work environment has never permitted them to show what they can really do. Many proposals for change strike them as frivolous—they do not address issues of boundedness, psychic rewards, time scheduling, student disruption, interpersonal support, and so forth. People interested in change should take such beliefs and preferences very seriously, for they reflect firsthand experience. If disruption is chronic, subtle differences in teaching technique will hardly make the difference. If teachers become discouraged because they are short of supplies or lack backing from key adults, they will not be enthusiastic over demanding new approaches.

The implications seem obvious: we must find out as much as we can about the relationship between the working conditions stressed by teachers and outcomes in the classroom. Large-scale projects should be undertaken in which teachers' preferences are scrupulously honored, and careful attention should be paid to their effects on teachers and students. Designs could be varied. In some instances, single-factor approaches could be used to test the importance of a particular condition. In others, various mixes could be instituted to find which combination is most productive. This kind of action and inquiry cannot be done cheaply or easily, and it will require deep commitment from participating school systems, teachers, parents, and others. Those conducting the project will have to be trusted as persons of extraordinary integrity and objectivity, since the findings will affect the interests of teachers and other parties. But we cannot know how significant teachers' beliefs are until they have received full and sustained testing. Furthermore, until advances in technical knowledge clearly make conventional approaches obsolete, we cannot ignore inquiry into the circumstances which influence learning under the usual conditions of schooling.

Teachers' Choice: The Question of Collegial Responsibility

The three scenarios project new demands on teachers as members of a common occupation. Cultural change will confront them with a plethora of possibilities; selections will somehow be made that will affect their work life. Changing reciprocities between school boards and teachers will produce demands for higher performance, and teachers will probably be pressed to participate in difficult personnel matters. Centralization would raise the issue of professional status and expectations for group self-control.

Teachers face dilemmas in these questions; they must choose which functions they will agree to perform and which they will leave to others. The decision to have others discharge these responsibilities is likely to produce greater exercise of vertical authority, challenging the autonomy they have fought so hard to attain. Yet more lateral control will also constrain individual freedom; group action will invariably mean less room for private choices. Willy-nilly, teachers will decide these questions in the years ahead; inaction will influence the course of affairs as much as positive programs.

These comments are addressed specifically to teachers and others who are interested in what would be required to move toward greater lateral organization of teaching. How could teacher individualism be modified to permit teachers, as members of a common group, to accept greater responsibility for the conduct of occupational and school affairs? What steps might assist such movement? I shall address two kinds of issues provoked by these questions. First, changes which might be made in the career system and, second, alterations in school organization which would reinforce conceptions of collegial responsibility and express it in action.

Teacher individualism is evident in the very inception of entry to the occupation; self-selection is a major feature of the recruitment system. Since entrants hold an image of the teacher based on earlier times, and since students see little of the informal collegial interactions which occur, entrants are likely to perceive teaching as a highly individualistic affair. To my knowledge, no special effort is made to offset that conception upon entry to teacher training, nor is effort made to identify which applicants have demonstrated capacity for efficacious peer relationships. Those who wish to populate teaching with more collegially oriented persons could begin at this point; special programs could be instituted in which would-be participants are screened along such lines. There are indications that personality and social experience play an important part in individual preferences for working alone, under close supervision, or alongside peers (Whyte 1955). Psychological testing and review of autobiographical data could be used to identify applicants who are most likely to favor collegial modes of operation. (As in screening for conservatism, research observations could play an important role in clarifying these issues.)

Collegial responsibility would require that working teachers come to trust one another—to be ready to put more of their fates into their colleagues' hands. One supposes that the capacity for such trust, and the correlated readiness to engage in decisions about peers, can be learned through programs directed toward those ends. Undergraduate and graduate preparation of teachers, for example, could be refashioned to give students more experience in group effort. Some professional schools rely heavily upon instruction of this sort; medical schools organize anatomy classes into small teams, architecture courses involve group projects, and military academies organize their instruction around extremely complex sets of peer relationships. The affective, experiential basis for later colleagueship is implied by the regular instructional program; intendedly or not, students learn to rely upon each other in the normal course of events. Such instructional modes could be introduced into schools of education. When the outcomes of group efforts have consequences for individual participants, a premium is placed on learning how to work effectively with others, how to select an effective leader, and so on. Conventional coursework in education, as in the arts and sciences generally, underscores individualistic modes of work in a zero-sum competitive race for grades; modifying such arrangements to include sharing of tasks and rewards could prepare teachers-to-be for closer working relationships in schools.

Collegiality may be induced through informal relationships brought about by tough faculty demands; my earlier comments on "shared ordeal" pointed up the solidarities encouraged by common confrontation of difficult tasks. Schools of education are rarely reported to demand difficult assignments and examinations; interesting research could be done on the apparent "softness" of their curricula and grading practices. Attempts to be considerate of students may sacrifice long-term benefits to current ease; value may lie in informal cooperation (e.g., study groups) stimulated by the necessity of meeting challenges posed by demanding professors. In times as permissive as ours (e.g., pass-fail grading), this is truly a countervailing suggestion; but people in schools of education who favor greater teacher collegiality might consider making sterner demands on their students.

The way most beginners are inducted into teaching leaves them doubly alone; they confront a "sink-or-swim" situation in physical isolation and get only occasional cultural support in the process. Teams seem particularly appropriate for inducting newcomers to classroom work; when neophytes learn to teach in the company of colleagues, sensitivity to the presence of other adults should decline. (I suspect that some of the teachers' preference for boundedness reflects lack of experience in working closely with other teachers in the classroom; we need research on this point.) The concept of sharing responsibility with colleagues could be underlined if *teams* were held accountable for producing particular results; experienced teachers would have a stake in the performance of newcomers and should be readier to help them improve their work. Induction as a member of a team is less wasteful than current arrangements in which beginning teachers who have trouble with discipline can be "written off"; working with supportive peers, some teachers might learn to handle classes after initial difficulties were overcome. Teams could help beginners ride out the rough spots while still holding them to group standards.

Teachers have historically held back from claiming jurisdiction over personnel decisions; Sharma (1955) found, for example, that very few teachers wanted to participate in decisions on promotion to tenure and allied matters. Such reluctance is understandable given the nature of relationships under cellular organization; teachers see little of one another's work and prefer to keep themselves free of collegial surveillance. But pressure to ensure adequate performance within the peer group will probably make it more difficult for teachers to avoid such responsibility (and vulnerability) in the future. Career changes of the sort we have described might make it easier for them to accept the dual obligation of submitting to collegial review and participating in it themselves.

Teachers could learn ways of dealing with these issues by examining practices in university faculties. Senior colleagues accept responsibility for assessing the work of juniors; their recommendations normally carry great weight, although they are usually reviewed by senior administrators. (Similar career mechanisms are found within medicine and law; senior practitioners mediate the careers of younger persons.) In public schools, however, it is not clear that experience carries deference from juniors; I mentioned that older teachers are sometimes depreciated (chapter 4). This problem suggests that career stages within teaching could help the occupation cope with questions of internal control; it would create an internal elite which could assume the burden of personnel judgments on behalf of the occupation.

Responsibility for the performance of peers will probably be more readily accepted where teachers work together in highly integrated teams. Members of teams have more at stake in the performance of fellow teachers and have considerable opportunity to observe their work activities. Although discharging a probationary teacher is undoubtedly difficult for team teachers, the consequences of failing to do so can be painful; there is motivation for making a difficult decision. The same principle applies to the issue of team leadership; I suspect that where teaming intensifies and persists, team teachers will claim the right to participate in the selection of their leaders. If boards hold teachers accountable for performance (on individual or group grounds), teachers will assert the right to some voice in conditions which affect their productivity; technical leadership will probably figure in such negotiations.

It appears that teacher organizations have refused to exercise discipline over members, alleging that this is the responsibility of management. Teachers can continue to take that stance, relying upon "due process" to protect themselves from arbitrary dismissal or other sanctions applied by management. But such a position reflects continuation of past traditions of negative power rather than the breaking of new ground and gives teachers little capacity to initiate improvements by assuming new functions. Should the trend toward collegiality take hold, some teachers will probably want to have more say in hiring and firing and promotion decisions. If they are highly invested in the organization, they will seek to advance their views in policy decisions. It is perhaps too soon to design ways to accomplish this, but teachers may find that they will need additional kinds of organization to achieve such purposes, particularly if leaders of bargaining units refuse to participate. Teachers might investigate faculty senates, medical executive committees, and other mechanisms designed to deal with policy rather than welfare issues; it is not clear that the adversary approach used in bargaining is well suited to policy-making on instructional issues. Various proposals have been developed for equivalent mechanisms for schools, and some school systems are trying to make them work (Benson 1961*b*, p. 316; Perry and Wildman, p. 236). They should be closely observed by educational researchers.

Some readers may feel that any modification of individualism is undesirable; we live in times when a frightening array of forces seems to threaten individuality. I understand that concern, for I share it. Care should be taken if teachers decide to move toward closer collegial relationships—ecstatic calls for "unity" and urgings to orthodoxy should be resisted. Teachers who prefer to work alone should be fully defended against the necessity of joining their peers; tendencies to enforce petty norms should be identified and rejected. But I prefer the vision of strong collegial ties over complete reliance on vertical authority; as Blau and Scott (1962) point out, lateral groups are more effective in finding fresh solutions and hammering out policies than are hierarchies. The strength of hierarchical organization lies in coordinating the efforts of diverse individuals. Although we will always need some coordination in public schools, my conception of education is that it should be closer to the deliberations of a legislature than the efficiency of an army or business enterprise. In the long run, schools will probably be more diversified and pluralistic if teachers play a major part in their operation.

Teachers and Technical Knowledge

Teachers have occupied a subordinate position in matters of technical knowledge. They are prepared for their work by professors, and once they are employed, major instructional decisions are made by school boards and administrators. Yet teachers are separating themselves into a distinct group by aggressiveness in collective bargaining and by loosening their associational ties with administrators and other school personnel. Our scenarios assume that these trends will continue and that teachers will be increasingly differentiated from others who work in schools.

It appears that technical knowledge will play a progressively more important part in the collective life of teachers. They will have to select from a growing number of options resulting from research and development and find ways to adapt and refine ideas and practices in light of their interests. More stringent expectations for teacher performance will place technique at the heart of many controversies. Teachers will have to find ways to bring expertise to bear on questions of their "accountability." The condition of teaching knowledge will affect their chances of weathering centralization without losing valued working conditions. Teachers face a sharp problem: How are they to overcome the record of intellectual dependency and adapt to changing needs? What steps might they take to prepare for independence in a future filled with controversy?

Action could take place on three levels: it could involve classroom teachers, specialists in inquiry, and teacher organizations. Efforts on these levels could get teachers started on the shift to more active participation in shaping their technical culture.

Movement to a greater degree of intellectual independence will confront internal obstacles; the ethos of the occupation is tilted against engagement in pedagogical inquiry. Reflexive conservatism implicitly denies the significance of technical knowledge, assuming that energies should be centered on realizing conventional goals in known ways. Individualism leads to distrust of the concept of shared knowedge; it portrays teaching as the expression of individual personality. Presentist orientations retard making current sacrifices for later gains; inquiry rests on the opposite value. Whatever changes in recruitment, socialization, and work organization may foster adaptability, a closer sense of guild and of commitment to the occupation's future will contribute to resolving the issue of teacher participation in building their knowledge base. Teachers' self-conceptions will have to change if they are to become more independent in their intellectual stance. We can see the years of dependency reflected in a shocking gap: How many famous teachers (classroom teachers, not professors or administrators) can the reader think of? I doubt that he can think of many; it is unlikely that the list will include any teachers who are remembered for technical contributions to the art of teaching. A teacher today can be considered outstanding by those who are familiar with his work without being thought to have made a single contribution to knowledge of teaching in general; the ablest people in the occupation are not expected to add to the shared knowledge of the group. There is, in short, no tradition honoring contributions to the craft; values supporting practitioner participation in development will have to be introduced and reinforced if intellectual autonomy is to get under way. Teachers will have to believe themselves capable of such work; they will have to surmount decades of subordination to academics and school officials. It is obvious that we cannot expect rapid or large-scale change in this domain; progress will probably be the work of a small but creative minority.

More teachers will take a hand in assessing pedagogical developments and advancing knowledge if selection and training are focused on such ends. Selection procedures could be adjusted to the need for inquiry-oriented teachers; entrants who show promise of making such contributions could be preferred. (Again, special training projects could center on this objective.) Instructors who are concerned with the state of technical knowledge in teaching could devise strategies for enhancing the relevant capacities; courses could concentrate on the intellectual skills needed for tough-minded assessment and imaginative inquiry. They might, for example, emphasize accurate observation, conscientious recording, habits of searching for alternative explanations, techniques for assessing data, and ability to write clearly. Students could be urged to examine various types of criticism, from literary criticism to social science methodology. They could be encouraged to range afield in search of useful kinds of conceptualization, as in the study of distributive justice, the analysis of communication, small group theory, leadership behavior, and any number of fields whose potential for understanding classrooms has been unrealized.

There are affinities between the analytic orientation I urged earlier and the preparation of critical, inquiring classroom teachers. Emphasis on observing teachers and students and reviewing one's impressions can serve to enlighten practice and can also lead to researchable ideas; seminars where students explore alternative solutions to problems can provoke hypotheses for investigation. Case analysis and review of microfilmed teaching can be used in research as well as in clinical preparation; rotating apprenticeships, in broadening the awareness of the student teacher, can serve inquiry as well as performance goals. This is not to say that there are no differences between analytic modes of practitioner preparation and research orientations. But the affinities are also genuine and can be capitalized upon; preparing critical, intellectually curious teachers is part of the process of producing practitioners who will be capable of contributing knowledge to the field.

There are probably school systems today which would welcome programs of inquiry in which teachers could play a part; government and foundation grants could facilitate their cooperation by releasing time for teachers and bringing scarce resources to bear on such efforts. Work schedules could be arranged to permit for planning inquiries, gathering data, and writing reports. Supportive school systems might be prepared to reorganize reward systems so that collegial contributions would be encouraged. Sponsors of such programs could help to link them for mutual support and stimulation and arrange for publication and dissemination of the results. Demonstration projects could offset the seeming utopianism of proposing that teachers could engage in direct efforts to improve the technical knowledge of the occupation.

Although one hesitates to propose creating another specialty, there are strong arguments for developing a cadre of teacher-researchers committed to working on classroom problems. Universities today draw off a considerable proportion of the research talent within teaching; graduate schools often serve to route able persons away from schools and into central offices of school districts and university posts. The doctorate usually signals the end of a teacher's involvement with classroom issues; it is as if the day-to-day problems of pedagogy were somehow less important than school operations or university interests. I suspect that much of what we hear from teachers about research being "impractical" and "irrelevant" is true; little educational inquiry is rooted in a concern for the actual difficulties facing classroom teachers.

Great care would have to be exercised in identifying and preparing people for the role of teacher-researcher; they could, if properly selected and prepared, become a corps of futurists within a present-oriented system. I conceive of the role as both practical and visionary; teacher-researchers would work directly on teaching problems while searching for better solutions. They could initiate inquiries of their own and assist teachers who wish to work on interests they may have. (I learned in Dade County that a surprisingly high proportion of teachers thought they would enjoy classroom-related research.[7]) Teacher-researchers could form a liaison between classroom teachers and outside researchers in research institutes and universities. They could channel ideas for research and disseminate useful findings.

Technical questions on the appropriate preparation of teacher-researchers could probably be resolved more easily than complex issues of role, school-university relationships, and personal commitment. Most universities today could assemble the needed content through a judicious blending of study in education and the disciplines.

The futures projected by the scenarios are complex; teachers will need knowledge and information attuned to their interests in what will likely be protracted periods of conflict and intellectual confusion. Although individual teachers and teacher-researchers could provide a steady stream of useful insights, the occupation will also need large-scale projects directed toward the assessment of novel instructional strategies, organizational changes, political movements, and the like. The logical candidates for performing this type of research and evaluation are teacher organizations. They are large enough to command the resources needed, stable enough to provide continuity, and, because of their membership, committed to the pursuit of teacher interests. Central units (e.g., state and national headquarters) will be called upon to provide essential information and scarce skills to local bodies of teachers; there will be ample demand for their services. I expect, therefore, that we shall see considerable growth in the research activities of teacher organizations in the years ahead.

Teacher organizations, moreover, could undertake long-range, technically oriented inquiries in which classroom teachers participate. Take, for example, the problem of inadequate codification we discussed in chapter 3. Who is better situated to initiate practice-oriented, large-scale inquiry than teacher organizations? They can solicit and organize contributions from their membership in the full expectation of cooperation; their purposes are not suspect. They need not be inhibited by the fear of being criticized for being "too practical": their constituency expects it. Since their working committees are composed of classroom teachers, they are not likely to support "irrelevant" or arcane investigations. Teacher organizations can perform research services in a variety of ways; they will serve teachers best if they attack technical as well as welfare issues.

Teaching is unique. No other occupation can claim a membership of over two million college graduates and tens of thousands with advanced degrees. To expect teachers to contribute to the development of their occupational knowledge seems reasonable; to the extent that they do, their future standing and work circumstances will benefit.

Appendix A
Sample Description

Five Towns

The ninety-four interviews which constitute the Five Towns sample were obtained through a two-step sampling procedure which combined judgment in the selection of school systems and randomness in the selection of respondents within those systems. The primary goal in designing the sample was to ensure a range of socioeconomic settings and grade level, as previous research indicated that both had significance for teacher roles. The design called for a five-cell sample (with equal numbers in each cell) of elementary and senior high school teachers from upper-income communities, junior high school teachers from the middle range, and elementary and senior high school teachers from lower-income settings. I decided that the systems involved should be participants in the New England School Development Council, since officials of the council could help me gain full cooperation in the study. This decision introduces an unknown bias, although the diversity of systems participating in the council suggests that the bias is limited.

In order to select school systems, all cities and towns (except Boston) in the Boston Metropolitan Area were arrayed in terms of household income (1960) from high to low, and the resulting list was divided into three equal parts. Two systems were chosen from the upper third, one from the middle (it was close to the median income for the Boston metropolitan area), and two from the lower part of the list. The system choices were based in part on the judgment of several consultants familiar with the area; I asked them to advise me on which systems were typical of their stratum. In three cells, teachers in all relevant types of schools were interviewed, but in two of them I made special provision to ensure that the schools involved were consistent with the socioeconomic criterion. This meant dropping one low-income school from the upper-income elementary cell and concentrating on three schools in the lower-income elementary cell; in the latter instance, the superintendent identified the three schools located in the lowest income neighborhoods. The teachers interviewed, therefore, came from thirteen schools which ranged across the income strata; they worked in six elementary, five junior high, and two senior high schools.

A strictly random procedure was used in selecting teachers within the schools. In the upper-income high school cell, twenty names were randomly selected from a container containing the names of all teachers. In the other cells, all teachers were listed alphabetically and selected on the basis of the interval which would produce twenty teachers from the system. The sample which was drawn included one hundred names; the final interviewing sample fell short by six persons.

Most of the interviews were conducted in the summer of 1963, although a few were done earlier and a few later. All were tape-recorded. Interviews were conducted, on the basis of respondent preference, in one of three places—the school, the respondent's home, or an office in Cambridge. The high yield (94 out of 100) was the result of cooperation from NESDEC, the help given by school administrators, careful efforts to prepare teachers for the interview through faculty meetings, and the persistence of the interviewers.

The sample design obviously limits its representativeness. It does not include teachers from rural settings or from the central city, although it does include teachers who work in industrialized areas. Senior high school teachers are overrepresented; consequently, elementary and junior high school teachers are underrepresented. Given these and other limitations, it is somewhat surprising how frequently the distributions found in Five Towns coincide with those reported in national probability samples. In any event, I recognize the limits imposed by the sample and have made serious efforts to honor those limitations in the text. Discussion there centers on the identification of themes; where distributions are referred to, it should be understood that they are tentative and require additional research. I have included only those which are, in my judgment, sufficiently provocative to merit attention as the basis for continued inquiry.

Dade County

In the course of a consultative project conducted in Dade County, Florida, it became necessary to conduct a survey of all professional staff in that large school system. It was possible to include some items which checked the earlier work done in Five Towns. The cooperation given by the school system was extraordinary; teachers, as well as administrators, librarians, and so forth, were gathered at twelve locations and filled out the questionnaire during school hours. The number of teachers filling out the questionnaire represented the normal attendance pattern of teachers during a work day. The survey was conducted in 1964.

The Miami area is a better-than-average site for ascertaining teacher attitudes in two major respects. First, over five thousand persons work as teachers throughout the various subcommunities in Dade County. Second, the characteristics of these teachers reflect the great migration into southern Florida. Fewer than 25 percent (23.7) of the respondents were born in Florida; 21.3 percent were born in other parts of the South, 5.2 percent in New England, 24.6 percent in New York, New

Jersey, Delaware, or Pennsylvania, and 6.8 percent in a state west of the Mississippi. This teaching staff probably has one of the most diverse regional origins among large school systems.

The questions alluded to in the text are presented in Appendix B.

Appendix B
The Questions

1. The Five Towns Interview Outline

(Quickly)   1. In what year were you born?
2. In what community were you born?
3. Where were you raised? (If any doubt on definition, accept as answer place where most years before sixteen were spent.)
4. In what occupation was your father engaged at the time that you began college?
5. (Ask of all except those with clear "Miss" designation.) Are you now or have you been married? Are there any children? If children, how many?

CHOICE   6. At what point did you make the definite decision to enter
(Not too   teaching?
slowly)   What were the circumstances at the time? (This is a "keep-going" probe to get the respondent going after the sharp question-answer opening. Be sure to slow down here.)
7. What were the major attractions that teaching held for you at the point where you decided to enter it?
8. What persons do you think influenced you in your decision to become a teacher? (Probes: Family...; Teachers...; Others...)
9. What other occupations did you consider seriously as possibilities?
10. Looking back today, what do you think were the most important factors in your decision to become a teacher?
11. Can you recall what you thought about yourself when you decided to enter teaching? What I mean is, Can you remember what qualities you felt would fit well with teaching as a line of work for you?

248

12. In what ways is teaching different from what you expected when you made the decision to go into the field? (How is it better than what you expected? How is it worse than what you expected?)
13. Where did you receive your secondary schooling?
14. What college(s) did you attend?   What course of study did
    (Undergraduate only)   you take there? In what year

    ————————————   did you get your B.A.?

    ————————————   —————   —————

15. How did you come to attend (*name of college*)? (Limited Probing)
16. Have you done any work since your bachelor's degree? (If yes) Where was that?

    ————————————   Degree and date if any.

    ————————————   —————

17. Are you taking any courses at the present time? (If yes) *Where* and *what*.
18. Could you list—we'll do this quickly—the positions (of any kind other than summer jobs)—that you have held since graduation from college?

School system and school or organization (Get community)	Specific Position (Subject, grade, level)	Years there
1. ———————————	———————	————
2. ———————————	———————	————
3. ———————————	———————	————
4. ———————————	———————	————
5. ———————————	———————	————

ETC.

19. (For current job only.)
    How did you come to leave ——— for ———?
    How did you hear of the opening at ——————?
20. Let's see, you began teaching here in ———. You mentioned that you came here because ———. Did anything else attract you to this system and school?
21. Would you describe your position here please? (Get as much as possible on grade, "level," etc., and any extracurricular activities.)
22. How important is it to you to teach (elementary) (junior high) (senior high) students? How would you feel about teaching (Omit own, of course)
    a. Adults in evening classes
    b. College (age) students
    c. Senior High
    d. Junior high
    e. Elementary
23. ELEMENTARY
    a. What part of the day do you consider the best for really getting something across to the students?

Appendix B

b. Do you tend to schedule any particular subject or activity at that time?

JUNIOR AND SENIOR HIGH

*How would you feel about teaching subjects other than — — —, — — —? Are there others you would like to teach?

(*If not clear* that teacher sees self a specialist or generalist, ask the following. Is it fair to say that you see yourself as a specialist in (subject)? Is it fair to say that you see yourself as a specialist in (age level of students)?

24. Of the various things you do as a teacher, which do you consider to be the most important?

25. To what extent are you free to do (above) more-or-less as you think best?

26. If you were to get a gift of ten more hours a week (with the provision that it be used for work), which of the following would you choose to spend that extra time on?

(CARD 1)

1. Curriculum committee
2. Private preparation
3. Public relations
4. In-class teaching
5. School operations
6. Parent conferences
7. Counseling

27. Since we're talking about time, I wonder if you could give me an approximate picture of how you distribute your time during an average school week?

First, how much time do you spend on the school premises?——
(How many hours?)

How do you distribute school time between:

1. Actual classroom teaching   ———
2. Direct preparation for class such as lesson
   planning, setting up equipment, etc.   ———
3. Grading papers, etc.   ———
4. Routine paper work (administrative)   ———
5. Seeing individual students   ———
6. Extracurricular and study halls, etc.   ———
7. Meetings of one kind or another   ———
8. Other—specify   ———

   ———   ———

   ———   ———

How much time, including weekends, do you spend working at home in the average week?   ———

How do you spend that time—on what tasks?

Do you spend time on school work other than at school or at home—such as at meetings of professional groups or at classes, for example? If yes, how many?   ———

That makes a total of — — — per average week. Does that sound about right?

250

28. How does your position compare with that of other teachers in the amount of work it calls for? Would you say that you work harder, about the same, or a little less than most teachers in the school? (Kinds of effort other than time)

(Crucial—
slow,
relaxed)

29. Of the teachers you had yourself at one time or another, which do you consider were outstanding? Could you describe one of them for me?

(Probe for outcomes, after general)

30. Of teachers you know who are working today, are there any you consider to be outstanding teachers? Would you describe one for me?

(Probe for outcomes, after general)

31. Every so often, teachers tell me, they have a really *good* day. Could you tell me what a good day is like for you? What happens?

(Probe for outcomes, after general)

32. Please recall some occasion when you felt especially proud of something you achieved as a teacher. Please tell me about it. Are there other things you have experienced which have made you feel especially proud?

33. Most of us have some occasions (we hope rare) when we feel ashamed about something we have done. What kinds of things may have happened which you regretted having done?

34. I know it's not easy to state clearly, but would you try to explain to me what you try most to achieve as a teacher? What are you really trying to do most of all?

(Full, neutral probing)

(Slow)

35. What changes—of any kind that occur to you—would allow you to do a better job of what you are really trying to do? (T.L.C.— "tender loving care")

36. Do you experience difficulty in assessing your own work? What I mean is, is it ever hard for you to tell how well you are doing as a teacher? Why is it difficult? What is difficult about it? Why do some teachers find it hard? (T.L.C.)

37. What are the major ways in which you tell whether you are doing the kind of job you want to do? What do you watch as indication of your effectiveness?

38. If you wanted to ask someone else to help you in your own *private* assessment of your work, who would you likely turn to?

39. We hear a lot these days about the problems teachers have, but there are a million and a half people working at teaching in the United States. What do you think attracts and holds people in public school teaching?

(Not too long)

40. As far as you personally are concerned, what are the really important satisfactions which you receive in your work as a teacher? (General, get as many as possible)

(Steady probing)

Of those you have mentioned, *which* do you feel *is the most important* satisfaction?

41. Have you found any satisfaction in teaching which you didn't expect to find when you made up your mind to enter the field?
42. What are the things which are "fun" in the course of your work?

(CARD 2)

43. Purely hypothetically, let's say that you have received a number of job offers at the same time. Which of these would interest you? Would you rank them in the order of their attractiveness? (1st, 2nd, 3d, etc.) (Ask *why* the first three choices are attractive.)
    1. Students and other conditions
    2. Salary
    3. Professional prestige
    4. Administrative influence
    5. Special need
    6. Professional freedom

    Are there any factors not on this list you might consider in looking at a new job?

(CARD 3)

44. Which of these statements (hand card to respondent) comes closest to describing your feelings about teaching.
    1. I am *extremely satisfied* with teaching as my occupation.
    2. I am *very satisfied* with teaching as my occupation.
    3. I am *more satisfied than not* with teaching as my occupation.
    4. I am equally satisfied and dissatisfied—I guess I'm in the middle.
    5. I am more dissatisfied than satisfied with teaching as my occupation.
    6. I am very dissatisfied with teaching as my occupation.
    7. I am extremely dissatisfied with teaching as my occupation.

    (Get respondent, if possible, to comment on his choice depending on the nature of the choice.)
45. Can you think of any changes—of any kind—which might increase your satisfaction with teaching as an occupation?
46. I guess no line of work is perfect. What are the things which you like least about teaching? What are the things which bother you most in your work?

    (*Full probing*)
47. What do you think you lose by being a teacher rather than in some other occupation?
48. What are the little things that irritate you in your work?
49. What kind of *knowledge* do you think a teacher must possess—what does he have to know—to be able to do a good job of teaching of the kind you do?

    What is *most* important?
50. What must a teacher be able to *do*—what skills must he or she possess—to do a good job of the kind of teaching you do? Which is *most* important?
51. What experiences do you think have been most influential in teaching you how to teach?
52. Have you ever experienced anything that might be called a "turning point" where you sort of knew you had become a "pro" as a teacher?

The Questions

(*Probe*)
53. What would you say are your greatest strengths as a teacher?
54. Some teachers seem to emphasize the importance of warmth and closeness to students while others seem to stress the importance of the teacher's getting students to work effectively. Which of the two (I imagine they're both important) do you consider *more* important?

Warmth and closeness . . . 1
Getting work done 2

(CARD 4)
55. If you could choose your students in the coming year, which of the following would you select? Why?
    1. A group of students whose emotional needs are a challenge to the teacher.
    2. A group of nice kids from average homes who are respectful and hard-working.
    3. A group of creative and intellectually demanding students calling for special effort.
    4. A group of underprivileged children from difficult homes for whom school can be a major opportunity.
    5. Children of limited ability who need unusual patience and sympathy—sometimes they're called "slow learners."
    Which would be your second choice? Why?
    Do you usually prefer ———?
56. What kind of reputation would you most like to have with the classes and students you deal with?
    (*Probe*)
57. What "facilities" are important to you in your teaching? What I mean is what "things"—books or equipment or labs or whatever —really make a difference in the kind of job you can do?
    (*Probe*)
58. What difference does the presence or absence of (above) make to you as a teacher?
59. Some teachers say that it is important to them to have a room which is theirs to deal with as they see fit. Is this true of you? Why is it important to have such a room?

PARENTS
60. How many parents, on the average, did you see in the course of a month last year? ——— What were the occasions on which you saw parents?
61. Would you like to see the parents of your pupils oftener or less often? Why is that?
62. What, from your point of view as a teacher, makes a "good parent?"

GUIDANCE, IF PRESENT (ELEMENTARY SUPERVISORS)
63. In what ways, if any, do (guidance people) really help you in your work as a teacher?
64. In what ways, if any, do (guidance people) make your work harder or less effective?

253

Appendix B

OTHER TEACHERS

65. Do you ever work together with other teachers, or do you teach
more-or-less alone?
(If together) On what sorts of things do you work with other
teachers? Would you like to do less, about the same, or more
work with other teachers? Why?
(If alone) Would you like to work more closely with other teachers?
Why? *(If yes)* On what sorts of things would you like to work with
other teachers?

66. Some teachers say that they prize their "autonomy." Is this something that is important to you? In what ways is it important?

67. Some teachers say that all members of a teaching staff should be
equals. Others say that there should be ranks of teachers from
"beginner" to "master"—similar to the university system of
lecturers, assistant, associate, and full professors. How do you feel
about this?

68. What, in your opinion, makes a teacher a really good "fellow
teacher"? How does a good fellow teacher act?

PRINCIPAL

69. Some people think that a school should be operated like a well-run
business or government agency where everyone's responsibility is
clearly stated and the lines of authority are sharp and clear. Others
think that schools should be organized loosely and that relationships among members of the staff should tend toward equality
rather than differences in authority. Which of these two views
comes closer to being yours?
Stated responsibility and clear authority 1
Looser organization tending to equality 2
Why do you choose (1) (2)?

70. What do you consider to be the major responsibilities of the
school principal toward you?

71. What do you consider to be your major responsibilities to the
school principal?

72. In one research project, it was found that teachers consider the
principal an important factor in choosing between possible
positions. What questions would you ask about the principal if
you were considering working in a new school?

73. Some say that our schools emphasize the traditions of our way of
life and that they should change very slowly. Others say that our
society is changing very rapidly and that our schools should adjust
to these changes and innovate constantly. Which of these two
positions comes closer to expressing your view?
Schools should change slowly 1
Schools should change constantly . . . 2
Could you tell me more about your views on this question?

74. If you had the opportunity to bring about change in our public
schools, what *single* change would you most like to see brought
about?

254

75. How do you feel about teaching machines? Do you think that they offer a great deal of promise, possibly some promise or no promise at all?
     Great deal... 1
     Some....... 2
     None....... 3
     Why?
76. How about television in the classroom? Do you think that it offers a great deal of promise, possibly some promise or no promise at all?
     Great 1
     Possibly some... 2
     None at all..... 3
     Why?
77. What is your opinion about these new curricula being worked out by college professors and teachers working together? I refer to the new curricula in physics, mathematics, and chemistry and to talk about the same thing in other fields on all levels. Do they hold great promise, possibly some promise or no promise at all?
     Great 1
     Possibly some... 2
     None 3
78. We hear a good deal these days about "merit pay." How do you feel about it?
     (Full Probing)
79. Perhaps you have heard some talk about team teaching. From what you have heard about it, does it appeal to you or not? Why?
80. Are you a member or at all active in professional organizations and other activities connected with teaching?
     (List memberships and indications of more than membership status.)
81. What are your major interests and activities outside of teaching?

CARD 5

82. Here's a card which, in rather crude fashion, is supposed to represent your total life interests. How many of the eight sections would you say "belong" to your work as a teacher? [Card bears a circle divided into eighths]
83. If you had it to do all over again, what occupation would you choose?
84. Where do you hope to be, professionally, in
     5 years?
     15 years?
     25 years? (Of those under 35 only)
85. All in all, how would you say that you have done in teaching?
     Would you say that you have enjoyed great success, some success, average success, or less-than-average success in your career as a teacher?

255

Appendix B

Great success 1
Above average success . . . 2
Average success 3
Below average success . . . 4
What went through your mind, if I may ask, as you chose one of the alternatives to my question?
I would like to end by asking you two factual questions . . .
86. What religion were you brought up in? Are you active in church (synagogue) affairs today?
87. What is your national origin on your father's side? Generation?
88. In special cases.
Do you happen to know what your father's annual income was when you entered college?

2. The Relevant Dade County Questions

13. Some school systems, eager to implement board policy with maximum efficiency, develop many rules and a definite system of authority. Other school systems, afraid that rules and authority may hamper creativity, emphasize freedom for members of their professional staff, sometimes at the expense of efficiency and the implementation of board policy.
In your opinion, what is the main emphasis in Dade County schools?
Board policy and efficiency through rules and authority are clearly emphasized 1
There is more emphasis on board policy and efficiency than on creativity 2
The two emphases are evenly mixed 3
There is more emphasis on creativity than on board policy and efficiency 4
Creativity through freedom for members of the professional staff is clearly emphasized 5

14. What do you think Dade County school *should* do? Do you think that they should put more emphasis on board policy and efficiency, do about what they are doing now, or put more emphasis on freedom and creativity?
More emphasis on board policy and efficiency 1
Do about what they are doing now 2
More emphasis on freedom and creativity 3

37. As far as getting ideas and insights on my work is concerned, I find that the following is the *most useful* of all.
In-service courses given by the school system 1
Informal conversations with colleagues and friends 2
Educational magazines and books 3
Courses I have taken in a college or university 4
Meetings I have attended in Dade County schools 5
Meetings I have traveled to attend outside of Dade County 6
My immediate superior 7

38. Persons in education sometimes complain that they must be careful not to do

256

things, publicly, which they themselves believe are acceptable but others might not. In terms of your experience in Dade County, which of the following comes closest to your feelings on this matter?

I feel I must be very careful 1
I feel some pressure to be careful 2
Sometimes I feel pressure, sometimes I do not 3
I feel relatively little pressure to be careful 4
I feel no special pressure to be careful 5

39. Teachers may receive assistance in curriculum and methods from a variety of sources. In your opinion, which of the following provides the *most* help to the classroom teacher? (Please circle only one.)

The principal 1
Central office supervisors 2
District director(s) 3
Assistant principal for curriculum or curriculum assistant 4
The department or grade chairman (or head) 5
Other teachers in the school 6
Other: please write in 7

40. Let's suppose there were effective arrangements in the Dade County schools for following up on research ideas you might develop. What do you think your reaction would be to such arrangements?

I would definitely be enthusiastic about doing some research 1
I might well be interested in participating 2
I might or might not be interested in participating 3
I probably would not be interested in participating 4
I would definitely be uninterested in doing research 5

43. Although it is difficult to know for sure how one is going to react, what do you think you would do if you were invited to accept a position *one step up* in the Dade County schools within the next five years?

I would accept eagerly and readily 1
I would probably accept 2
I would hesitate and wonder what to do 3
I would probably refuse 4
I would definitely refuse 5

44. Quite apart from whether you are interested in promotion or not, do you think it is likely that you will be invited to consider it within the next five years?

Yes, I think it is very likely 1
Yes, I think it is somewhat likely 2
Chances are around 50-50 3
No, it is somewhat unlikely 4
No, it is entirely unlikely 5

T 1 How do good teachers, in your opinion, gauge the effectiveness of their teaching? Which of the following is the good teacher most likely to rely on as

Appendix B

indication? Good teachers rely *most* on:

The reactions of other teachers who are familiar with their work and
their students 1
The opinions expressed by the students generally 2
Their general observation of students in light of the teacher's conception
of what should be learned 3
The assessments made by the principal 4
The assessments made by a special "supervisor" or similar person 5
The results of objective examinations and various other tests 6
The reactions of students' parents 7
Other: please write in: 8

T 3 If I had to describe myself as tending toward more emphasis in my teaching,
I would say ...

I'm pretty much the "no-nonsense, get-the-learning-of-subject-matter-
done" kind of teacher 7
I tend toward the subject matter emphasis, but think other things are
important, too 8
I guess I'm about 50-50 on this 9
I tend away from emphasis on subject matter, as I consider other things
more important 0
I think that emphasis on subject matter is the mark of a poor teacher ... X

T 4 If you were to receive a gift of ten hours more a week, but with the provision
that it be spent on work, which of the following would you choose to spend
that time on *first* (Please circle only one.)

Service on a school curriculum committee 1
Preparing lessons, reading and studying, and reviewing student work ... 2
Enhancing the community's assessment of the school by working on
exhibits, parent meetings, etc. 3
Teaching students either in groups or in individual conferences 4
Improving school operations by work on scheduling, discipline, student
government or similar matters 5
Discussing student work and problems with their parents 6
Counseling individual students on problems they consider important ... 7

T 5 Some teachers think they can assess how their teaching is going. Others feel
that it is very difficult. What do you think?

I believe that it is relatively easy to know when one is really teaching
effectively 1
I believe that it is possible to know one's own effectiveness *at times* 2
I believe that it is *relatively difficult* to know when one is really
teaching effectively 3

T 7 Some teachers think it would be a genuine loss for them to leave the
classroom to enter administrative work in schools. Other teachers feel that it
would be a gain in that it would broaden the part they play in instruction.
Which of the following comes the closest to expressing *your* feeling on the
matter?

I would feel real loss if I left the classroom for administration 1
I would feel some loss if I left the classroom 2
I would have mixed feelings if I left the classroom 3
I would feel some gain if I left the classroom 4
I would feel real gain if I left the classroom for administration 5

T 8 Although few would call school teachers a "privileged class," they do earn money, receive a certain level of respect from others, and are in a position to wield some influence. Of these three, from which do you derive the most satisfaction?
The salary I earn in my profession 7
The respect I receive from others 8
The opportunity to wield some influence 9
I receive no satisfaction at all from these things 0

T 9 Teachers can enjoy a variety of things in their work. Which of the following is the most important source of satisfaction for you?
The opportunity teaching gives me to study, read, and plan for classes .. 1
The chance it offers to develop mastery of discipline and classroom management 2
The times I know I have "reached" a student or group of students and they have learned 3
The chance to associate with children or young people and to develop relationships with them 4

T 10 Which of the following things do you like best about teaching?
The relative security of income and position 7
The time (especially summer) which can permit travel, family activities, etc. 8
The opportunity it offers to earn a living without much rivalry and competition with other people 9
Its special appropriateness for persons like myself 0
None of these afford me satisfaction X

T 11 Of the features grouped below, I think that the following (circle one) is most important to me:
The salary and respect received and the position of influence 1
The opportunities to study, plan, master classroom management, "reach" students, and associate with colleagues and children 2
The economic security, time, freedom from competition, and appropriateness for persons like me 3

Notes

Chapter One

1. Although the emergence of public schools in colonial New England is a well-told story, we know considerably less about fee-for-service instruction during that period. Individual teaching enterprises did exist, especially in cities, but historians have yet to explore the full extent of such arrangements. See Cremin (1970), Kaestle (1973), and Middlekauff (1963).

Chapter Two

1. This chapter was planned and written before the publication of the 1972 report from the National Education Association (*Status of the American Public-School Teacher, 1970-71* [Washington, D.C.: Research Division, National Education Association, research report 1972-R3]). It is based primarily on two earlier reports (NEA 1963-M2 and 1967-R4); I have, however, added observations from the later report in the notes where it seems appropriate.

2. The wording of the questions can be found in Appendix B; for Five Towns, see Appendix B-1. In this instance, the two questions are numbers 8 and 10 in the Five Towns interview. Henceforth, I shall indicate the relevant question in parentheses in the text.

3. On question 8 (attractions to teaching), 14.4 percent of the respondents made reference to teaching as valuable service. On question 10 (most important factors in your decision), 17.3 percent responded in this fashion.

4. 6.7 percent said they "liked school" and wished to continue in work related to it; 12.2 percent said they were interested in a particular subject. The last NEA survey (1972-R3) asked specifically about "interest in a subject-matter field," and 34.5 percent of the respondents selected it as one of *three* reasons they decided to become teachers. Men chose it more often than women (46.6 percent

versus 28.2 percent) and high school teachers more often than elementary teachers (57.0 percent compared with 14.3 percent). The survey does not break data down by sex within level of schooling, but it appears that interest in a particular subject is highly associated with level of schooling.

5. References to material benefits total 16.7 percent including money, prestige, and security in the attractions question and 6.2 percent in the key factors question.

6. The mean number of days teachers reported as scheduled for their regular school year in 1970-71 was 181 (National Education Association 1972, p. 134). Americans who work five days a week with three weeks vacation and eight holidays annually put in 237 days a year.

7. Although 13 percent included work schedule among the attractions, only 4 percent listed it among the major factors influencing their decision to enter teaching.

8. The most recent NEA survey included a reference to ''long summer vacation''; 14.4 percent of all respondents included it as one of three reasons for entering teaching (NEA 1972, p. 160).

9. A refined estimate of social mobility would have to include measurement of *net* upward mobility—some teachers occupy statuses lower than their parents'. Given the data in hand, it is not wise to undertake anything more precise than the discussion in the text. Farmer fathers, for example, can be owners or renters, prosperous leaders in their communities or impecunious sharecroppers. The same problems hold for self-employed fathers, who can own major or minor enterprises.

10. In 1971, 43.9 percent of men in teaching had fathers who were unskilled, semiskilled, or skilled workers compared with 29.0 percent of the women (NEA 1972, p. 61).

11. In one of the pilot interviews I conducted, one teacher told of a fisherman father who, after four days at sea, was forced to sell his share of the catch for twenty-five cents.

12. In the 1963 study, 8 percent of women compared with 2.9 percent of men referred to ''a tradition in my family,'' a difference which suggests that family influences perpetuate feminine composition of the teaching force (NEA 1963, p. 47). In the different question asked in the later survey, 25.7 percent of the women cited family influence on their decision compared with 10.5 percent of the men (NEA 1972, p. 52).

13. The study undertaken in 1971 reveals that 17.9 percent of respondents considered the influence of an elementary or secondary teacher one of three main reasons for entering the occupation (NEA 1972, p. 159).

14. In the 1971 sample 21.1 percent of women and 10.5 percent of men selected ''never really considered anything else'' as one of the three main reasons for becoming a teacher—this is normally the response of those who made an early commitment. 21.4 percent of elementary versus 13.0 percent of secondary teachers gave the same response (NEA 1972, p. 159).

15. The information following each excerpt from the interviews includes the interview number and the sex and age of the respondent. The last entry refers to grade for elementary teachers and subject (or subjects) taught for secondary teachers.

16. In a question asking respondents to recall an outstanding teacher, women

teachers tended to recall women, men to recall men. Wright found the same tendency in his data (personal communication).

17. It may be that special programs (such as the Teacher Corps) recruit counteridentifiers to the occupation, a point which could be researched. We might expect to find such counteridentifiers active in the alternative schools movement as well.

18. I recall reading a story in the *New York Times* some years ago reporting that the ablest students from Albany State College (now the State University of New York at Albany) were electing to go into graduate school in fields other than education. As state colleges become "multipurpose" institutions and recruit more faculty from the disciplines, fewer able students will probably be encouraged to enter classroom teaching.

19. The term "conservative" has been used in this chapter to refer to orientations toward the occupation. It is interesting, however, that teachers classify themselves as more *politically* conservative than liberal; 16.9 percent say their political philosophy is conservative and 43.6 percent say they tend to be conservative, a total of 60.5 percent. And 39.5 percent classify themselves as liberal or tending to be liberal (NEA 1972, p. 158).

Chapter Three

1. Those interested in examining such studies will find excellent bibliographies in Blau and Scott (1962), Gross (1958), and Taylor (1968).

2. The first public normal school was established in Lexington, Massachusetts, in 1839 (Elsbree 1939, p. 146).

3. This estimate is based on multiplying 180 days per year by 6 hours, yielding 1,080 hours per year. Twelve years of schooling thus produces 12,960 hours, exclusive of any out-of-class contact such as occurs in extracurricular activities.

4. "Favorable votes" refers here to ratings of "excellent" or "satisfactory."

5. There were fourteen teachers in the Five Towns sample who had begun to teach in the same year in which they were interviewed. All fourteen alluded, at some point, to this problem.

6. I wish to acknowledge Mario Fantini's courtesy in letting me have these diaries.

7. I first learned to look for such exchanges from Everett Hughes during classroom discussion at the University of Chicago.

8. These observations should be qualified, of course, where team teaching is the mode of instruction. The last available information (NEA 1972) indicates that 12.4 percent of teachers are members of teams; I have no idea, however, how many teachers *begin* to teach under such arrangements.

9. Responses to the other alternatives were: "the results of objective examinations and other tests," 13.5 percent; "the reactions of other teachers," 11.5 percent; "the opinions expressed by the students," 7.3 percent; "the assessments made by the principal," 2.9 percent; "the assessments made by a special 'supervisor' or similar person," 1.0 percent; and "the reactions of students' parents," 1.2 percent.

Chapter Four

1. It is true, of course, that older teachers working today earn more than twice their initial salary in real income terms. It is unlikely that their earlier decisions,

however, were based on the expectation of a general rise in income. Nor is there cause to believe that teachers beginning today expect an equivalent rise in the future, although it would be an interesting point for research.

2. The root of the word career is the same as that of *car* (*Shorter Oxford English Dictionary*).

3. This is conjectural and should be the object of inquiry. Married women who return after a protracted absence could, of course, be trained into newer techniques; this necessity, however, would increase the overall cost of employing older married teachers compared with younger single or married teachers.

4. The terms "involvement" and "engagement" are used interchangeably in this discussion. In both instances, I am referring to the Lewinian concept of life space and the proportion individuals allocate to their work.

5. The 1972 NEA report unfortunately fails to break down the results on this question by marital status. The figures for men and women are presented; 33 percent of the men chose "certainly would teach" and 27.8 percent "probably would teach," while 51.1 percent of the women chose the former and 30.4 percent the latter. The sex differential remained similar, therefore, in the most favorable responses to teaching (21.4 percent in the earlier report, 20.7 percent in the later).

6. Level of satisfaction was divided into four possibilities (1-4), repeat readiness into four, and presence/absence of costs into two; scores could range, therefore, from 3 to 10.

7. E. C. Hughes developed the ideas of facets and phases in a memorandum written in the 1950s. Work can be seen as one facet of a person's life which, like other facets, takes on different meanings in various life phases. I do not believe that the memo was published.

8. Some of the older women teachers varied markedly from this depiction. Their interviews were characterized by repeated complaints about fatigue—they mentioned time and again how tired they were. Some, for example, said they went to bed as soon as they got home from school. One got the distinct impression that they were looking forward to retirement.

9. Dade County respondents were asked whether they thought it likely that they would be asked to take a position one step up within the next five years (question 44, App. B-2). Of men in their thirties, 43 percent thought it likely, 34 percent unlikely. Men in their fifties, on the other hand, had quite different expectations; 21.7 percent thought it likely, 61.1 percent unlikely. Asked how they would react to such an invitation, 9.5 percent of men in their thirties would refuse while 29 percent of men in their fifties signaled unwillingness to be promoted (question 43, App. B-2).

10. That such controls continue to exist—even in urban areas—is indicated by responses to the Dade County questionnaire. Asked whether they felt they had to be careful about doing things publicly which they considered acceptable but others might not, 45.2 percent of Dade County teachers replied either "I feel I must be very careful" or "I feel some pressure to be careful" (question 38, App. B-2).

11. One could understate the influence administrators have in salary matters. They have some discretion, I understand, in a teacher's initial placement on the salary schedule; they can also influence a teacher's mobility potential through the power of recommendation.

12. This is based on classroom discussion at the University of Chicago.

Chapter Five

1. This definition is from the *American Heritage Dictionary of the English Language* (Boston: Houghton-Mifflin, 1969).
2. Question 30, App. B-1, is an example. The respondent has selected an "outstanding" teacher to describe; descriptive statements, therefore, reveal the characteristics which the respondent associates with superior performance. This indirect approach discloses the evaluative criteria used without asking for them explicitly.
3. The term *sentiment* denotes an affective dimension. The *American Heritage Dictionary*, for example, defines sentiment as "a thought, view or attitude based on feeling or emotion instead of reason." The last phrase, "instead of reason," involves an inference which is hazardous and, I believe, unnecessary. One way of summarizing my conception of sentiment is to define it as a cathected attitude.
4. See question T-3, App. B-2; 73.7 percent of the respondents selected the response "I tend toward the subject-matter emphasis, but think other things are important, too." Only 5.6 percent chose the first response, "I'm pretty much the 'no-nonsense, get-the-learning-of-subject-matter done' kind of teacher."
5. The question of equality of educational opportunity has, of course, become a major issue in the past few years. See, for example, the Coleman Report or Arthur Wise's work. James S. Coleman, et al., *Equality of Educational Opportunity* (Washington, D.C., Office of Education, 1966) and Arthur Wise, *Rich School, Poor School* (Chicago: University of Chicago Press, 1968).
6. Such pluralism was evident in the department of social studies in one of the high schools where research was conducted. Three men were interviewed. One, the chairman, stressed intellectual, college preparatory goals and depicted himself as countervailing the dominant (Republican) orthodoxy in the community. The second talked at length about the importance of teaching reading to high school students and of his interest in helping adolescents think about issues like man's place in the universe. The third grew most excited as he described the informal counseling he did with students in extracurricular activities; himself of lower-class origin, he enjoyed advising students who were ignored by their $60,000-a-year fathers.
7. Instructional outcomes were mentioned ninety times, relational seventy-three.
8. Cognitive and affective references were roughly equal—forty-eight and forty-two.
9. Mentions of these three kinds of relational outcomes were, respectively, thirty-two, twenty-seven, and fourteen.
10. I am not sure if Everett Hughes ever made this point in print, but I recall it from class discussion.
11. Relational outcomes were mentioned sixty-three times, compared with thirty references to instructional outcomes.
12. Twenty-five percent of high school teachers gave a similar response.
13. Sixteen of the eighteen respondents who mentioned the appreciation of former students were over forty.
14. This point is based on exploratory interviews which preceded the Five Towns interviews.

15. Twenty percent of the respondents mentioned evidence of special interest by students.

Chapter Six

1. Anesthesiologists are likely to feel that surgeons underutilize their capacities (Lortie 1949). Staff experts complain that line officials make too many decisions without their guidance (Gardner and Moore 1955).

2. Although there are numerous definitions of craft, one I find useful is that a craft is work in which experience improves performance—the job cannot, like many unskilled or semiskilled types of work, be fully learned in weeks or even months.

3. Seniority rights of transfer affect the *type* of students a teacher works with, but they do not involve choice of individual students. We need inquiry, in fact, into the informal understandings which influence how principals allocate particular students to particular teachers. There seems to be a norm of equity at work which leads to rotating difficult students among teachers, but this has not (to my knowledge) been investigated.

4. My data provide some leads on this question of which teachers find it relatively easy to assess their work. One is role; teachers who teach highly specific skills (e.g., first-grade reading, typing, athletics) have greater confidence in their capacity to assess outcomes. Another variable may be personality; respondents who sounded high on authoritarianism also seemed dogmatic on this question. Experience may be another factor, for in Dade County teachers with more experience were more likely to find assessment easy. The latter, curiously, was true for women teachers but not for men. This entire area obviously begs for research.

5. These probes constituted a series of questions based on various dimensions of intangibility.

6. Writers, for example, are protected by copyright laws, and claims of scientists are adjudicated by date of publication.

7. This observation is based on the testimony of substitutes who report wide fluctuations in the expected level of discipline within the classes they visit—even in the same school.

8. An elementary teacher working with thirty students for six hours could, at the very most, spend twelve minutes with each child. A high school teacher working five hours with one hundred and fifty students would have no more than two minutes to spend with each.

9. In school systems where students are subjected to external examinations, the temptation facing the teacher is to "use" the students for self-advancement and, possibly, to press them hard. The image of the harsh teacher found in European films, for example, may reflect this pressure. Relatively few American teachers face this contingency; perhaps their characteristic temptation is to seek affective responses from students at the cost of not making unpopular demands on them.

10. Twenty-six chose "expressive only" compared with twelve choosing "task only."

11. The other sources of shame mentioned by respondents were behavior connected with disciplinary actions (15.4 percent), personal inadequacies in instruction (15.4 percent), overt conflict with other staff members (8.8 percent), issues of student promotion and grading (5.5 percent), "apprenticeship guilt"—

that is, worry over mistakes made as a new teacher (5.5 percent)—and miscellaneous, don't know, and no response (14.2 percent). For an analysis of these responses see Lortie 1967*a*.

Chapter Seven

1. It is ironic that high school teachers would opt for more time counseling students—about 24 percent, compared with 15 percent for elementary teachers. Counseling is more institutionalized as a specialized role in high schools, and this points to conflict between teachers and counselors on these tasks.

2. Questions 13 and 14, App. B-2, dealt with this issue; the responses presented here are to question 14.

3. Shirley Stokes found that elementary teachers in Ontario, Canada, placed loyalty to students and peers considerably ahead of loyalty to administrators (undated, p. 68).

4. In Five Towns, one teacher went on at great length about an incident where her recommendation on the promotion of a child was overruled by the principal. It was obviously a seriously disturbing event for her.

5. The coding here was done in a highly conservative fashion. Only those cases where definite cause and effect language was used were included.

6. I am well acquainted with one teacher who decided to leave teaching after a year in which one disturbed child constantly disrupted classroom work. The child was later placed under psychiatric care, but that one year alienated a teacher who had ranked first in her graduating class and had received high commendation for her earlier teaching.

Chapter Eight

1. Such power used to be possessed essentially on social class grounds, but today the militancy of minority-group members has extended it to include blacks, Chicanos, and so forth.

2. Fifty-six percent of the senior high school teachers, compared with 11 percent of the elementary teachers, mentioned technical performance. I suspect that this may be due to the greater task interdependency of high school teachers, who share students and therefore suffer the consequences of inferior instruction in other classes.

3. Five Towns teachers were asked what constituted fun in their work (question 42, App. B-1). Many talked of those moments when teacher and students could act together in a spirit of relaxed rapport, sharing jokes and such. Yet the pathos of teaching asserted itself; many added that one had to avoid prolonging such moments lest the students "take advantage" and the teacher lose control.

4. In Chicago (and I suspect other large cities), pressure from minorities has led to the formation of local school councils which have, in some instances, addressed themselves aggressively to the local school and principal. Such councils certainly have a hand in the formation of local school policy, but the legitimacy of this influence has not yet received general recognition.

5. There is some indication that principals yield to that influence over time. Bridges (1964) found that more experienced principals were more likely to approximate teacher expectations on how they should wield authority.

6. Albert Shanker made these observations in a lecture given at the University of Chicago in April 1965.

Chapter Nine

1. This observation is based on conversation with Bruce Cooper, who is conducting research on free schools.
2. The sources for these data are Tyack (1967, p. 468), Campbell, Cunningham, and McPhee (1965, p. 94), and a pamphlet issued by the National Center for Educational Statistics, Office of Education (Washington, D.C.: DHEW publication no. (OE) 72-97, 1972). The mean size of school districts in 1948 was approximately 253, and in 1970, 2,930. This is a rough statistic which does not differentiate between operating and nonoperating districts, but it does give some indication of the magnitude of this trend.
3. Personal communication from Alan Thomas.
4. Adaptation is seen in these pages as an *active* process in which members of a group choose to change their behavior to adjust to new circumstances.
5. Members of the medical profession have learned to bring a variety of specialized viewpoints to bear on a particular problem. One thinks, for example, of the clinical pathological conference where failure is explored fully and openly by various specialists.
6. School boards seem to feel that teachers should show their "dedication" by carrying on such activities on their own time. Yet a counterargument can be posed; where boards refuse to pay for such activities, they are telegraphing a low opinion of their worth.
7. In response to question 40 (App. B-2), 67 percent of Dade teachers chose either "I would definitely be enthusiastic about doing some research" (26.7 percent) or "I might well be interested in participating" (40.3 percent).

References

Bailyn, B. 1960. *Education in the forming of American society.* Chapel Hill: University of North Carolina Press.

Bales, R. F. 1956. Task status and likeability as a function of talking and listening in decision-making groups. In *The state of the social sciences,* ed. L. D. White, pp. 148-61. Chicago: University of Chicago Press.

Becker, H. 1951*a.* The professional dance musician in Chicago. *American Journal of Sociology* 57:136-44.

———.1951*b.* Role and career problems of the Chicago public school teacher. Ph.D. thesis, University of Chicago.

Benson, C. 1961*a. The economics of public education.* Boston: Houghton Mifflin.

———. 1961*b. The economics of public education.* 2d ed. Boston: Houghton Mifflin.

Berg, I. E. 1970. *Education and jobs: The great training robbery.* New York: Praeger.

Berg, P. C. 1973. The impact of collective bargaining on the principal. *Administrator's Notebook* 21:1-4.

Bidwell, C. 1965. The school as a formal organization. *Handbook of organizations.* Chicago: Rand McNally.

Blau, P. 1955. *The dynamics of bureaucracy.* Chicago: University of Chicago Press.

Blau, P., and Scott, W. R. 1962. *Formal organizations.* San Francisco: Chandler.

Blumer, H. 1947. Sociological theory in industrial relations. *American Sociological Review* 12:271-78.

———. 1957. Collective behavior. In *Principles of sociology,* ed. A. M. Lee, pp. 167-222. New York: Barnes and Noble.

Bridges, E. 1964. Teacher participation in decision making: Interaction of personal and situational variables. *Administrator's Notebook* 12:1-4.

References

Brophy, J. E., and Good, T. L. 1970. Teachers' communication of differential expectations for children's classroom performance: Some behavioral data. *Journal of Educational Psychology* 61:365-74.

Butts, F., and Cremin, L. A. 1953. *A history of education in American culture.* New York: Holt.

Callahan, R. E. 1962. *Education and the cult of efficiency.* Chicago: University of Chicago Press.

Campbell, R. F.; Cunningham, L. L.; and McPhee, R. 1965. *The organization and control of American schools.* Columbus, Ohio: Charles E. Merrill.

Campbell, R. F., and Lorion, J. E. 1972. *Performance contracting in school systems.* Columbus, Ohio: Charles E. Merrill.

Caplow, T. 1954. *The sociology of work.* Minneapolis: University of Minnesota Press.

Charters, W. W., Jr. 1963. The social background of teaching. In *Handbook of research on teaching,* ed. N. L. Gage, pp. 715-813. Chicago: Rand McNally.

———. 1970. Some factors affecting teacher survival in school districts. *American Educational Research Journal* 7:1-27.

Cole, S. 1969. *The unionization of teachers.* New York: Praeger.

Coleman, J. S., et al. 1966. *Equality of educational opportunity.* Washington, D.C.: Office of Education.

Conant, J. B. 1963. *The education of American teachers.* New York: McGraw-Hill.

Cooley, C. H. 1956. *Human nature and the social order.* Glencoe, Ill.: Free Press.

Corwin, R. G. 1965. *A sociology of education.* New York: Appleton-Century-Crofts.

Cremin, L. A. 1961. *The transformation of the school.* New York: Alfred A. Knopf.

———. 1970. *American education: The colonial experience 1607-1783.* New York: Harper and Row.

Dahlke, H. O. 1958. *Values in culture and classroom.* New York: Harper.

Dreeben, R. 1968. *On what is learned in school.* Reading, Mass: Addison-Wesley.

———. 1970. *The nature of teaching.* Glenview, Ill.: Scott Foresman.

Edgar, D. E., and Warren, R. L. 1969. Power and autonomy in teacher socialization. *Sociology of Education* 42:386-99.

Elsbree, W. S. 1939. *The American teacher.* New York: American Book Co.

Fantini, M. D. 1972. Review of *Teachers and power,* by R. J. Braun. *New York Times Book Review,* May 3 and 12.

Festinger, L. 1962. *A theory of cognitive dissonance.* Stanford: Stanford University Press.

Gallup, G. 1969. *How the nation views the public schools.* Princeton: Gallup International.

Gardner, B. B., and Moore, D. G. 1955. *Human relations in industry.* 3d ed. Homewood: Richard D. Irwin.

Getzels, J. W., and Jackson, P. W. 1963. The Teacher's personality and characteristics. In *Handbook of research on teaching,* ed. N. L. Gage, pp. 506-82. Chicago: Rand McNally.

Ginzberg, E.; Ginzberg, S. W.; Axelrad, S.; and Herma, J. L. 1951. *Occupational choice.* New York: Columbia University Press.

270

References

Gold, R. L. N.d. In the basement: The apartment-building janitor. In *The human shape of work*, ed. P. Berger, pp. 1-49. New York: Macmillan.

Goodlad, J. I., et al. 1970. *Behind the classroom door.* Worthington, Ohio: Charles A. Jones.

Griffiths, D. E.; Goldman, S.; and McFarland, W. J. 1965. Teacher mobility in New York City. *Educational Administration Quarterly* 1:15-31.

Gross, E. 1958. *Work and society.* New York: Thomas Y. Crowell.

Hall, D. T. 1967. Peer relationship during the initiation phase of an academic role transition. Paper presented at the American Educational Research Association, 17 February 1967, New York.

Hall, O. 1944. The informal organization of medical practice in an American city. Ph.D. thesis, University of Chicago.

————. 1948. The stages of a medical career. *American Journal of Sociology* 53:327-36.

Haller, E. J. 1966. Teacher socialization: Pupil influences on teachers' speech. Ph.D. thesis, University of Chicago.

Halpin, A. W., and Croft, D. B. 1963. The organizational climate of schools. *Administrator's Notebook* 11:1-4.

Havighurst, R., and Neugarten, B. 1957. *Society and education.* Boston: Allyn and Bacon.

Hermanowicz, H. J. 1966. The pluralistic world of beginning teachers. In *The real world of the beginning teacher*, pp. 15-25. Report of the nineteenth national TEPS conference. Washington, D.C.: National Educational Association.

Hiller, E. T. 1928. *The strike.* Chicago: University of Chicago Press.

Hodge, R.; Siegel, P. M.; and Rossi, P. 1964. Occupational prestige in the United States, 1925-63. *American Journal of Sociology* 70:286-302.

Hofstadter, R. 1963. *Anti-intellectualism in American life.* New York: Random House.

Hollingshead, A. B. 1957. Human ecology. In *Principles of sociology,* ed. A. M. Lee, pp. 67-118. New York: Barnes and Noble.

Holt. J. C. 1964. *How children fail.* New York: Pitman.

Hoy, W. K. 1969. Pupil control ideology and organizational socialization. *School Review* 77:257-65.

Hughes, E. C. 1958. *Men and their work.* Glencoe, Ill.: Free Press.

Hughes, M. 1959. *Development of the means for the assessment of the quality of teaching in elementary schools.* Salt Lake City: University of Utah Press.

Illich, I. 1971. *De-schooling society.* New York: Harper and Row.

Jackson, P. 1968. *Life in classrooms.* New York: Holt, Rinehart and Winston.

Jackson, P., and Belford, E. 1965. Educational objectives and the joys of teaching. *School Review* 73:267-91.

Jersild, Arthur T. Behold the beginner. In *The real world of the beginning teacher*, pp. 43-53. Report of the nineteenth national TEPS conference. Washington, D.C.: National Educational Association.

Kaestle, Carl F. 1973. *The evolution of an urban school system, New York City, 1750-1850.* Cambridge: Harvard University Press.

Kaufman, H. 1960. *The forest ranger: A study in administrative behavior.* Baltimore: Johns Hopkins Press.

Keppel, F. 1961. *Personnel policies for public education.* Pittsburgh: University of Pittsburgh.

References

Kronus, C. 1969. Occupational career decisions: Temporal patterns and sociological correlates. Ph.D. dissertation, University of Chicago.

Ladd, Edward T. Interpretation and perspectives. In *The real world of the beginning teacher*, pp. 75-83. Report of the nineteenth national TEPS conference. Washington, D.C.: National Educational Association.

Lévi-Strauss, C. 1967. *Structural anthropology*. Garden City, N.Y.: Doubleday.

Lieberman, M. 1956. *Education as a profession*. Englewood Cliffs, N.J.: Prentice-Hall.

Lindesmith, A. R. 1947. *Opiate addiction*. Bloomington, Ind.: Principia Press.

Linton, R. 1936. *The study of man*. New York: Appleton-Century.

Lortie, D. C. 1949. Doctors without patients: The anesthesiologist—a new medical specialist. Master's thesis, University of Chicago.

———. 1958. The striving young lawyer: A study of early career differentiation in the Chicago bar. Ph.D. dissertation, University of Chicago.

———. 1959. Laymen to lawmen: Law school, careers, and socialization. *Harvard Educational Review* 29:352-69.

———. 1967a. The teacher's shame: Anger and the normative commitments of classroom teachers. *School Review* 75:155-71.

———. 1967b. Towards educational equality: The teacher and the educational park. In *Education parks*. United States Commission on Civil Rights, clearinghouse publication no. 9.

———. 1968. Shared ordeal and induction to work. In *Institutions and the person*, ed., H. S. Becker et al., pp. 252-64. Chicago: Aldine.

———. 1969. The balance of control and autonomy in elementary school teaching. In *The semi-professions and their organization*, ed. A. Etzioni, pp. 1-53. New York: Free Press.

———. 1970. The cracked cake of educational custom and emerging issues in evaluation. In *The evaluation of instruction: Issues and problems*, ed. M. C. Wittrock and D. E. Wiley, pp. 149-64. New York: Holt, Rinehart and Winston.

———. 1973. Observations on teaching as work. In *Second handbook of research on teaching*, ed. R. M. W. Travers, pp. 474-97. Chicago: Rand McNally.

McDowell, H. D. 1954. The principal's role in a metropolitan school system: Its functions and variations. Ph.D. thesis, University of Chicago.

Maguire, T. F. 1970. Exchange and interaction in academic departments. Ph.D. thesis, University of Chicago.

Mallery, D. 1962. *High school students speak out*. New York: Harper.

March. J. G., and Simon, H. A. 1958. *Organizations*. New York: Wiley.

Mason, W. S. 1961. *The beginning teacher*. Washington, D.C.: U.S. Department of Health, Education, and Welfare, Office of Education, circular no. 644.

Mayer, M. 1961. *The schools*. New York: Harper.

———. 1969. *The teachers' strike, New York, nineteen sixty-eight*. New York: Harper and Row.

Mead, G. H. 1934. *Mind, self, and society*. Chicago: University of Chicago Press.

Middlekauff, Robert. 1963. *Ancients and axioms: Secondary education in eighteenth-century New England*. New Haven: Yale University Press.

Miller, D. C., and Form, W. A. 1951. *Industrial sociology*. New York: Harper and Bros.

272

References

Mitchell, D. P. 1972. *Leadership in public education study.* Washington, D.C.: Academy for Educational Development.

Naegle, K. D. 1956. Clergymen, teachers, and psychiatrists. *Canadian Journal of Economics and Political Science* 22:46-62.

National Education Association. 1963. *The American public-school teacher, 1960-61.* Washington D.C.: Research Division, research monograph 1963-M2.

———. 1967. *The American public-school teacher, 1965-66.* Washington, D.C.: Research Division, research report 1967-R4.

———. 1972. *Status of the American public-school teacher, 1970-71.* Washington, D.C.: Research Division, research report 1972-R3.

National Opinion Research Center. 1953. Jobs and occupations: A popular evaluation. In *Class, status, and power,* ed. R. V. Bendix and S. M. Lipset, pp. 411-25. Glencoe, Ill.: Free Press.

Ogburn, W. F. 1933. The family and its functions. *Recent Social Trends in the United States* 1:661-708.

Park, R., and Burgess, E. 1924. *Introduction to the science of society.* Chicago: University of Chicago Press.

Parsons, T. V. 1958. Some ingredients of a general theory of organization. In *Administrative theory in education,* ed. A. W. Halpin, pp. 40-72. Chicago: Midwest Administration Center, University of Chicago.

———. 1959. The school class as a social system. *Harvard Educational Review* 29:297-318.

Parsons, T. V., and Bales, R. F. 1955. *Family socialization and interaction process.* Glencoe, Ill.: Free Press.

Parsons, T. V., and Shils, E. A., eds. 1952. *Toward a general theory of action.* Cambridge: Harvard University Press.

Pedersen, K. G. 1973. *The itinerant schoolmaster: A socio-economic analysis of teacher turnover.* Chicago: Midwest Administration Center, University of Chicago.

Perry, C. R., and Wildman, W. A. 1970. *The impact of negotiations in public education: The evidence from the schools.* Worthington, Ohio: Charles A. Jones.

Peterson, W. 1956. Career phases and inter-age relationships: The female high school teacher in Kansas City. Ph.D. thesis, University of Chicago.

Rainwater, L.; Coleman, R. P.; and Handel, G. H. 1959. *Workingman's wife: Her personality, world, and life style.* New York: Oceana.

Rist, R. C. 1970. Student social class and teacher expectations: The self-fulfilling prophecy in ghetto education. *Harvard Educational Review* 40:411-51.

Rosenberg, M. 1957. *Occupations and values.* Glencoe, Ill.: Free Press.

Rosenthal, A. 1969. *Pedagogues and power.* Syracuse, N.Y.: Syracuse University Press.

Sharma, C. L. 1955. Practices in decision-making as related to satisfaction in teaching. Ph.D. dissertation, University of Chicago.

Silberman, C. E. 1970. *Crisis in the classroom.* New York: Random House.

Simmel, G. 1950. *The sociology of Georg Simmel.* Trans. and edit. Kurt Wolff, Glencoe, Ill.: Free Press.

Smith, L. M., and Geoffrey, W. 1968. *The complexities of an urban classroom: An analysis toward a general theory of teaching.* New York: Holt, Rinehart and Winston.

References

Stokes, S. N.d. The shortest shadow. Multilithed. Toronto: Federation of Women Teachers' Associations of Ontario.

Stonequist, E. V. 1930. The marginal man: A study in the subjective aspects of cultural conflict. Ph.D. thesis, University of Chicago.

Stouffer, S. A., et al. 1949. The American soldier. Princeton: Princeton University Press.

Stout, R. T. 1966. Education as a social mobility route for children of suburban blue collar workers. Ph.D. thesis, University of Chicago.

Sullivan, H. S. 1953. The interpersonal theory of psychiatry. New York: Norton.

Sumner, W. G. 1906. Folkways. Boston: Ginn.

Sykes, G. 1953. The P.T.A. and parent-teacher conflict. Harvard Educational Review 23:86-92.

Taylor, L. 1968. Occupational sociology. New York: Oxford University Press.

Tocqueville, A. 1954. Democracy in America. Vol. 1. New York: Vintage Books.

Trask, A. E. 1964. Principals, teachers, and supervision: Dilemmas and solutions. Administrator's Notebook 13:1-4.

Tyack, D. B. 1967. Turning points in American educational history. Waltham, Mass.: Blaisdell.

Vidich, A. J., and Bensman, J. 1958. Small town in mass society. Princeton: Princeton University Press.

Waller, W. 1961. The sociology of teaching. New York: Russell and Russell.

Watson, B. 1967. The national teacher corps: A tale of three cities. Administrator's Notebook 16:1-4.

Whyte, W. F. 1955. Money and motivation. New York: Harper and Bros.

Wilson, L. 1942. The academic man: A study in the sociology of a profession. London: Oxford University Press.

Wise, A. 1968. Rich school, poor school. Chicago: University of Chicago Press.

Wright, B. D., and Tuska, S. A. 1968. From dream to life in the psychology of becoming a teacher. School Review 76:253-93.

X, Dr. 1965. Intern. New York: Harper and Row.

Yee, A. H. 1968. Source and direction of causal influence in teacher-pupil relationships. Journal of Educational Psychology 59:275-82.

Index

Index

Index

Index

Index

Public sector employment, 6, 7
Punishment, 3, 4. *See also* Control, classroom

Qualifications, 17, 18-19, 23-24
Questionnaires, 110, 248-59

Rainwater, L., 188
Rapport, 173-74. *See also* Mood; Students, relationships with
Ratio, teacher-student, 15, 23
Reassurance, need for, 140-41, 142-44, 149-50, 161, 185, 196, 210. *See also* Support, need for
Recognition, scarcity of, 130, 133, 161
Recruitment: necessity for, 25, 83, 99; resources for, 26-54, 236; and socialization, 56
Relational outcomes, 117-20, 123, 131. *See also* Students, relationships with
Religion, relation to teaching, 10-11, 28
Research, 70, 214, 216-20; by classroom teachers, 212-13, 232, 240-43
Resources, allocation of, 184-86, 197, 198, 199, 201
Responsibility, collegial, 222-24, 235-39
"Revolution," educational, 214, 217-18
Rewards, ancillary, 101, 103-5; contingent, 223, 224-25; extrinsic, 101-5; intrinsic (*see* Rewards, psychic); material, 30-31, 33, 82-83 (*see also* Income); psychic, 101, 103-4, 105, 116, 119-25, 161, 164, 181, 187-200, 210, 211; relation to occupations, 101-2; variability of, 103, 168, 181, 210
Rist, R. C., 148
Role-taking, 62-63
Rosenberg, M., 28
Rosenthal, A., 203
Rossi, P., 13
Rules, necessity for, 70, 138-39, 151, 164, 189. *See also* Control, classroom

Salaries. *See* Income

Sampling procedure, 245-46
Satisfaction, work, 89-99; and extrinsic rewards, 96, 101-5, 183; and goals, 103-4; and involvement, 89-99; and isolation, 96-97; and psychic rewards, 103-4, 105, 106
Scenarios for change, 215-28
Schedules, school, 16-17, 31-33, 103, 182. *See also* Hours worked
School boards: authority of, 5-6, 7, 22, 196; future of, 22, 221-24; history of, 2-6, 22; teachers' relations to, 21
Schools: assignment to, 4-5, 137, 138-41, 196, 197; criticism of, 222-23; ecological patterns in, 13-16; expansion of, 15, 19; public's expectations of, 133, 134, 218. *See also* Education
Schoolwide concerns, 163-64, 170-71, 174, 175, 185, 193, 194
Scientific thought, 212-13, 230-31, 241-42
Scott, W. R., 239
Screening of trainees, 39, 51, 56, 230-31, 236, 241-42
Secondary teachers: hours worked by, 89-90; social status of, 12, 48; time allocation of, 147
Second careers, 51
Secularization of schools, 12
Security, employment, 6, 7-8, 13, 30-31, 36-37, 103
Self-fulfilling prophecy, 85-86
Self-image, 28, 76, 148, 160-61, 241. *See also* Status
Seniority, 5, 99, 161, 205; and income, 60, 83-84, 102
Service ideal, 28-29, 52, 53, 102, 103
Sex of teachers, 8, 9-10, 33, 52, 204. *See also* Marriage; Men teachers; Women teachers
Shame, sources of, 156-59
Shanker, Albert, 207
Shared culture, lack of, 67, 70, 73-74, 76, 80-81
Shared ordeal, 73-74, 160, 237
Sharma, C. L., 238
Shils, E. A., 152
Siegel, P. M., 13